Beware the People Weeping

Benn Pitman, the court stenographer, originally published this print. Although he placed Mrs. Surratt at the center of the conspirators, he omitted Dr. Mudd, since he felt proof was lacking that the doctor was involved.

Beware
the People Weeping

Public Opinion
and the Assassination
of Abraham Lincoln

THOMAS REED TURNER

Louisiana State University Press

Baton Rouge and London

Designer: Albert Crochet
Typeface: Galliard
Typesetter: Graphic Composition, Inc.
Printer and binder: Thomson-Shore, Inc.

LIBRARY OF CONGRESS CATALOGING IN PUBLICATION DATA

Turner, Thomas Reed, 1941–
    Beware the people weeping.

    Includes index.
    1.   Lincoln, Abraham, 1809–1865—Assassination—
Public opinion.   2.   Public opinion—United States.
I.   Title.
E457.5.T96   973.7′092′4   81–14252
ISBN 0–8071–0986–X   AACR2

For Lois, Amy, Melissa, and Jennifer

Contents

Illustrations

Preface

The most common assumption about the historiography of the assassination of Abraham Lincoln is that it is so voluminous and complete that no further need for research exists in this area. At a factual level, although with some notable and controversial exceptions, this assertion is fairly accurate.[1] However, even a cursory examination of assassination historiography reveals that, while historians have adequately explained many facets of Lincoln's death, they have been so involved with interpretation that they have given too little attention to understanding events adequately as they occurred. Facts have merely been used to bolster preconceived theories.

The first major historical emphasis was an attempt to defend alleged victims of military justice, such as Mrs. Mary Surratt and Dr. Samuel Mudd, and to portray Secretary of War Edwin M. Stanton and the Radical Republicans as using the assassination to conduct a reign of terror that served the substitution of their own harsh Reconstruction policy for that of the benevolent and martyred Lincoln. This view was then elaborated upon by the suggestion, with no offer of definite proof, not only that Stanton had acted vindictively but also that many unexplained events surrounding the assassination might indicate that the secretary of war and other Radicals had hated Lincoln and his policies enough to have engineered his murder. More recent authors have attempted to substantiate these allegations and claim to have proved definitively, through the discovery of new documents, that not only Stanton but head of the National Detective Police, Lafayette Baker, and a host of other northerners were indeed responsible for Lincoln's murder.

---

1. For example, a survey of the literature will enable one to comprehend even such remote details as why the bullet entered the left side of Lincoln's head despite the fact that Booth fired from the right. Otto Eisenschiml, *The Case of A. Lincoln, Aged 56* (Chicago: Abraham Lincoln Book Shop, 1943). However, other "facts," such as exactly what occurred at Garrett's barn, are not so readily apparent and have produced much historical controversy.

This methodology has been an extremely easy one for historians to use because there were undeniable irregularities in the treatment of prisoners and in the proceedings of the military commission. If one possesses enough imagination, it is also easy to discover gaps in the record and to raise unanswerable questions that might indicate there was a larger and as yet unsolved conspiracy. Unfortunately, these more obvious aspects of the assassination have received undue attention, while other, perhaps more significant points have been glossed over. Critics saw no point in investigating such questions as whether the outcome would really have been different in a civil instead of a military trial, how contemporaries viewed the trials, or whether the deadlocked jury in the John Surratt trial really signified an acquittal of his mother. The answers to these questions appeared either self-evident or unimportant.

Events may, and have, come to light that were completely unknown to contemporaries and that may greatly alter our views. Until the 1930s historians did not even have complete access to the vast file of archival material that has been so important in yielding increased knowledge about the assassination. Although the historian has gained much information from these sources and cannot help being influenced by the standards of his own era, he must not do so to the exclusion of the views of contemporaries. Such a distortion has apparently occurred regarding the Lincoln assassination.

There is, therefore, a need for a complete reexamination of Lincoln's assassination and the conspiracy trials which attempts to discover what really happened and how and why people reacted the way they did. This will reveal exactly where historians have been faithful to events as they transpired and where they have distorted, or presented a shifted and exaggerated emphasis that may never have existed. Further, it will allow a testing of the various conspiracy theories to see if there is any truth in such charges or whether they are largely the product of historians' overactive imaginations.

The recent outbreak of assassinations in the United States in the last two decades adds further urgency to the task. The assassination of John F. Kennedy reveals some interesting parallels to the Lincoln assassination, especially in the reactions of the people. The feelings of sorrow and vengeance and the irrational behavior were all quite similar.

When people take action on such views, even if they appear irrational and erroneous, historians have no right to dismiss them as they have been so prone to do.

There is further similarity in the growth of a conspiracy literature about the Kennedy assassination which rivals, if it does not surpass, that about Lincoln. This has occurred despite an official government investigation and an attempt to allay people's suspicions. It is important to note that people cannot conceive of a president being killed except by a wide-ranging conspiratorial group.

No serious student of the Kennedy assassination would think of writing about that event without attempting to place it in its historical context. Yet before this occurrence, assassinations were apparently so remote from the experience of historians that there was a tendency to view them in a vacuum. Only by combining what is valid in the views of contemporaries with what is valid in recently discovered materials will the assassination of Lincoln once again be placed in its proper historical setting.

Acknowledgments

I wish to acknowledge the assistance of the many people who contributed to the completion of this project. To Professor Kenneth A. Bernard, who introduced me to the joys and rigors of historical research and writing and who has remained my teacher and friend, I am profoundly indebted. Professor Robert V. Bruce of Boston University also provided many helpful insights and suggestions.

I am grateful to the staffs of several libraries, including those at Boston University, Duke University, and Harvard University and at the Library of Congress, and the National Archives, who provided invaluable assistance. Mr. Elmer Parker of the National Archives deserves a special thanks for making my work there most enjoyable and for willingly sharing his own research on the assassination with me.

I am also grateful to the administration of Bridgewater State College, through the Scholarly Support Committee, for funds to defray part of the cost for typing the manuscript, as well as for a sabbatical leave that enabled me to complete necessary changes. Mrs. Barbara Doten typed the manuscript in final form, employing her usual professional and critical eye.

Photographs were generously supplied by the Library of Congress, National Archives, and the Louis A. Warren Library and Museum, in Fort Wayne, Indiana. Mark E. Neely, Jr., director of the Louis A. Warren Library, was particularly helpful in making available many items from his library's excellent collections.

On a personal note, I wish to thank my parents, Brenton and Irene Turner, who have constantly supported me in my scholarly endeavors and fostered my interest in history and Abraham Lincoln. My wife and daughters have also genially tolerated the long hours necessary to bring this manuscript to completion.

Acknowledgments

I also appreciate the help and support of the editors of Louisiana State University Press, particularly Martha L. Hall and Catherine Barton, who have guided me expertly through the hitherto unfamiliar territory of preparing a manuscript for publication.

Beware the People Weeping

I.

The Historical Problem

This study is not meant to be a complete overview of the voluminous literature dealing with the Lincoln assassination; in fact, a fairly sizable volume would be needed to begin to do justice to assassination historiography. However, there is a need to survey briefly the major historiographical trends, since they reveal very clearly the failure of historians to place the events in their historical context and also their tendency to distort what really happened.

The first major historical effort to defend victims of military justice was begun by David DeWitt in *The Judicial Murder of Mary E. Surratt* (1895). A sequel, *The Assassination of Abraham Lincoln and Its Expiation* (1909), has long been regarded as one of the classic works on the assassination. While DeWitt was a pioneer in the field, and in many respects a careful historian, his work is nonetheless marred by an extreme animosity toward the military trial and particularly toward Edwin M. Stanton. The title of Chapter 3 in his second volume, "The Reign of Terror—Capture and Death of Booth," clearly reveals the direction of his bias. By the severest standards, the pursuit of the conspirators could hardly be equated with the French Revolution's reign of terror, which he suggests. Since DeWitt was by training a lawyer, his background undoubtedly influenced his feelings of outrage against what had been done to Mrs. Mary Surratt and Dr. Samuel Mudd.[1]

DeWitt's basic weakness, however, is in his methodology, for he freely admits that he based his study on three sources—Perley Poore's *Conspiracy Trial for the Murder of the President*, the impeachment investigation proceedings, and the John Surratt trial testimony. He then excluded everything else, no matter from what source, if it could not be verified in these documents. In this manner DeWitt felt he might dis-

---

1. David M. DeWitt to John T. Ford, December 9, 1890, in Ford's Theatre Collection, Maryland Historical Society.

cover the truth beneath the mountains of falsehood where it had lain buried.[2]

Because of this narrow approach, however, what DeWitt manages to do is produce a factually sound but lifeless polemical tract against military tribunals. While he cannot be generally faulted for his history, except insofar as everything about the assassination cannot be discovered in his three sources, he isolates Lincoln's murder in the stream of time. He apparently saw no connection between an assassination following the close of a bloody civil war and the seeming correctness of a military trial as it appeared to people in 1865. Rather, he judges all events by an arbitrary standard derived from his own legal background, with no allowance for the tensions of the historical situation.

What is also wrong with DeWitt's approach, as well as that of other historians who have followed his lead, has been the tendency to belabor the obvious. Military trials for civilians had been rather universally condemned by Americans throughout our history, as were the hooding and handcuffing of prisoners and other obvious irregularities that occurred in connection with the trial of the conspirators. Therefore, it is important to try to understand why, in 1865, Americans abandoned their normal tradition and such irregularities could and did occur.

Far more insidious than attacks on military tribunals and their victims have been attempts, beginning with Otto Eisenschiml's, to imply that northern leaders were behind the assassination. He states quite succinctly, "There was one man who profited greatly by Lincoln's death; this man was his Secretary of War, Edwin M. Stanton."[3]

Eisenschiml used a very clever methodology of proving his thesis by raising a series of provocative questions. Even though in many cases he is forced to admit that the orthodox answer is still correct until proven otherwise, he creates unwarranted doubts. With this technique the question oftentimes becomes more important than the answer. It is also easy for the author to maneuver out of tight spaces by claiming that he merely asked the question while refusing to take credit for the implied answer.[4]

2. David M. DeWitt, *The Assassination of Abraham Lincoln and Its Expiation* (New York: MacMillan, 1909), Preface.
3. Otto Eisenschiml, *Why Was Lincoln Murdered?* (Boston: Little Brown, 1937), 396.
4. For searching reviews of Eisenschiml's technique, see Edgar J. Rich, "Review of

Eisenschiml's suspicions about Stanton fall into several major areas. From a story told by telegraph operator David Homer Bates that Lincoln had requested Stanton's assistant, Major Thomas Thompson Eckert, to accompany him to the theater on the night of the assassination but had been refused by the war secretary because of a heavy workload, he infers that Stanton took such action so that Lincoln might be left unguarded. The refusal meant that the president was accompanied only by Metropolitan Police Force guard John F. Parker, who had an unsavory record and at the critical moment was evidently not in the proper place to stop Booth from entering the president's box, although he was apparently never punished for his negligence. He also suggests that Parker's retention on the force until 1869 (when he lost his job over a type of infraction he had committed for years with impunity) might be connected with Stanton's dismissal from office a few weeks earlier.[5]

Further, he feels that the pursuit of the assassins was misdirected, since the one road the murderers were bound to take out of Washington was not properly guarded. Also, events such as the loss of commercial telegraph service on the night of the assassination, April 14, might indicate that Booth and his coconspirators had inside help.[6]

In addition, he wonders about the killing of Booth, indicating that he might have been shot by a member of the National Detective Police, Everton Conger, rather than Boston Corbett, in order to prevent the assassin from telling what he knew. Eisenschiml also casts doubt about missing pages in Booth's diary and naïvely raises the possibility that Booth might not have been killed in Garrett's barn but that someone else died in his place. The hooding and mistreatment of the other prisoners, coupled with their rapid execution, could also be viewed as an attempt to insure their silence and to eliminate any loose ends.[7]

Why Was Lincoln Murdered?" and James G. Randall to E. J. Rich, September 21, 1939, both in Stone Collection, Boston University, and William Hanchett, "The Eisenschiml Thesis," *Civil War History*, XXV (1979), 197–217. For Eisenschiml's defense of his work, see *Reviewers Reviewed: A Challenge to Historical Critics* (Ann Arbor: William L. Clements Library, 1940).

5. Eisenschiml, *Why Was Lincoln Murdered?*, 19, Chap. 5; David Homer Bates, *Lincoln in the Telegraph Office: Recollections of the United States Military Telegraph Corps During the Civil War* (New York: Century, 1907), 367–68. For a refutation of charges that Lincoln was allowed to go to the theater unguarded, see George S. Bryan, *The Great American Myth* (New York: Carrick and Evans, 1940), 219–27.

6. Eisenschiml, *Why Was Lincoln Murdered?*, 80–82, 96.

7. Otto Eisenschiml, "Addenda to Lincoln's Assassination," *Journal of the Illinois State*

Finally, he charges that the government made little attempt to return and try the one alleged conspirator who had escaped, Mrs. Surratt's son, John. When he was ultimately brought to trial, the government, despite the weakness of its case, still hounded him unmercifully, apparently out of fear of what he might be able to disclose.[8]

In one instance in which Eisenschiml falls back on the traditional answer, he wonders why General Ulysses S. Grant and his wife did not accompany the Lincolns to Ford's Theatre, indicating that an ordinary criminologist would have been very interested in this point. He then notes that Mrs. Lincoln and Mrs. Grant had recently argued at City Point—a reasonable explanation for the Grants' absence that evening. Similarly, he muses about a statement made by Stanton, on learning of Booth's death, that Corbett had saved the government considerable bother, and then goes on to state lamely, "Yet, there is nothing conclusive in all this."[9]

Although Eisenschiml's methodology is clever, it hardly proves his thesis. One major problem is that his basic view of the Radical Republicans is outmoded. He, in fact, devotes a considerable part of *Why Was Lincoln Murdered?* to charges that the Radicals did not even wish victory in the Civil War to come too quickly, since it would deprive them of the chance to institute a harsh reconstruction. Recent scholarship has revealed, of course, that the Radicals were anything but monolithic in outlook and were not all motivated by a desire to bring devastation to the South. The latest Lincoln biography argues forcefully that this dichotomy between Lincoln and the Radicals never existed and that, particularly regarding the question of race, the so-called Radicals considered Lincoln to be sound.[10]

While Eisenschiml merely raised questions, recent authors have attempted to provide definite answers. Such efforts received a decided

---

Historical Society, XLIII (1950), 218, *Why Was Lincoln Murdered?*, 142–44, 150, and *In The Shadow of Lincoln's Death* (New York: Wilfred Funk, 1940), 33, 56, 75, 79–80.

8. Eisenschiml, *In the Shadow of Lincoln's Death*, 256, 285, 306.

9. Eisenschiml, *Why Was Lincoln Murdered?*, 58–59, 64, 185.

10. Eisenschiml, *Why Was Lincoln Murdered?*, 309–71. For a discussion of recent trends in Reconstruction historiography, see Richard O. Curry, "The Civil War and Reconstruction, 1861–1877: A Critical Overview of Recent Trends and Interpretations," in Robert P. Swierenga (ed.), *Beyond the Civil War Synthesis: Essays of the Civil War Era* (Westport, Conn.: Greenwood Press, 1975), 33–56; Stephen B. Oates, *With Malice Toward None: The Life of Abraham Lincoln* (New York: Harper & Row, 1977), 183.

boost in 1961, with the publication, in *Civil War Times*, of the discovery by chemist Ray Neff of a volume of *Colburn's United Service Magazine*, which contained a cipher message and the signature of Lafayette Baker, head of the National Detective Police. This enigmatic message read in part:

> I am constantly being followed. They are professionals, I cannot fool them. 2–5–68. In new Rome there walked three men, a Judas, a Brutus, and a spy. Each planned that he should be the kink [*sic*] when Abraham should die. One trusted not the other but they went on for that day, waiting for that final moment when with pistol in his hand, one of the sons of Brutus could sneak behind that cursed man and put a bullet in his brain and lay his clumsey corpse away. As the fallen man lay dying, Judas came and paid respects to one he hated, and when at last he saw him die, he said 'Now the ages have him and the nation now have I.' But alas [as] fate would have it Judas slowly fell from g[r]ace, and with him went Brutus down to their proper place. But lest one is left to wonder what has happened to the spy, I can safely tell you this, it was I. Lafayette C. Baker 2–5–68.[11]

This, if it could be relied on, would seem to offer verification for what Eisenschiml had hinted at.

The material appeared to be authentic, because Neff not only was able to verify that the signature was Baker's but also discovered rather conclusive corroborating evidence. In 1872, at a hearing over an unprobated codicil to Baker's will, it was revealed that although he had supposedly died poor, he in fact had $275,000 that had been appropriated after his death by his sister without anyone's knowledge. Most interesting of all was the testimony of William Carter, a former detective, who had seen Baker, his ex-boss, on June 30, 1868, just shortly before his death. Baker, who was writing in an English military journal, told Carter that he was writing his memoirs and offered him the volume.[12]

One of the most commendable things about this material at the time, however, was the fact that both Neff and *Civil War Times* editor Robert H. Fowler were very cautious in their estimates of what the cipher message might mean. Fowler reminded his readers that the mere writing of the message hardly substantiated the allegations against Stanton,

11. Robert H. Fowler, "Was Stanton Behind Lincoln's Murder?" *Civil War Times*, III (August, 1961), 10.
12. *Ibid.*, 16–23.

and Neff added, "One can readily imagine the pleasure Baker would have gotten from the knowledge that one day he would again be in the national spotlight, although dead more than ninety years, pointing the accusing finger at his 'old friends.'" It was refreshing not to see extravagant claims made over a piece of evidence the meaning of which is so difficult to determine.[13]

I have uncovered one more bit of information about this matter that, while interesting, still leaves it unexplained. Otto Eisenschiml, in the *Journal of the Illinois State Historical Society* (Summer, 1950), revealed his discovery of the May 2, 1868, *People's Weekly*, published in Baltimore by Ben Green. An article printed in that issue described Stanton's difficulties with Lincoln over the convening of the Virginia legislature. On the day after the fall of Richmond Lincoln had met with Confederate judge John Campbell and agreed that the Virginia legislature should be allowed to assemble to withdraw that state's troops from the rebellion. General Godfrey Weitzel was instructed to give the legislators the necessary protection. Stanton, however, was upset that a rebel legislature might be given official status by such action, and gave orders to disobey Lincoln's instructions as well as obtained Lincoln's consent to withdraw the permission he had given. The article then goes on to charge that Stanton, Judge Advocate Joseph Holt, Pennsylvania Congressman Thaddeus Stevens, and other Radicals engineered the elimination of Lincoln because he was too lenient.

> We have no time or space in this number to continue this subject; but our belief is that Stanton, after forcing the well meaning but too yielding, Lincoln to recall that order to Gen. Weitzell, determined to get rid of him, as an obstacle to his game of rebel hanging and plundering; and that he accomplished his purpose through that infamous adjunct of the War Department the Bureau of Military Injustice. We will explain the process in our next. If the theory of our stenographic friend be correct, then Thad Stevens, whose vindictive fury gave life to the embryo spirit of assassination in Stanton and Holt, and by the murder of Lincoln, made Johnson the 'offspring of assassination,' is now seeking to renew the old mythological fable, by 'devouring his own offspring.' Our Washington editor

13. *Ibid.*, 5, 13. Unfortunately Neff has abandoned some of this caution; he is one of the leading consultants and suppliers of documents for the book and the film entitled *The Lincoln Conspiracy*, both of which are misleading, erroneous, and sensationalist. The book is by David Balsiger and Charles E. Sellier, Jr. (Los Angeles: Schick Sunn Classic Books, 1977) and the film was released by Schick Sunn Classic Pictures, 1977.

says last week that Stanton has 'disclosed the secrets of his prison house' to an editor of the New York *Tribune*. If the secrets of his administration of the War Department and Holt's management of the Bureau of Military Injustice are ever truthfully disclosed, they will be enough to make one's hair stand on end.

Unfortunately, in the light of Green's promise to divulge further secrets, no extant copy of the next edition has ever been discovered.[14]

The striking thing is the date of May 2, 1868, for Baker's cipher message was dated 2/5/68. While this might mean February 5, 1868, it could also be taken to be May 2, 1868, if the day and month were arranged in that order. If Baker's date is taken as May 2, this might be a coincidence, but it may well have been this article that was the catalyst for Baker's writing the cipher message. The probability of the correctness of this interpretation is further reinforced by the internal evidence of the message, for the second part read:

> On the thirteenth he [Stanton] discovered that the President had ordered that the legislature of Virginia be allowed to assemble to withdraw that states troops, from action against the U. S. He fermented immediately into an insane tyrade. Then for the first time I realized his mental disunity and his insane and fanatical hatred for the president. There are few in the War Department that respect the president or his strategy but there [are] not many who would countermand an order that the pres[ident] had given. However during that insane moment he sent a telegram to Gen. Weitzel countermanding the presidents order of the twelfth. Then he laughed in a most spine chilling manner and said, "If he would to know who rescinded his order we will let Lucifer tell him. Be off Tom [Eckert?] and see to the arrangements."[15]

While Baker was mistaken about dates and certain aspects of these events, the article in *People's Weekly* shows the same stress on the difficulties between Lincoln, Campbell, Weitzel, and Stanton over the convening of the Virginia legislature. This seems to be a further suggestion of the connection between the newspaper and Baker's cipher message.

14. Eisenschiml, "Addenda to Lincoln's Assassination," 96. Interestingly, Green himself had been charged in 1865 with having prior knowledge of the assassination. See N. A. Patterson to Andrew Johnson, May 18, 1865, in Letters Received, File P 514, Judge Advocate's Office (hereinafter cited as JAO), 1865, RG 153, "Records of the Office of the Judge Advocate General, Investigation and Trial Papers Relating to the Assassination of President Lincoln," National Archives (hereinafter cited as NA).
15. Fowler, "Was Stanton Behind Lincoln's Murder?," 10.

However, even if this interpretation is correct, one still wonders what Baker had in mind when he left the message and why he attempted to give a volume containing part of it to one of his former agents. Was it anything more than a malignant joke against Stanton after reading a derogatory newspaper article, or was there indeed some truth behind it? Or was Baker really so afraid about attempts against his life that he feared imminent death and decided that his old friends should not escape unscathed if they were responsible? In some ways his allegations would appear to be weakened by his statement that over one hundred high-ranking northerners were involved. Secrecy on the part of so many individuals seems doubtful, and if someone was really trying to kill Baker, there might have been many who thought they had good reason to do so.[16]

It is also strange that Baker, at least in an indirect manner, would implicate himself so strongly in the conspiracy. He was undoubtedly aware that had such evidence come to light in his own lifetime, his part in the affair would have brought him just as much difficulty as it would have brought to Stanton, whereas revelations after his death would have tarnished his historical image.

However, this was far from the final shot in the escalation of the conspiracy controversy for, in 1965, Vaughan Shelton wrote *Mask for Treason*, which attempted to alter radically the entire conception of the conspiracy. One of Shelton's key allegations was that Lewis Paine (whose real name was Louis Thornton Powell) had not really been Secretary William H. Seward's assailant. In his view, the youthful giant who had stumbled into Mrs. Surratt's parlor on April 17 was, in fact, Powell's third cousin, Hugh Louis Payne. According to Shelton, Powell was an agent of Lafayette Baker, and his job was to see that Booth carried out Lincoln's murder in the proper manner. The assault on Seward was not even a direct part of the Lincoln conspiracy, in which plot Seward himself was very likely involved. But since many people had knowledge of the plot, someone, probably Major Eckert, saw an opportunity to eliminate the secretary of state and contracted with Powell to kill Seward also. When look-alike cousin Louis Payne showed up at the Surratt house, Baker seized the opportunity and had him arrested.

16. *Ibid.* Balsiger and Sellier, *The Lincoln Conspiracy*, charge that Baker was poisoned by his brother-in-law.

Baker then masterminded the trial, giving the public the scapegoats for whom they clamored, while protecting his own treachery and that of other northern officials and allowing his hired assassin to escape.[17]

Shelton tries to bolster his thesis by arguing that handbills described Paine so completely they could only have been produced after the government had someone in custody. He also claims that witnesses who could have confirmed the existence of two separate individuals were coerced to support the government version of events. Thus Margaret Branson, at whose mother's home Paine had stayed in Baltimore, was frightened into verifying the prosecution story. Furthermore, the existence of her sister, Mary, who was romantically linked with Paine, was not even made known.[18]

His strongest attack, however, centers on the discrepancies he feels he sees in the testimony of members of the Seward household involving the assassination events. Shelton arrived at his view by comparing Benn Pitman's version of the trial testimony, which he considered to be the government's edited version, with T. B. Peterson's version, which he feels is independent and unbiased. By making this comparison he discovered that Seward's servant, Bell, and Seward's son, Augustus, supported the orthodox historical version that Augustus had been aroused by the commotion and entered his father's room, first believing himself to be grappling with Seward's nurse, George Robinson, who he thought had lost his mind and was assaulting his father, and then helping Robinson to eject the assassin. Since Robinson, however, was rather vague in his testimony on the subject, merely referring to someone coming to his aid, Shelton concluded that his helper was Emrick Hansell of the State Department, who was also wounded in the assassination attempt. Shelton believed it was very likely that Augustus Seward was not even in the house, since no one mentioned seeing him there. He further believed that Augustus' own statement belied the fact that he believed himself grappling with the nurse, for Robinson was a

17. Vaughan Shelton, *Mask for Treason* (Harrisburg: Stackpole Books, 1965), 401–403; Robert H. Fowler, "New Evidence in Lincoln Murder Conspiracy," *Civil War Times Illustrated*, III (February, 1965), 4–11.

18. Shelton, *Mask for Treason*, 40–42, 47, 213. He erroneously claims that depositions of Mary and Margaret Branson were destroyed, but they still remain in the NA files. See Mary and Margaret Branson, May 1, 1865, in Statements, Letters Received, File B 428, JAO, 1865, RG 153, NA.

black man and Augustus could not have possibly mistaken him for the assassin in the lighted hallway. Shelton also implies that Secretary Seward may not have been seriously injured in the fall from his carriage but was using this to cover his own involvement in the Lincoln assassination.[19]

Of such stuff is historical myth made, however, for Shelton was not aware that George Robinson was white, not black. Also there is indisputable evidence that the events at the Seward house transpired pretty much the way the participants recounted them and that the assailant was Lewis Paine or Powell, not some mythical cousin.

Despite all the obvious errors in Shelton's book he did uncover one very disturbing piece of evidence, the R. D. Watson letter, which was mentioned during the conspiracy trial and which reads: "New York, March 19th, 1865 Mr. J. H. Surratt Dear Sir I would like to see you on important business, if you can spare the time to come to New York. Please Telegraph me immediately on the reception of this whether you can come or not and much oblige Yours tr—— R. D. Watson P. S. Address Care Demill and Co. 178½ Water Street." The disturbing thing about this letter is that Shelton claimed to have discovered that its author was none other than Lafayette Baker.[20] While *Civil War Times Illustrated*'s handwriting expert could not be so positive that the Watson letter was written by Baker, the magazine did manage to tie the address on the letter to Baker, claiming that this was a company with which both Baker and Booth had dealings.

As to why Baker was in touch with Surratt, to Shelton the answer seems obvious—to arrange the details of the assassination. Shelton lets Stanton off with only possessing some knowledge of the plot but claims that Baker was the prime mover.[21]

Shelton makes other charges, for he believes that Mrs. Surratt may well have had some role in the assassination. According to him the field glasses that she carried to her tenant, John Lloyd, contained poison that David Herold was to slip into the whiskey that Booth drank. Since

19. Shelton, *Mask for Treason*, Chap. IX, 435–48.
20. R. D. Watson to John H. Surratt, March 19, 1865, in Letters Received, File H 398, JAO, RG 153, NA; Shelton, *Mask for Treason*, 322, 424. Balsiger and Sellier, *The Lincoln Conspiracy*, refer to the shipping company as the Chaffey Shipping Company.
21. Fowler, "New Evidence in Lincoln Murder Conspiracy," 9; Shelton, *Mask for Treason*, 135, 322, 432.

Booth did not drink deeply enough, he lingered on in agony but did not die. Shelton suggests that when the fugitives met Confederate soldiers William Jett, A. R. Bainbridge, and Mortimer B. Ruggles at the Rappahannock, Herold informed them concerning what he had on his hands and the fifty-thousand-dollar reward they might earn. They then decided to hide Booth with farmer Richard H. Garrett while Jett hastened to Richmond to attempt to contact the authorities. Meanwhile, the detectives stumbled on Booth's track and took care of all future difficulties with a bullet. Shelton does admit that there is a mystery as to why Mrs. Surratt and Herold did not talk but concludes that Mrs. Surratt acted to protect her daughter, Anna, and Herold was afraid to admit his own guilt and the attempt to poison Booth. Shelton never really does make it clear why Herold would still refuse to talk when he was about to die anyway.[22]

Shelton attempts to prove too much without possessing the necessary depth of historical background to deal with his topic. His claims that Herold attempted to poison Booth are little more than unsubstantiated conjecture based largely on Booth's supposed illness at this period, coupled with the fact that Dr. Mudd had said that the leg wound was really not dangerous. However, while Mudd had made such a statement, he also admitted in the next breath that he really did not know much about that type of wound. On the other hand the New York *Tribune* reported on April 29, 1865, "The surgeons who held the autopsy upon Booth assert that he must have endured untold anguish of body, as well as of mind, from the nature of the fracture of his leg, the small bone having cut its way through the flesh and protruded." Ruggles, who was an experienced soldier and had examined the injury at Garrett's, believed that even amputation might not have saved Booth from death by gangrene. If true, this would seem to weaken Shelton's poison theory.[23]

---

22. Shelton, *Mask for Treason*, 276, 310–11, 317–19, 419–21. Viewing Mrs. Surratt as perhaps involved is unusual, since most conspiracy writers see her as an innocent victim. For another argument of her possible involvement, see Theodore Roscoe, *The Web of Conspiracy* (Englewood Cliffs, N.J.: Prentice-Hall, 1959), 250.

23. Samuel Mudd, April 21, 1865, Statement, in Record Book, File M, p. 66, JAO, RG 153, NA; New York *Tribune*, April 29, 1865, p. 5; Prentiss Ingraham, "Pursuit and Death of John Wilkes Booth," *Century Magazine*, XXXIX (1890), 444, 446; Stanley Kimmel, *The Mad Booths of Maryland* (Indianapolis: Bobbs Merrill, 1940), 251.

It was unfortunate that Shelton lacked a deeper background, for despite his erroneous assumptions, the Watson letter remains, and so does the alleged connection of John Wilkes Booth and Lafayette Baker with a New York shipping company. In the light of one piece of evidence, another piece that before seemed meaningless may take on added significance. Henry Ste. Marie, John Surratt's old schoolmate and fellow Papal Zouave, said of one conversation with Surratt in a statement dated July 10, 1866: "He says he does not regret what has taken place, and that he will visit New York in a year or two, as there is a heavy shipping firm there who had much to do with the South, and he is surprised that they have not been suspected." On June 21, Ste. Marie had already written to Rufus King, American minister to Rome, that Surratt claimed to have acted on the instructions of certain persons, whom he did not name, some of whom were in New York and others in London. While this is hardly conclusive, it suggests the question as to whether Surratt was hinting at the involvement of DeMill and Company.[24]

Also, despite overwhelming evidence that Paine and Powell were the same person and Seward's assailant, Shelton might have discovered other evidence to bolster his case, and it is not inconceivable that there were some yet undiscovered conspirators involved. The Washington *Evening Star* of April 18, 1865, for example, carried the following description of Seward's assassin, which was supposed to have been given by George Robinson: "The villain was about six feet in height, of medium-sized round face, of extremely light complexion, with light sandy hair, and whiskers and moustache, both light in color and in growth, and was broad shouldered." While this was apparently merely an erroneous report, as it was carried by no other source, the similarity of the description to John Surratt is striking.[25]

If inclined to Shelton's view about Paine and Powell, one might ponder the meaning of the following from the Missouri *Republican*. "At

24. Lee F. Stock (ed.), *United States Ministers to the Papal States: Instructions and Despatches, 1848–1868* (2 vols.; Washington: Catholic University Press, 1933), I, 368; United States Court of Claims, *Henry B. Ste. Marie v. the United States Amended Petition No. 6415, May 6, 1873,* 20–23.

25. Washington *Evening Star*, April 18, 1865, p. 1. See also Hartford *Daily Courant*, April 19, 1865, p. 2, which carries the same interview with Robinson but lacks his assailant's description.

the evidence of one witness, who testified that Payne was a man named Wood [one of Paine's aliases], Harrold [Herold] thought it so good a joke that he laughed outright in court." This could be supported by a New York *Times* article on January 19, 1869, containing an alleged confession by George Atzerodt in which he said that he saw on the assassination night "Booth, Wood and Payne in Wood's room." While this might be nothing more than a typographical error and the *Times* does not reveal the source of this confession, the statement does provide some food for speculation.[26]

This is not to argue too strongly for any of the foregoing points, all of which are very far from proven, but merely to show that while authors like Shelton have been busy stretching dubious material to fit their theories, there exists other material that makes even the serious historian pause to wonder. Although many points in the conspiracy theories are obviously false, others cannot be dismissed without further investigation. This is still an area where more research needs to be done, although the very nature of the subject makes the task slow and the results far from certain.

This call for additional careful research has hardly been met in the latest and in many ways the most unfortunate work ever undertaken on the assassination, *The Lincoln Conspiracy*, in both the book and movie versions. Severe doubt has already been cast on several of its major assumptions, but the wide circulation it has received has established an image in the public mind that will be difficult to erase.

The Lincoln Conspiracy authors make the modest claim to have advanced research more in twelve months than in the last 112 years and they proceed, using new documents, including the recently discovered "missing pages" of Booth's diary to give us the truth about the assassination. In their view, the assassination was the culmination of several plots occurring simultaneously with the purpose of kidnapping or eliminating the president. Booth was at the center of three of these groups: (1) Maryland planters who included Dr. Mudd; (2) Confederate agents Jacob Thompson and Clement Clay, who were based in Canada and had commissioned Booth a colonel in the Confederate de-

26. Missouri *Republican*, quoted in New Orleans *Times-Picayune*, May 19, 1865, p. 4; New York *Times*, January 19, 1869, p. 8. A similar undated copy of the confession is found in the papers of George P. Fisher, LC.

tached service; and (3) a group of northern businessmen and bankers that included people like Jay Cooke and even Lincoln's friend, Ward Hill Lamon. There was a natural tie between the latter two groups, since the businessmen's motivation was their own enrichment through cotton speculation. In addition, there was a northern plot, led by the Radical Republicans to get rid of Lincoln, Andrew Johnson, and Seward, making it appear to be the work of the Confederacy so that the Radicals could seize power and carry out their vindictive policies.[27]

Such maneuverings could hardly be kept secret, however, and Lafayette Baker learned of Booth's involvement in the plots. He also noticed the suspicious transfer of Captain James W. Boyd to Old Capitol Prison, which he felt might be part of the conspiracy. Indeed, he proved to be a good prophet, as Booth was fired as head of the bankers and speculators' plot and replaced by Boyd. But Booth was not one to be dismissed so easily, and when he persisted in his own attempts, he was visited by Baker and Colonel Everton Conger. Conger warned Booth that he and his group had been acting like fools and that he should either stay out of the way or end up in the Potomac.

Baker ultimately confronted Secretary Stanton with his discoveries and indicated his belief that Major Eckert had made arrangements for Lincoln's assassination. This caused Stanton to produce a document that would prove that Baker and Vice-President Johnson were plotting to kidnap Lincoln. Baker later told one of his detectives that it was Stanton who had rescinded Lincoln's order regarding the convening of the Virginia legislature and had sent Eckert off to make the assassination arrangements.

Before any of these plots could come to fruition, however, Booth in his own desperation had decided upon murder. To aid him in this scheme he enlisted Ed Henson who, like Booth, had been engaged in smuggling for the Confederacy. While not revealing his intentions directly to Henson, Booth told him that if he was looking for excitement he should meet him at Good Hope Hill, Maryland, near midnight on April 14. Henson kept the appointment and it was he, not David Herold, who escaped with Booth.

David Herold, who had been involved with Booth's kidnapping

27. Balsiger and Sellier, *The Lincoln Conspiracy*, 38–62.

schemes, innocently entered the picture when, having ridden down into Maryland with a sixteen-year-old neighbor to do some drinking, he was discovered asleep on a porch by Baker's detectives. He was taken back to Washington where he and James Boyd, who had also been captured, were told by Baker that they must lead him to Booth or their own lives were forfeit. Baker was in charge of the pursuit, having been summoned to Washington by Stanton, who was in near panic for fear his own involvement in the kidnappings and assassination might be revealed.

Baker put his best detectives on the trail, including ace Indian tracker, Whippet Nalgai. Nalgai discovered Booth's diary, which Booth had lost, and the detectives noticed all the damaging entries. The diary was returned to Stanton, who ordered Eckert to place it in a safe; the damaging pages were apparently then removed.

Meanwhile, other Baker detectives who were escorting Herold and Boyd through Maryland in search of Booth carelessly allowed them to escape. It was Boyd and Herold who met the three Confederate soldiers and were led to Garrett's barn, where Boyd was killed and Herold captured. When Baker informed Stanton of the error, it was decided to accept the corpse as Booth and to silence the other alleged conspirators by holding a military trial and executing them.

Baker's detectives had surmised by now that Ed Henson was accompanying Booth and that the pair was probably trying to escape by giving a false trail and going north. While the detectives came close to finding Booth, he escaped, going to England and perhaps even India. Lafayette Baker was ultimately silenced when he was secretly poisoned by his brother-in-law.[28]

On the face of it much of this sounds like a wildly improbable tale that a careful historian would probe and test before rushing into print. The major contentions of *The Lincoln Conspiracy* have already been called into question, thanks to the work of William C. Davis, *Civil War Times Illustrated*'s editor. Davis points out that none of these new documents have been independently verified and that many are certainly suspicious. As he notes, Booth's so-called diary was in reality an appointment book, and there is no good evidence that Booth kept a diary

28. *Ibid.*, 54–302 *passim*.

or even had the temperament to be a diarist. Also while eighteen missing pages have supposedly been found, a check at the museum in Ford's Theatre reveals that thirty-six pages are missing.

Similar doubt is cast on the papers of the shipping firm of Chaffey and Biggs, which is not listed in any New York directory or newspaper and whose ledgers are illegible in an era when mercantile firms employed scribes specifically for their permanship. In addition, the diary of Indiana Congressman George W. Julian, which purportedly mentions a meeting where the Radicals discussed the finding of Booth's diary and the damaging revelations, was previously published in 1924 by a historian who had no love for the Radicals and hence no motivation to suppress anything damaging to them. It contained no such entry.[29]

The most damaging discovery, however, concerns the alleged substitution of Boyd for Booth. Davis noted that a number of careful investigators had laid the myth of Booth's escape to rest and that it would be difficult to believe that Booth, who was twenty-five, 5'8" tall, and had black hair and dark eyes, could be mistaken for Boyd, who was forty-two, 6'2" tall, with grey hair and blue eyes. The most conclusive evidence, though, was Davis' discovery and verification through family records and obituaries that Boyd was killed while a member of a posse, in January, 1866, eight months after he supposedly died in Garrett's barn.[30]

If this central claim is wrong, then most of these new documents that are so intricately linked together to prove this thesis seem to be part of an elaborate forgery. While the authors of *The Lincoln Conspiracy* may themselves have unwittingly taken a part in this duplicity, because of their uncritical acceptance of such dubious material, they must still bear a large responsibility for perpetrating this fraud on the American public.

This brief survey of the historiographical trends reveals that histori-

29. William C. Davis, "Behind the Lines: Caveat Emptor," *Civil War Times Illustrated*, XVI (August, 1977), 33–37.
30. William C. Davis, "Behind the Lines: 'The Lincoln Conspiracy'—Hoax?," *Civil War Times Illustrated*, XVI (November, 1977), 47–49. For another important critique of *The Lincoln Conspiracy*, as well as a discussion of the major exploitation literature, see Harold M. Hyman, *With Malice Toward Some: Scholarship (or Something Less) on the Lincoln Murder* (Springfield, Ill.: Abraham Lincoln Association, 1978).

ans have tended to distort what really happened in 1865 and 1867. Historians have belabored the obvious, raised false issues, and proposed fantastic conspiracy theories that do not stand up to careful scrutiny. Such distortions will become even more evident in the following examination of assassination events.

2.

A Brief Era of
Good Feeling

And maybe, too, it is good for us now and then to put ourselves back in the places of the people who had to live through these terrible moments, so that we can understand that history does not usually make real sense until long afterward.

Dorothy M. Kunhardt and Phillip B. Kunhardt, Jr., *Twenty Days*

On the evening of April 14, 1865, John Wilkes Booth assassinated Abraham Lincoln as he sat in Ford's Theatre watching the play *Our American Cousin*. At the same time, Lewis Paine attempted unsuccessfully to kill Secretary of State William Seward, wounding him and several other members of his household. These events produced shock waves among the American people that were to be deep and lasting. The celebration of the war's end ceased and the national mood turned to despair and anger.

The early days of this same month witnessed the beginning of the end of the Confederate States of America. On the evening of April 2, President Jefferson Davis departed the city of Richmond by train, along with most of his cabinet. The next day Union troops under General Weitzel replaced the Confederate Flag with the Stars and Stripes. Tuesday, April 4, the New York *Times* carried the following headlines: THE GLORIOUS NEWS, ENTHUSIASM SOLEMNITY AND THANKSGIVING, BUSINESS SUSPENDED AND FLAGS DISPLAYED, THE PRAISE OF THE ARMY ON EVERY TONGUE, GREAT MASS MEETINGS IN WALL STREET AND AT UNION SQUARE, PATRIOTIC SPEECHES AND PATRIOTIC SONGS, and WHOLE CITY AGLOW WITH EXCITEMENT ILLUMINATIONS AND FIREWORKS.[1]

Three thousand miles away in San Francisco, the citizens received the news with a similarly festive attitude. "Some huzzaed and t'rew up

---

1. New York *Times*, April 4, 1865, p. 1.

their hats; some drank brandy-punche and champagne cocktails; some commenced kindling bonfires and discharging rockets." In Philadelphia, a citizen aptly expressed the views of many when he exclaimed to the editor of the Philadelphia *Evening Bulletin*, "It sounds like hell let loose, but it feels like paradise regained."[2]

Rapidly following the news of Richmond's fall came word of the surrender of Robert E. Lee to Ulysses S. Grant at Appomattox Court House, on April 9, producing unabashed jubilation. The Reverend A. L. Stone told his congregation of April 13, a day set aside for fasting, "Last week we could not restrain our joy; but this week the tide is higher." Again the New York *Times* announced in bold headlines UNION VICTORY PEACE. Editorially, a hope was expressed that the profound joy of the nation would not be shown merely in effervescent enthusiasm and huzzahs but would "appear in the form in which it is so fitly and opportunely proclaimed by the Secretary of War—ascriptions of praise to Almighty God and offering of honor to the great leader of our armies whom he has used as his instrument to save the nation."[3]

At Washington some people did respond in the prescribed manner, when two thousand people under the lead of Mr. Sipes united with impressive effect in singing the doxology "Praise God from Whom All Blessings Flow." The procession then proceeded to the White House, where President Lincoln told the crowd: "I have always thought Dixie was one of the best tunes I had ever heard. Our adversaries over the way, I know, have attempted to appropriate it, but I insist that on yesterday we fairly captured it. (applause). I referred the question to the Attorney General and he gave it as his legal opinion that it was now our property (laughter and loud applause). I now ask the band to favor us with its performance."[4]

Most people, while undoubtedly thankful to God for delivering them, were more influenced by the feeling of levity that seized the crowd listening to the president and, despite the Lenten season, pre-

2. San Francisco *Chronicle*, April 4, 1865, p. 2; Philadelphia *Evening Bulletin*, April 4, 1865, p. 4.
3. A. L. Stone, *Fasting and Feasting: A Discourse Delivered Before the Park Street Congregation on the Occasion of the Annual State Fast, Thursday, April 13, 1865* (Boston: Henry Holt, 1865), 4; New York *Times*, April 10, 1865, p. 4.
4. Washington *Evening Star*, April 14, 1865, p. 2.

ferred to celebrate in a more boisterous manner. At Harvard College, student J. L. Sibley jotted in his diary: "The people are wild with enthusiasm at the news of the surrender of the rebel General Lee. It exceeds anything I have ever known. The papers will be full of details. Another holiday in college. Illuminations, speeches, all round the country." The celebration at Wilmington, Delaware, was typical of the celebrations that occurred in hundreds of other communities, with guns firing, bells ringing, a large procession through the streets, and such excitement as was never before witnessed in that city. At the nation's capital the celebration rivaled if it did not surpass them all. "The very heavens seemed to have come down, and the stars twinkled in a sort of faded way, as if the solar system was out of order, and earth had become the great illuminary. Everybody illuminated. Every flag was flung out, windows were gay with many devices, and gorgeous lanterns danced on their ropes along the walls in a fantastic way, as if the fairies were holding holiday inside." Even Secretary Stanton, intoxicated with the happiness of victory, thought to hang over his portico a cunning arrangement of gas jets that spelled PEACE.[5]

This outpouring of joy seemed to many to be the preview for an era of renewed brotherhood. The New York *Times* reminded its readers that "the hour of victory is always the hour for clemency—always the hour for the easiest winning of the hearts of the vanquished." On Lee's surrender the Philadelphia *Evening Bulletin* added that Grant had given terms more generous than those usually given to a defeated enemy, but the country was ready to acquiesce in anything the general directed.[6]

Such views were certainly widespread; the New York *Tribune* headline read MAGNANIMITY IN TRIUMPH, and the editors went on to say they had hoped to print the president's amnesty proclamation and thus record the final chapter of the battered rebellion. It had not yet been received, but they still had hopes of obtaining it before press time.

---

5. W. G. R., '09, (ed.), "Harvard and the Tragedy of 1865: Diary of John Langdon Sibley," in *Harvard Alumni Bulletin*, April 26, 1940, p. 899; New York *Times*, April 10, 1865, p. 1; Washington *Evening Star*, April 14, 1865, p. 1; Lloyd Lewis, *Myths After Lincoln* (New York: Harcourt Brace, 1929), 49. Although historians have neglected this vast outpouring of emotion, Lewis was one of the few to capture it adequately and to sense something of its importance.

6. New York *Times*, April 5, 1865, p. 4; Philadelphia *Evening Bulletin*, April 10, 1865, p. 4.

Reverend Samuel T. Spear, in a discourse after the assassination, re-called that he had heard a loyal gentleman propose that Robert E. Lee be made a major general in the United States Army, as the best way to relieve the mortification of defeat and conciliate the southern mind. He added, "Public opinion was drifting in this direction." The Reverend Henry Ward Beecher preached a sermon entitled "Love Your Neighbor, the Nation's Motto," in which his major theme was that Jefferson Davis should be allowed to go away into exile and in which he warned against employing vengeance in the guise of justice.[7]

On the surface, one might get the impression that with this era of renewed brotherhood at hand, the assassination was the major, if not the only, reason that this feeling was dispelled. Many historians have completely forgotten the bitterness engendered by four years of war, as well as the events leading up to the war. Their view was that once the war was over, there should have been a mild peace, with the nation entering on a tranquil course almost immediately. However, it seems more realistic to view such conciliatory expressions as merely a first exuberant outbreak, with the understanding that the nation would have been faced with harsher realities before long, even if the assassination had not occurred. Although Lincoln would undoubtedly have at-tempted to impose a lenient peace, and with more skill than Johnson, forces for a harsh reconstruction would still have been at work. Even while these expressions of good feeling were being uttered, an under-lying hostility was still apparent. It was little wonder that such feelings of violence and vengeance immediately surfaced after the assassination.

Hostile sentiments were especially reserved for the rebel leaders, wherever they might be found. On two separate occasions, the New York *Times* criticized the New York *Tribune* because the latter had called for a free pardon for Jefferson Davis. If he managed to get away, said the *Times*, that was all right, but if he were captured, the only fitting penalty was for him to be hanged. Some sermons also revealed vindic-tive feelings on the part of ministers even before the assassination oc-curred. The Reverend Thomas Laurie reminded his congregation of the harsh treatment of Union prisoners by the South and said that

7. New York *Tribune*, April 11, 1865, p. 4; New York *Times*, April 6, p. 8, April 11, 1865, p. 4; Samuel T. Spear, *The Punishment of Treason* (Brooklyn: *Union* Steam Presses, 1865), 13.

while he knew that Scripture said vengeance belonged to the Lord, he was not calling for vengeance but for justice.[8]

Hints of future violence were also clearly visible. A crowd outside Stanton's window at the War Department on the fall of Richmond heard the secretary beg Providence "to teach us how to be humble in the midst of triumph"; but when someone said Richmond was in flames, the crowd roared "Let 'er burn." A vindictive speech by Vice-President Johnson, in which he called for the hanging of Jefferson Davis twenty times over because treason is the greatest of crimes, brought a call of "Hang him!" from the crowd. After Lincoln's rather moderate speech to a crowd gathered at the White House on Tuesday, April 11, the second speaker, Iowa Senator James Harlan, made the mistake of asking what should be done with the rebels. Again came the cry of "Hang him!" And when Harlan suggested that the president might use the pardon power, the crowd roared as one, "Never!"[9]

The foregoing "era of good feeling," with certain minor exceptions, might almost be regarded as unimportant and not really connected with the assassination, except that it brings into sharp relief the revulsion that occurred after Lincoln's death. In fact, there is a good deal of evidence that the violence which the country underwent was much more severe because of the kindly sentiments, however transient, that had preceded it. The nation seemed to experience a feeling of betrayal. It was as if the prodigal son had been about to be welcomed home with celebration and the killing of the fatted calf, when suddenly it was discovered that the prodigal not only was not penitent but had suddenly seized a dagger and plunged it into his father's back. Many people felt, with apparent justification, that the assassination might revive the dying Confederacy.[10]

The number of commentators who mentioned this rapid change from joy to despair is eloquent testimony to the influence the assassi-

---

8. New York *Times*, April 12, 1865, p. 4; Thomas Laurie, *Three Discourses Preached in the South Evangelical Church, West Roxbury, Mass., April 13th, 19th, and 23rd, 1865* (Dedham, Mass.: John Cox Jr., 1865), 10. See also Stone, *Fasting and Feasting*, 12–13.

9. Jim Bishop, *The Day Lincoln Was Shot* (New York: Harper and Bros., 1955), 44, 46, 53.

10. Abott A. Abott, *The Assassination and Death of Abraham Lincoln, President of the United States of America, at Washington, on the 14th of April, 1865* (New York: American News, 1865), 11.

nation had. The New York *Herald* said, on Sunday, April 16: "The sun set last night upon a jubilant and rejoicing people. The whole nation was exhilirated with the success which had attended our armies in the field and the final overthrow of the rebellion. But it rose this morning upon a sorrow-stricken people." In Columbus, Ohio, Senator John Sherman wrote: "The change from joy to mourning that day in Columbus was marked and impressive. No event of my life created a more painful impression than this news following the rejoicings of the day before."[11]

A rapid revulsion also set in against what many people now considered to have been Lincoln's too lenient policy towards rebels and traitors. The Chicago *Tribune* said that "yesterday we were with the late President, for lenity; he had been so often right and wise; he had so won our confidence that we were preparing to follow and support him in a policy of conciliatory kindness; today we are with the people for justice." One anonymous writer, who claimed to have been a copperhead, advised the government that its duty was to hang every rebel caught. He could have felt no worse had his own mother or father been slain and would personally volunteer to shoot every southern man. This ex-copperhead closed by saying, "Although I was a Copperhead, I can safely say that you cannot find a Copperhead in the whole North today." In New York, George T. Strong wrote in his diary that public feeling had reverted to what it had been four years ago when the news of Fort Sumter had aroused the North to the danger it faced.[12]

The views of many who had previously been moderate changed. William Lloyd Garrison, the famous abolitionist who had previously opposed capital punishment, called during a speech in New York for the hanging of Jefferson Davis. The Boston *Evening Transcript* allowed, however, that in this case few would be disposed to blame Mr. Garrison for his inconsistency.[13]

11. New York *Herald*, April 16, 1865, p. 1; John Sherman, *Recollections* (2 vols.; Chicago: Warner, 1896), I, 354.

12. Chicago *Tribune*, April 17, 1865, p. 2; Anonymous to Edwin Stanton, April 15, 1865, in Letters Received, File A 81, JAO, RG 153, NA; Allan Nevins and Milton Thomas (eds.), *Diary of George T. Strong* (4 vols.; New York: MacMillan, 1952), IV, 583. Strong was a New York lawyer, trustee of Columbia College, and a member of the Sanitary Commission during the Civil War. The diary he kept between 1835 and 1875 presents a stirring national record of the Civil War period.

13. Boston *Evening Transcript*, May 10, 1865, p. 2.

Similarly, ministers who had spoken of love and conciliation on the preceding fast day, April 13, were now often more vindictive than the members of their congregations. Reverend Maxwell P. Gaddis, only a few hours after a moderate sermon, went on to preach one of the bitterest sermons produced on the assassination.[14]

It is apparent that John Wilkes Booth's pistol ball entered the heart of the nation just as surely as it pierced Lincoln's body. Where previously there had been hope of conciliation and a feeling of celebration, there was now only despair. This despair rapidly turned to anger and thoughts of vengeance. What was to occur in the future was well foreshadowed in "The Martyr" by Herman Melville:

> He lieth in his blood—
> The Father in his face;
> They have killed him, the forgiver—
> The Avenger takes his place. . . .
>
> There is sobbing of the strong,
> And a pall upon the land;
> But the people in their weeping
> Bare the iron hand:
> Beware the People weeping
> When they bare the iron hand.[15]

---

14. Charles J. Stewart, "The Pulpit and the Assassination of Lincoln," *Quarterly Journal of Speech*, L (1964), 299; Maxwell P. Gaddis, *Sermon Upon the Assassination of Abraham Lincoln, Delivered in Pikes Opera House, April 16, 1865* (Cincinnati: *Times* Steam Book and Job Office, 1865), 4.

15. Hennig Cohen (ed.), *The Battle-Pieces of Herman Melville* (New York: Thomas Yoseloff, 1964), 130.

3.

Good Feeling Turns to Fury

In the theater the reaction to the assassination was swift and elemental. The screams of Mrs. Lincoln and the cry of Major Rathbone to "stop that man" echoed in the hushed theater, but the momentary silence was shattered by awful pandemonium as people instinctively began to realize what had occurred. Walt Whitman, though not present at the assassination, nonetheless described very well the tumultuous nature of the scene.

> A moment's strange incredulous suspense and then the deluge—people burst through chairs and railings and break them up—there is inextricable confusion and terror—women faint—quiet, feeble persons fall and are trampled on—many cries of agony are heard—the broad stage fills to suffocation with a dense and motley crowd like some horrible carnival—two or three manage to pass up water from the stage to the President's box—others try to clamber up.
>
> In the midst of all this the soldiers of the President's Guard, with others, suddenly drawn to the scene, burst in (some two hundred altogether); they storm the house, through all the tiers, especially the upper one, inflamed with fury, literally charging the audience with fixed bayonets muskets and pistols, shouting 'Clear out! Clear out!'[1]

Almost immediately there were cries to hang the assassin and burn the theater. Calls for destruction of the theater were a natural result of the assassination having occurred there, as well as the fact that Booth was an actor. Antitheatrical sentiment was to swell in the following weeks. Henry Hawk, a member of the cast of *Our American Cousin*, feared for his safety so much that he attempted to leave Washington for Philadelphia but was unsuccessful because the trains were not running. His fears were not groundless since a storekeeper near Ford's Theatre who defended the theatrical people found himself with a rope around

---

1. Richard M. Bucke, Thomas B. Harned, and Horace L. Traubel (eds.), *The Complete Writings of Walt Whitman* (10 vols.; New York: G. P. Putnam's Sons, 1902), V, 250–51; Lloyd Lewis, *Myths After Lincoln* (New York: Harcourt Brace, 1929), 54.

his neck and was just barely rescued by authorities from the angry mob. Even as far away as Columbus, Ohio, actress Clara Morris reported that the police feared that theaters and actors might be the subject of mob violence.[2]

The suspicion also began to grow that Booth must have had help in the theater to succeed. The New York *Herald* on April 23 reported that all the other boxes in the theater were purposely empty to aid Booth's escape, and Captain George Bell reported to Secretary Stanton that at the time Booth fired, the passageway through which he escaped was less crowded than at almost any other time during the play. Corporal James Tanner, who had taken the initial testimony on the assassination night, wrote on April 17, "I have an idea, which is gaining ground here, and that is that the assassin had assistance in the theatre, and that the President was invited there for the express purpose of assassinating him." It was apparently under the sting of such criticism that John T. Ford felt compelled to write the *Herald*, saying how pained he was to learn that people who should know his loyalty were criticizing him because a rebel band had played at his theater in Baltimore.[3]

Outside of Ford's Washington theater on the assassination night, there was a terrible storm of emotion as the dying president was carried across the street to the Petersen House. Correspondent George Alfred Townsend captured it vividly in his usual purple prose, "A conflagration of fire is not half so terrible as the conflagration of passion that rolled through the streets and houses of Washington on that awful night."[4]

To those who spoke ill of Lincoln, vengeance was swift and irreversible. On the street a man shouted, "I'm glad it happened." In a moment, he was scuffed underfoot, had most of his clothes torn from his body, and was barely rescued by three policemen with drawn revolvers as he was being hustled to a nearby lamppost. Senator William Stewart,

2. Boston *Herald*, April 11, 1897, p. 28; W. J. Ferguson, *I Saw Booth Shoot Lincoln* (Boston: Houghton Mifflin, 1930), 58; Clara Morris, "Some Recollections of John Wilkes Booth," *McClure's Magazine*, XVI (1901), 303.

3. New York *Herald*, April 23, 1865, p. 8; George Bell to Edwin Stanton, April 26, 1865, in Letters Received, File B 579, JAO, RG 153, NA; James Tanner, "Letter to Henry F. Walch, Washington, April 17, 1865," *American Historical Review*, XXIX (1884), 517.

4. George A. Townsend, *The Life, Crime and Capture of John Wilkes Booth with a Full Sketch of the Conspiracy of Which He Was the Leader, and the Pursuit, Trial and Execution of His Accomplices* (New York: Dick and Fitzgerald, 1865), 10.

who walked the streets that night, fully expected to see the soldiers fall on unarmed paroled southerners and slay them. "A bloody battle which would have shocked humanity was averted a thousand times that night by a miracle." Charles Sabin Taft, one of the attending physicians, recorded the ugly mood of the crowd as the hearse bearing Lincoln's body made its way to the White House. "One man who ventured a shout for Jefferson Davis was set upon and nearly torn to pieces by the infuriated crowd."[5]

The response of one group of people to the assassination was particularly touching—that of the blacks, to whom Lincoln had been the Emancipator, Father Abraham. Navy Secretary Gideon Welles said that the sight of their anguish touched him most of all and that strong and brave men wept when he met them.[6]

A personal hardship also fell with terrible swiftness on the members of the assassin's family. Booth's sister, Asia Booth Clarke, recalled for the rest of her life the stigma her brother's deed had caused. "The tongue of every man and woman was free to revile and insult us, every man's hand was raised against us; if we had friends they condoled with us in secret; none ventured near."[7]

Other members of the Booth family feared for their lives and faced accusations of possible involvement in the assassin's deed. In Cincinnati, where Junius Brutus Booth was appearing, mobs tore down his playbills all over the city. A mob of over five hundred gathered at the hotel where he was staying, bent on violence. He was saved by the hotel clerk claiming that he had left the city, but the hotel was watched by crowds for four or five days before he could be spirited away. Junius later found himself in the Old Capitol Prison on suspicion of being involved with his brother, because of a letter he had sent urging him to give up the "oil business," which was misconstrued as a code word for the murder. However, investigation revealed to the authorities that

5. Jim Bishop, *The Day Lincoln Was Shot* (New York: Harper and Bros., 1955), 213; George Rothwell Brown (ed.), *Reminiscenses of Senator William M. Stewart* (New York: Neale, 1908), 193; Charles Sabin Taft, "Abraham Lincoln's Last Hours," *Century Magazine*, XLV (1893), 636.

6. Howard K. Beale (ed.), *Diary of Gideon Welles* (3 vols.; New York: W. W. Norton, 1960), II, 290. See also William E. Doster, *Lincoln and Episodes of the Civil War* (New York: G. P. Putnam's Sons, 1915), 36.

7. Asia Booth Clarke, *The Unlocked Book: A Memoir of John Wilkes Booth by His Sister Asia Booth Clarke* (New York: G. P. Putnam's Sons, 1938), 131.

John Wilkes Booth was actually engaging in oil speculation, and they became convinced that Junius had no role in the assassination.[8]

Secretary Stanton was also informed that another brother, Joseph Booth, had left San Francisco on one of the last steamers and that he was aware of the conspiracy against the president. Edwin, who was appearing in Boston, was absolutely crushed. Because of his well-known devotion to the Union and his influential friends like Governor John Allison Andrew, however, he avoided much of the criticism that fell on other members of his family. Writing to Adam Badeau on April 16, he said, "Oh! how little did I dream my boy, when on Friday night I was as Sir Edward Mortimer exclaiming 'Where is my honor now? Mountains of shame are piled upon me!' that I was not acting but uttering the fearful truth."[9]

Despite the instantaneous outbursts of violence, still the hope was often expressed that there might be moderation. On April 15, the Philadelphia *Evening Bulletin* said: "There must be no mobbing, no rioting, in short, no anarchy. The law must reign supreme or in this great crisis chaos will overwhelm us, and our own maddened feeling bring upon us national wreck and ruin which traitor arms have failed to accomplish." In San Francisco, for a time, there was almost a tolerance of illegal deeds, as when General Irvin McDowell admitted that the destruction of certain newspaper offices might have saved him the trouble of having to close these treasonous presses. The *Chronicle*, while it administered a mild rebuke, pointed out that the people had performed certain acts of irregular justice "which though not sanctioned by the courts will not be severely condemned by the most moderate and law-abiding citizens." However, by April 20, violence had proceeded too far for the *Chronicle* and it cautioned, "Now let law and order resume their sway."[10]

8. Osborn H. Oldroyd, *The Assassination of Abraham Lincoln, Flight, Pursuit, Capture, and Punishment of the Conspirators* (Washington: O. H. Oldroyd, 1901), 96–97; Unidentified newspaper clipping, N.d., in Letters Received, File E 57, H. S. Olcott to Henry L. Burnett, April 27, 1865, in Letters Received, File O 112, both in JAO, 1865, R.G. 153, NA.

9. J. H. Brown to Edwin Stanton, May 17, 1865, in Letters Received, File B 580, JAO, RG 153, NA; "Edwin Booth and Lincoln, with an Unpublished Letter by Edwin Booth," *Century Magazine*, LXXVII (1909), 920.

10. Philadelphia *Evening Bulletin*, April 15, 1865, p. 4; San Francisco *Alta Californian*, April 16, 1865, p. 1; San Francisco *Chronicle*, April 17, p. 3, April 20, 1865, p. 4.

John Wilkes Booth has been viewed by several historians as a tool of the Radical Republicans. It seems highly unlikely that northern officials would hire a well-known actor to kill Lincoln in a theater where chances of capture were great.

Courtesy of National Archives, Civil War, No. 198

Unlike many contemporary prints, this is a fairly accurate representation of how Booth carried out the assassination.

Booth leaps to the stage while Lincoln is incorrectly shown rising and holding his head. The orchestra and audience begin to react to the attack on the president.

The large rewards offered for the murderers have been criticized by historians and did cause a lack of cooperation on the part of those pursuing Booth. However, contemporaries felt that large rewards were the surest means of apprehending the assassins.

While many historians have criticized Secretary of War Edwin M. Stanton for conducting a reign of terror and have hinted that he engineered Lincoln's death, contemporaries believed that he acted responsibly under very trying conditions.

Courtesy of National Archives, Civil War, No. 190

In this inaccurate portrayal of federal troops surrounding Garrett's barn, Herold surrenders to the authorities while Boston Corbett places his pistol to the door to slay the assassin. There is some evidence that Booth might have committed suicide.

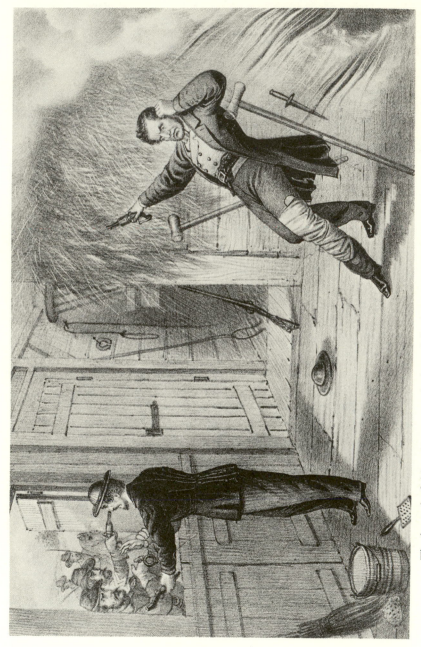

The legend of this cartoon reveals the satisfaction some contemporaries felt at Booth's agony, though many felt that his death would deprive the public of ever knowing the full extent of his plot.

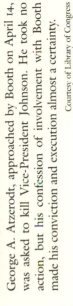

George A. Atzerodt, approached by Booth on April 14, was asked to kill Vice-President Johnson. He took no action, but his confession of involvement with Booth made his conviction and execution almost a certainty.

The trial and execution of Mary E. Surratt were controversial both in 1865 and since. The military commission recommended clemency because of her age and sex, though President Johnson claimed that Judge Advocate Holt withheld that plea from him. She thus became the first woman hanged by the federal government.

David Herold, a former drugstore clerk who was also involved in the kidnapping plot, allegedly guided Paine to Seward's home and then joined Booth in his flight. His capture with Booth at Garrett's barn meant that he was almost certainly doomed to conviction and exe-

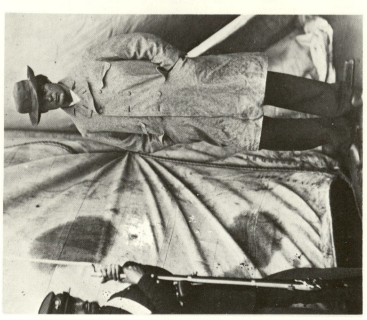

A giant of a young man, Lewis Paine (Louis Thornton Powell) assaulted Secretary of State Seward and several members of his household. Because he seemed to show no remorse for his actions, many people in 1865 considered him to be the prime villain of all the conspirators.

36

This illustration of the proceedings of the military commission shows the eight prisoners seated in the dock. When first brought before the court, they were forced to wear hoods, but protests by several commission members caused this practice to be discontinued.

Courtesy of Louis A. Warren Lincoln Library and Museum

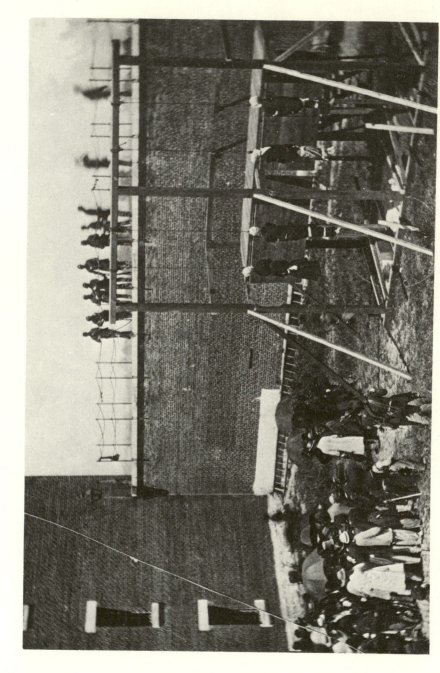

The execution of Mrs. Surratt, Paine, Herold, and Atzerodt, on July 7, 1865, as photographed by Alexander Gardner.

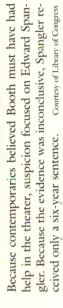

Because contemporaries believed Booth must have had help in the theater, suspicion focused on Edward Spangler. Because the evidence was inconclusive, Spangler received only a six-year sentence. Courtesy of Library of Congress

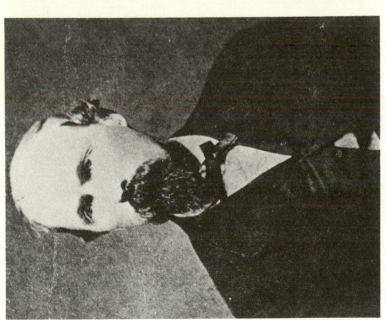

Defenders of Dr. Samuel A. Mudd argue that he became innocently involved in the assassination by setting Booth's leg, as any doctor would have done. President Carter, before leaving office, expressed his belief in Mudd's innocence but did not issue the full pardon sought by his grandsons. Courtesy of Louis A. Warren Lincoln Library and Museum

Michael O'Laughlin, Booth's boyhood friend, enlisted in a plot to kidnap the president. He was sentenced to life imprisonment and died at Fort Jefferson during a yellow fever epidemic.

Samuel B. Arnold, another boyhood friend and classmate of Booth's, was also involved in the kidnapping plot. He was sentenced to life imprisonment but was freed by Andrew Johnson in 1869.

Surratt fled to Europe and enlisted as a Papal Zouave. He is shown here in uniform. However, he was recognized by a former classmate who wished to claim a share of the reward money. Surratt was arrested and returned to the United States for trial.

John H. Surratt, the son of Mary Surratt, was accused of complicity in the assassination but was not brought to trial until 1867. Since a civil jury could not agree, he was set free, causing historians to consider the fairness of this civil trial versus the biases revealed by the military trial.

Many prints appeared showing Booth being tempted by Satan. To contemporaries the devil that had stirred Booth to action was the Confederacy, as well as subversive organizations in the North.

THEORY. PRACTICE. EFFECT.

BICKLEY.
Head of the Knights of the Golden Circle.

BOOTH.
The Assassin.

THE
MARTYR PRESIDENT.

This print represents the prevailing view that subversive northern groups such as the Knights of the Golden Circle inspired Booth to carry out the assassination.

Courtesy of Louis A. Warren Lincoln Library and Museum

43

This cartoon depicting the apotheosis of Lincoln is typical of many that portrayed him as a martyr and contributed to his transformation into a folk hero.

Courtesy of Louis A. Warren Lincoln Library and Museum

The ship of state might have received a severe jolt, but as the Washington *Evening Star* reported, "President Johnson has the helm steadily in hand." Several newspapers pointed with pride to the fact that the price of national securities had not fallen, as proof of the government's stability. Another indicator, though one might debate whether it was as significant as stock market prices, was George T. Strong's assertion that arrests for drunkenness and disorder were fewer during the week following Lincoln's murder than in any week for many years.[11]

To many observers, the assassination seemed to have produced a new unity among the people. George A. Townsend remarked that the scenes he had witnessed revealed as never before the worthiness and magnanimous power of the people, and H. L. Burnett, who was to serve as one of the judge advocates in the conspiracy trials, noted a pale, determined expression and set of the jaw that seemed to say, "We will stand guard and the government shall not die."[12]

If people had confidence in Johnson, it was because of his often repeated sternness. Some Radicals were particularly pleased that, if Lincoln had to die, at least Andrew Johnson would succeed to the presidency. Congressman George W. Julian mentioned that at a Radical caucus after the assassination, everybody was still shocked, though "the feeling was nearly universal that the accession of Johnson to the Presidency would prove a godsend to the country." When Julian and fellow Radical Ben Wade went to call on the new president, the latter said, "Johnson, we have faith in you. By the Gods, there will be no trouble now in running the government."[13]

A great deal of evidence illustrates Johnson's bitter frame of mind. Captain William Williams, who was sent to guard the president at the Kirkwood House hotel, reported him as pacing the floor, constantly

11. Washington *Evening Star*, April 17, 1865, p. 2. Similar views abounded; for example, see *Lincoln Lore*, No. 1478 (April, 1961), Lincoln National Life Foundation, Fort Wayne, Indiana. Hugh McCulloch, *Men and Measures of Half a Century* (New York: Charles Scribner's Sons, 1900), 226, and Katie Van Winden, "The Assassination of Abraham Lincoln: Its Effect in California," *Journal of the West*, IV (1965), 222, offer other possible reasons for the stable price of securities. Allan Nevins and Milton Thomas (eds.), *Diary of George T. Strong* (4 vols.; New York: MacMillan, 1952), IV, 388.

12. Townsend, *Life, Crime and Capture*, 18; Henry L. Burnett, "Assassination of President Lincoln and the Trials of the Assassins," in James H. Kennedy (ed.), *History of the Ohio Society of New York, 1885–1905* (New York: Grafton Press, 1906), 592.

13. George W. Julian, *Political Recollections, 1840–1872* (Chicago: Jensen, McClung, 1884), 255, 257.

wringing his hands, and saying, "They shall suffer for this, they shall suffer for this." General Grant later recalled Johnson's mood. "He seemed to be anxious to get at the leaders to punish them. He would say that the leaders of the rebellion must be punished, and that treason must be made odious."[14]

Before a group of Washington ministers, Johnson himself said, "In my opinion the time has come when you and I must understand and must teach that treason is a crime, and not a mere difference of political opinions." In reply to a committee of the New York Union League the president said the individuals who sought to take the nation's life should receive an even more severe punishment than the assassin. A similar speech to an Illinois delegation produced an editorial in the *Times* praising Johnson's firmness.[15]

It has seemed to puzzle modern historians that anyone could seriously believe that the South was involved in the assassination, but for most contemporaries, including President Johnson, this was the only possible conclusion. Several men made diary entries that were strikingly similar. Former Attorney General Edward Bates wrote, "Sic semper tyrannis is the motto on the shield of Virginia—and this may give a clue to the unravelling of a great conspiracy, for this assassination is not the act of one man; but only one scene of a great drama." Mrs. Gideon Welles, wife of the secretary of the Navy, said she heard a phrase uttered from her husband's lips that she had never heard before or since— "Damn the rebels, this is their work."[16]

Newspapers fully echoed these sentiments. On April 17, the New York *Times* cataloged the list of horrible deeds perpetrated by the rebel-

14. John E. Buckingham, *Reminiscences and Souvenirs of the Assassination of Abraham Lincoln* (Washington: Press of R. H. Darby, 1894), 63; U.S. Congress, House, Committee on the Judiciary, *Impeachment Investigation, Testimony Taken Before the Judiciary Committee of the House of Representatives in the Investigation of the Charges Against Andrew Johnson*, 39th Cong., 2nd Sess., 40th Cong., 1st Sess. (Washington: Government Printing Office, 1867), 827.

15. *Proceedings of a Called Meeting of Ministers of All Religious Denominations in the District of Columbia . . . and the Reply of the President* (Washington: McGill and Witherow, 1865), 13; New York *Times*, April 20, April 21, 1865, p. 4.

16. Howard K. Beale (ed.), *The Diary of Edward Bates, 1859–1866*, Vol. IV of the Annual Report of the American Historical Association, 1930 (Washington: Government Printing Office, 1933), 473; Mrs. M. J. Welles's impression of the assassination (Typescript in Gideon Welles Papers, LC), April 14, 1865. See also Adam Gurowski, *Diary, 1863–1864–1865* (3 vols.; Washington: W. H. and O. H. Morrison, 1866), III, 397.

lion, and the Washington *Evening Star* reported that it was conclusively known that the plot was a deeply laid conspiracy including members of the Knights of the Golden Circle. Others traced a link from Jefferson Davis and Robert E. Lee to Booth. This inclusion of Lee was interesting, for previously, military men had been largely exempt from the animosity heaped on rebel leaders, as merely having carried out their duty.[17]

On April 25, the *Times* printed Stanton's dispatch to General John Adams Dix, announcing that the War Department had evidence that the president's murder was organized in Canada and approved at Richmond and that Seward's assailant was believed to be one of the Saint Albans raiders. The *Times* added that should the facts be established on competent proof, it would surprise no one.[18]

Extremely severe proposals were made for dealing with rebels. Senator Orville H. Browning had heard Britten A. Hill and others propose that the South be depopulated and repeopled with another race and that in the North all copperheads should be dragged from their houses and summarily disposed of. After Davis' capture one Pennsylvania gentleman made an interesting offer to the government. "Will you give me the liberty of executing him if condemned? I will travel at my own cost to wherever it may be necessary for the purpose."[19]

The leading journals even began to launch attacks on each other for supposed leniency to rebels. The *Times* took the New York *World* to task for saying that even if Seward recovered, he should resign from the cabinet because his views were so repugnant to the South. The *Times* said the only person who would applaud this was the assassin, who had such sentiments in mind when he used his dagger to cut Seward very severely on his face and neck. On two separate occasions *Harper's Weekly* criticized the New York *Tribune* for calling persons involved in arson certain distinguished Americans of the other party to the Civil War; while the Easton (Pa.) *Free Press* criticized the Easton (Pa.) *Argus*

17. New York *Times*, April 17, 1865, p. 4; Washington *Evening Star*, quoted in New York *Times*, April 27, 1865, p. 1; Philadelphia *Evening Bulletin*, April 17, p. 4, April 27, 1865, p. 4.

18. New York *Times*, April 25, 1865, p. 1.

19. James G. Randall and Theodore C. Pease (eds.), *Diary of Orville Hickman Browning* (2 vols.; Springfield, Ill.: Jefferson's Printing and Stationery, 1933), II, 21; William Hampshire to Edwin Stanton, May 16, 1865, in Letters Received, File H 303, JAO, RG 153, NA.

for its southern tenderness. George T. Strong went so far as to cancel his copy of the New York *Tribune* because editor Horace Greeley's views had become so unpopular.[20]

In Washington, rebel prisoners, no matter what their offense, were in grave peril, for suspicion was aroused that they were involved in the murder. As several prisoners were being taken to the Old Capitol Prison, reports were circulated that they were Booth and Surratt. This brought cries of "Hang them!" "Kill them!" and a volley of rocks was thrown. Another report that a man in woman's clothing had broken from his captors and entered the Kirkwood House caused a crowd of several thousand to surround the building.[21]

Several prisoners have left vivid accounts of their experiences. When Virginia Lomax was at the provost marshal's office, a rumor that Booth was inside brought a large crowd with rocks and sticks to kill him. On seeing her, someone asked if she were one of the conspirators, and the crowd began to eye her in a manner that gave her a few anxious moments. Thomas Nelson Conrad and some other prisoners were followed from General Christopher Colon Augur's office by a crowd crying, "There is Booth; seize him and gibbet him!" Even released prisoners were in jeopardy; several had been attacked and severely injured, some escaping death only by the interference of the soldiers. The Old Capitol itself also became a special target for the mobs. Several prisoners expressed anxiety for fear the mob might storm the prison and take them out to execute them. However, the authorities took precautions to double the guard, and the danger finally passed. Captive rebel soldiers also received the fury of the mob, for a crowd threatened to burn the section of Old Capitol where one hundred rebel officers were quarantined en route to Fort Warren in Boston Harbor.[22]

20. New York *Times*, April 20, 1865, p. 4; *Harper's Weekly*, April 29, p. 258, May 13, 1865, p. 290; Easton (Pa.) *Free Press*, May 4, 1865, p. 2; Nevins and Thomas (eds.), *Diary of George T. Strong*, IV, 586.

21. New York *Times*, April 18, 1865, p. 1; New York *Tribune*, April 27, 1865, p. 5.

22. *The Old Capitol and Its Inmates: By a Lady Who Enjoyed the Hospitality of the Government for a Season* (New York: E. J. Hale, 1867), 52, 167. Author unknown but generally said to be Virginia Lomax. Thomas N. Conrad, *The Rebel Scout* (Washington: National, 1904), 150; Thomas N. Conrad, *A Confederate Spy: A Story of the Civil War* (Lynchburg, Va.: Artcraft Printing, 1961), 82; Harry Ford, in New York *Post*, July 8, 1884, p. 3; William Garrett, "True Story of the Capture of John Wilkes Booth," *Confederate Veteran's Magazine*, XXIX (1921), 130; Seaton Munroe, "Recollections of Lincoln's Assassination," *North American Review*, CLXII (1896), 426.

Even inside Old Capitol, Miss Lomax and her fellow prisoners suffered some discomfort as one minister harangued them for their complicity in the deed. "I would now, in conclusion, say to every Southern man and woman (looking up at the windows) before me, that on the head of each, mark me, each one of you, rests the blood of the martyr Abraham. Your very presence in this prison proclaims your guilt. Wherefore are you here? Because you have aided and abetted the rebellion, and every rebel, therefore, of either sex, is a murderer."[23]

The government, aware of the potential danger to the prisoners, took measures to protect them. On April 17, Charles A. Dana, assistant secretary of war, gave orders to Marshal James L. McPhail to bring conspirator Michael O'Laughlin to Washington: "Have him in double irons and use every precaution against escape, but as far as possible avoid everything which can lead to suspicion on the part of the people on the train and give rise to an attempt to lynch the prisoner." Christian Rath, later the executioner of the conspirators, said that he took similar precautions when ordered to transport Jefferson Davis' secretary, Burton Harrison, from prison, because the times were so unsettled.[24]

The lack of concern expressed over the violence is also striking. William Daggett wrote to his mother of a Union soldier shooting a man dead on the spot for saying he was glad Lincoln had been assassinated, and added, "My seven shooter is in my pocket and I shall not fail to use it should I hear any such remark." Melville E. Stone, general manager of the Associated Press, described an equally gripping scene. "I made my way around the corner to the Matteson house . . . very soon I heard the crack of a revolver, and a man fell in the centre of the room. His assailant stood perfectly composed with a smoking revolver in his hand, and justified his action by saying: 'He said it served Lincoln right.' There was no arrest, no one would have dared arrest the man. He walked out a hero. I never knew who he was."[25]

---

23. *Old Capitol and Its Inmates*, 185–86.

24. *The War of the Rebellion: A Compilation of the Official Records of the Union and Confederate Armies* (130 vols., Washington: Government Printing Office, 1880–1901), Ser. I, Vol. XLVI, Pt. 3, p. 821; hereinafter cited as *OR*; John A. Gray, "The Fate of the Lincoln Conspirators: The Account of the Hanging, Given by Lieutenant-Colonel Christian Rath, the Executioner," *McClure's Magazine*, XXXVII (1911), 629–30.

25. *Lincoln Lore*, No. 1478 (April, 1961). Unidentified newspaper clipping, in Truman H. Bartlett Collection, Boston University.

At the very least, treasonable utterances were liable to land the speaker in prison. In New York, several people got stiff fines and up to six months in jail for such an offense. In the Pewter Mug Saloon on Nassau Street, Henry Lee was struck over the head with a bottle for expressing gratification at Lincoln's death. In reporting the case to the inspector, the police sergeant declared, "Served him right."[26]

One of the most widely reported occurrences was the killing in Maryland of Joseph Shaw, the editor of the Westminster (Md.) *Democrat*. Shaw had been ordered out of town by citizens because of disrespectful language to Lincoln in his paper. He left but returned, and a group of irate citizens called on him. Shaw emerged and fired into the crowd, wounding Henry Bell, whereupon the townspeople fell on him and killed him on the spot.[27]

There was difficulty in Baltimore because of photographs of rebel soldiers in the windows of certain photographers' establishments, but the military and police authorities were reported to be making every effort to preserve order. Such trouble apparently led to an order by General Lew Wallace forbidding sale of portraits of any rebel officers or of John Wilkes Booth and threatening arrest and imprisonment for repeated violations. However, on May 27, Assistant Adjutant General Edward D. Townsend sent the following order to General Dix, General George Cadwalader, and General Wallace: "If you have prohibited the sale of photograph likenesses of J. Wilkes Booth the Secretray of War directs that the prohibition be removed."[28]

At Fort Jefferson, Dry Tortugas, where four of the conspirators were to be imprisoned, a prisoner who cheered the assassination was strung up by his thumbs for so long that he died shortly after being cut down; but as the guard, Henry Whitney, said "I honestly confess that I have very little sympathy for him or every man who is punished for such expressions."[29]

The widespread nature of the violence in some ways tends to slightly

26. New York *Times*, April 16, p. 5, April 19, p. 2, April 26, 1865, p. 2; New York *Herald*, April 18, 1865, p. 8.
27. *The Terrible Tragedy at Washington: Assassination of President Lincoln* (Philadelphia: Barclay, 1865), 113.
28. New York *Times*, April 16, 1865, p. 5; *OR*, Ser. I, Vol. XLVI, Pt. 3, pp. 1072, 1227.
29. Henry B. Whitney Diary (MS in Henry B. Whitney Papers, Duke University Library), April 22, 1865.

exaggerate the numbers of people in the North who rejoiced over Lincoln's death, because oftentimes people who were innocent became suspected of treasonable sentiments. At Rochester, New York, D. L. Hunt, who was supposed to have said, "He ought to have been assassinated," was chased by a howling mob and escaped with his life only by being placed in jail. Hunt, who claimed to be a Republican and to have voted for Lincoln, explained that what he had meant was what a waste to kill Lincoln now when the war was over and that if the rebels had attempted it four years ago, they might have had a chance to end the war. Even more bizarre was the fact that a man who reported the case to General John Ellis Wool was overheard using Hunt's words and in turn was reported to the mayor.[30]

Ministers also had to weigh their words carefully. A minister at the Mission Church near Camp Fry was arrested for saying, "If Johnson pursues the same course as Lincoln, he will meet the same fate." He then had to explain to the authorities that what he had meant was that if President Johnson pursued the same lenient policy towards rebels as President Lincoln had, he would meet the same fate at their hands. The Reverend Mr. Massey, preaching a sermon at the Baptist Church in Medway, Massachusetts, made no mention at all of the assassination and for this omission was given fifteen minutes by the congregation to get out of town.[31]

Even months later the sentiments aroused had not completely died down. Former Alabama Senator Clement C. Clay, who was imprisoned at Fortress Monroe with Jefferson Davis and was himself charged with complicity in the murder, recorded that while the Third Pennsylvania Artillery was on duty he could not walk outside without hearing cries of "Shoot him!" "Hang him!" "Bring a rope!" "The damned rascal!"[32]

The long list of violent actions and their wide geographic distribution clearly illustrate that people did not view the assassination as merely the isolated act of a few assassins but as a natural result of several years of southern treachery. On Tuesday, April 18, the New York *Tribune*

30. Albany *Atlas and Argus*, April 20, 1865, p. 3.
31. Washington *Evening Star*, April 17, 1865, p. 3; *Terrible Tragedy at Washington*, 114–15.
32. Ada Sterling (ed.), *A Belle of the Fifties: Memoirs of Mrs. Clay of Alabama, Concerning Social and Political Life in Washington and the South, 1853–1866* (New York: Doubleday, 1904), 346.

commented very perceptively: "The deeds of last Friday night were the work, let us still hope, of a few insignificant wretches; but the frenzy which impelled them pervades many breasts, and is liable at any moment to blaze out into crimes the most execrable. Hence the indignation, now so general, has quite other aliment than the special atrocities which aroused it, and it is destined to have results which those atrocities standing alone, would hardly produce or justify."[33]

The sorrow created by the assassination is too well remembered and documented to require much comment. Scores of groups met and passed resolutions of condolence and sympathy that were conveyed to the widow and family. The outpouring of the people as the casket bearing Lincoln's remains was borne slowly home to Springfield was magnificent and truly touching. In pulpit after pulpit, ministers expressed the idea that it was as if in each household the father had been slain.[34]

If the sorrow has been remembered, the accompanying violence has either been played down by historians or else treated as a phenomenon fostered by northern radicals to suit their own political purposes. However, violent deeds and expressions were so much at the heart of public reaction and apparently arose so spontaneously that it is difficult to see how anyone could have controlled them if he had wished. People honestly believed that the South was involved, and sometimes vengeance was visited upon innocent and guilty alike. This terrible whirlwind of opinion was greatly to affect the pursuit of the conspirators and their trials.

33. New York *Tribune*, April 18, 1865, p. 4.
34. For a typical example of resolutions passed, see New York *Tribune*, April 17, 1865, p. 3; Philadelphia *Evening Bulletin*, April 22, 1865, p. 1. For a sermon typical of the many preached on the theme of the death of a father, see John Farquhar, *The Claims of God to Recognition in the Assassination of President Lincoln* (Lancaster, Pa.: Pearsol and Geist, 1865), 6. See also James F. Kirkham, Sheldon G. Levy, and William J. Crotty (eds.), *Assassination and Political Violence: A Report to the National Commission on the Causes and Prevention of Violence* (Washington: Government Printing Office, 1969), 70–73, for argument that the president is seen by the public as a father figure and that this is why presidential assassination is always so traumatic. The data herein seem to bear out this contention.

4.

Secretary Stanton

The part played by Secretary of War Stanton on the assassination night and during the pursuit and trial of the conspirators has become one of the central issues surrounding the assassination of Abraham Lincoln. Many historians have argued that such a tense situation called for a man with a cool head and calm hand. A leader was needed to step forth and allay people's fears; yet, in their view, Stanton lacked all the required attributes and could not calm his own terror. During such a crisis in American history, they argue, probably no man more unfit could have been chosen to hold the reins of the government.[1]

Stanton has been charged with an almost criminal negligence for his slowness in organizing pursuit measures to capture the assassin, and he is particularly chided for not rapidly informing the public who the assassin was. Through a procedure established earlier in the war, dispatches of a crucial nature were first sent to General Dix in New York, from whose headquarters they were given to the press. The first dispatch, written about 1:30 A.M. on April 15 but not sent until 2:15 A.M., made no mention of the assassin's name. Not until 3:20 A.M. did a telegram inform General Dix that "investigation strongly indicates J. Wilkes Booth as the assassin of the President. Whether it is the same or a different person that attempted to murder Mr. Seward remains in doubt." At 4:44 A.M. it was definitely stated that there had been two assassins involved.[2]

L. A. Gobright of the Associated Press, who found Booth's derringer in Ford's Theatre, also sent a short special dispatch. "The President was

1. David M. DeWitt, *The Assassination of Abraham Lincoln and Its Expiation* (New York: MacMillan, 1909), 55–56; Lloyd Lewis, *Myths After Lincoln* (New York: Harcourt Brace, 1929), 56–58.
2. *The War of the Rebellion: A Compilation of the Official Records of the Union and Confederate Armies* (130 vols., Washington: Government Printing Office, 1880–1901), Ser. I, Vol. XLVI, Pt. 3, pp. 780–81, hereinafter cited as *OR*.

shot in a theater tonight and perhaps mortally wounded." This dispatch also made no mention of Booth, and in fact, when he later followed it with another message ordering the story stopped, the New York *Tribune* reported, "Nothing is said about the truth or falsity of that [first] dispatch."[3]

Although there was some delay in officially notifying the newspapers, the news was hardly suppressed, as some newspapers did receive the name of the assassin from private dispatches. The announcement of the assassin's name in the newspapers, in any case, should hardly have been a government priority, for it could have little bearing on the pursuit. The government's primary responsibility was to notify its military commanders and detectives who would be engaged in tracking the assassins, and this was fairly rapidly accomplished.[4]

Rapid and ill-thought-out dispatches to the newspapers might have had the very effect on people that Stanton has been accused of fostering anyway, of arousing them to frenzy, especially the army. That the army did not get out of hand, except for minor incidents, is no indication that this might not have occurred, and it should have been a legitimate consideration on the part of public officials. The fact that the government took precaution initially not to have the news published in certain commands shows that they were aware of this possibility.[5]

The government had good reason to fear army violence, and several military men acknowledged this possibility. Smith Stimmel, who had commanded the president's cavalry escort, recorded the desire of his men to plunge into a fight. Similarly General George A. Custer believed he expressed the universal opinion of the army when he wrote, "Extermination is the only true policy we can adopt toward the political leaders of the rebellion, and at the same time do justice to ourselves and posterity." In General W. T. Sherman's army there was reported to be great excitement, with one citizen having been killed for expressing

3. L. A. Gobright, *Recollections of Men and Things in Washington During Half a Century* (Philadelphia: N.p., 1869), 348; New York *Tribune*, April 15, 1865, in Otto Eisenschiml, *Why Was Lincoln Murdered?* (Boston: Little Brown, 1937), 75. Eisenschiml, of course, implies some sinister censorship in all of this.

4. Washington *Chronicle*, April 15, 1865, p. 1; New York *Tribune*, April 15, 1865, p. 1. See George S. Bryan, *The Great American Myth* (New York: Carrick and Evans, 1940), 190, for a list of newspapers that did receive the name of the assassin.

5. *OR*, Ser. I, Vol. XLVII, Pt. 3, p. 239. Similarly, announcement of the news in places like Richmond, which Eisenschiml called for, could have brought about a violent disaster.

approval of the deed. Sherman himself telegraphed General Henry Halleck: "The news of Mr. Lincoln's death produced a most intense effect on our troops. At first I feared it would lead to excesses, but now it has softened down and can be easily guided."[6]

Instead of being criminally slow in reacting to the assassination events, Stanton was the one man who actually did take charge of the situation, while others around him were immobilized. Men like Senator Sumner could do little more than sit and sob at the dying Lincoln's bedside, but it was Stanton, virtually alone, who directed whatever investigation and pursuit there was. Contemporaries, who judged his performance in the light of their own fears, immobility, and despair, heaped upon Stanton almost undimmed praise.[7]

Charles Dana, the assistant secretary of war, who, when he arrived at Petersen House (the boarding house across from Ford's Theatre), was pressed into service in writing dispatches, spoke admiringly of Stanton's activity that night as compared with the inactivity of the other cabinet members present.

> They seemed to be almost as paralyzed as the unconscious sufferer within the little chamber. Mr. Stanton alone was in full activity. . . . Then he began and dictated orders, one after another, which I wrote out and sent swiftly to the telegraph. All these orders were designed to keep the business of the government in full motion until the crisis should be over. It seemed as if Stanton thought of everything, and there was a great deal to be thought of that night. The extent of the conspiracy was, of course, unknown, and the horrible beginning which had been made naturally led us to suggest the worst. The safety of Washington must be looked after. Commanders all over the country had to be ordered to take extra precautions. The people must be notified of the tragedy. The assassins must be captured. The coolness and clearheadedness of Mr. Stanton under the circumstances were most remarkable. I remember that one of the first telegrams was to General Dix, the Military Commander of New York, notifying him of what had happened. No clearer brief account of the

6. New York *Times*, April 24, p. 5, May 7, 1865, p. 2; *OR*, Ser. I, Vol. XLVII, Pt. 3, p. 245; William T. Sherman to Henry Halleck, N.d., in Edwin M. Stanton Papers, LC. Eisenschiml, *Why Was Lincoln Murdered?* 89, denied there was any possibility the soldiers might get out of control.

7. For historians who have agreed with the contemporary views, see Bryan, *Great American Myth*, 186, and Jim Bishop, *The Day Lincoln Was Shot* (New York: Harper and Bros., 1955), 240. While admitting that Stanton may have committed certain errors, they argue that he did better than most people could have under such difficult circumstances.

tragedy exists today than this, written scarcely three hours after the scene in Ford's Theater, in a little stand in the room where, a few feet away, Mr. Lincoln lay dying.[8]

Surgeon Charles A. Leale, who attended the dying president, also praised Stanton.

On that awful memorable night the great War Secretary, the Honorable Edwin M. Stanton, one of the most imposing figures of the nineteenth century, promptly arrived and recognized at that critical period of our country's history the necessity of a head to our Government and as the President was passing away established a branch of his War Department in an adjoining room. There he sat, surrounded by his counsellors and messengers, pen in hand, writing to General Dix and others. He was soon in communication with many in authority and with the Government and army officials. By Secretary Stanton's wonderful ability and power in action, he undoubtedly controlled millions of excited people. He was then the Master, and in reality Acting President of the United States.

Corporal Tanner, who was pressed into service to record the testimony, summed up Stanton's performance succinctly. "Through all that awful night Stanton was the one man of steel." Praise for Stanton also found its way into the press, with the New York *Times* correspondent describing Stanton as issuing order after order with the remarkable determination and foresight for which he was noted.[9]

It is not certain just how quickly it became known that Booth was the assassin. Although Tanner did write, "In fifteen minutes I had testimony enough down to hang Wilkes Booth, the assassin, higher than ever Haman hung," he also added: "No one said positively that the assassin was John Wilkes Booth, but all thought it was he. It was evident that the horror of the crime held them back. They seemed to hate to think that one they had known at all could be guilty of such an awful crime." The fact that Stanton had to investigate the attempted assassi-

---

8. Charles A. Dana, *Recollections of the Civil War with the Leaders at Washington and in the Field in the Sixties* (New York: D. Appleton, 1898), 274. His ordering of priorities of what had to be done is interesting, with capturing the assassins quite a way down on the list. Even Eisenschiml grudgingly agrees with Dana's appraisal of Stanton's dispatches in *Why Was Lincoln Murdered?*, 6. However, in Eisenschiml lurks the idea that clear dispatches are easier to write if one knows what is going to happen. Vaughan Shelton, *Mask for Treason* (Harrisburg: Stackpole Books, 1965), 38, says that the inordinate amount of attention devoted to the Seward assassination in the dispatches shows that this event was a mystery to Stanton, whereas Lincoln's assassination was not unexpected.

9. New York *Sun*, April 16, 1905, p. 7; New York *Times*, April 21, 1865, p. 1.

nation of Seward, together with performing other duties that night, does not make the four and a half hours from time of murder to positive identification of the assassin seem an inordinately long amount of time.[10]

If there was any inaction on the part of the authorities, a clue to it can be found in Charles Dana's statement that the first priority of the government was the safety of Washington. New York *World* correspondent George Townsend presented his view of the confusion that the assassination had caused. "On the Friday night of the murder the departments were absolutely paralyzed. The murderers had three good hours for escape; they had evaded the pursuit of lightning by snapping the telegraph wires, and rumor filled the town with so many reports that the first valuable hours, which should have been used to follow hard after them, were consumed in feverish efforts to know the real extent of the conspiracy."[11] With Lincoln dying and apprehension that Seward's wounds might prove fatal, frightened government officials were obviously interested in preventing more bloodshed, including their own.

The following dispatch to the New York press reveals the extent of the rumors circulating: "The wildest excitement prevailed in all parts of the city. Men, women, and children, old and young, rushed to and fro, and the rumors were magnified until we had nearly every member of the cabinet killed. Some time elapsed before authentic data could be ascertained in regard to the affair." Among the rumors that quickly became prevalent was one that General Grant had been shot on his way to Philadelphia, but the New York *Times* correspondent reported in a 2 A.M. dispatch that it was not true. Grant's son, Jesse, recounts the tale of someone peering into his father's carriage and said that years later his mother received a letter from someone claiming he was sup-

10. James Tanner, "Letter to Henry F. Walch, Washington, April 17, 1865," *American Historical Review* XXIX (1924), 516; Eisenschiml, *Why Was Lincoln Murdered?*, 71.

11. New York *World*, May 4, 1865, p. 1; George A. Townsend, *The Life, Crime, and Capture of John Wilkes Booth with a Full Sketch of the Conspiracy of Which He Was the Leader, and the Pursuit, Trial, and Execution of His Accomplices* (New York: Dick and Fitzgerald, 1865), 49. For historians supporting this view, see Bishop, *Day Lincoln Was Shot*, 234, and John Cottrell, *Anatomy of an Assassination* (New York: Funk and Wagnalls, 1966), 128. Eisenschiml, *Why Was Lincoln Murdered?*, 172–73, ridicules the conspiracy plot and says there was no danger to Stanton, Grant, or even Johnson; but how could contemporaries know this, unless, as he surmises, they were involved in the plot.

posed to assassinate Grant, but had failed and been glad of it ever since. The general himself referred to a similar letter he received after the assassination, but he could not determine if it was genuine or not.[12]

It also appeared that Johnson had been destined for assassination. Detective John Lee, sent to guard the new president, was informed by bartender Michael Henry of a suspicious stranger—George Atzerodt—and in checking Atzerodt's room, Lee discovered weapons and a coat containing a bank book belonging to Booth. The discovery of the enigmatic card, which said: "Don't wish to disturb you. Are you at home?— J. Wilkes Booth," also led contemporaries to the conclusion that Johnson had been among Booth's intended victims, even though it has since been argued that the card may really have been left for Johnson's secretary.[13]

There were also rumors of attempts against Stanton's life. The New York *Times* of April 16 reported that two gentlemen hastening to the house of the secretary to inform him of the attack on Mr. Lincoln met a man outside muffled in a cloak, who, when accosted by them, ran away. Stanton recounted a similar story, only in his version it was a young man who had encountered the intruder after running from the theater to inform him.[14]

A mysterious stranger outside Stanton's house was by no means unusual, for such individuals were also reported in other locations. On Saturday, April 22, it was noted that a guard had been placed around Senator Charles Sumner's house, because he was discovered to have been one of the projected assassination victims. On April 29, he was

12. Abott A. Abott, *The Assassination and Death of Abraham Lincoln, President of the United States of America, at Washington, on the 14th of April, 1865* (New York: American News, 1865), 3; New York *Times*, April 15, 1865, p. 1; Jesse Grant, *In the Days of My Father, General Grant* (New York: Harper Brothers, 1925), 41; Ward H. Lamon, *Recollections of Abraham Lincoln, 1847–1865* (Chicago: A. C. McClung, 1895), 273–74; Philip Van Doren Stern, *The Man Who Killed Lincoln* (New York: Random House, 1939), 124, has John Surratt boarding the train to assassinate Grant, despite the fact there is no very good ground for this assertion.

13. Benn Pitman, *The Assassination of President Lincoln and the Trial of the Conspirators* (New York: Funk and Wagnalls, 1954), 70, 144.

14. New York *Times*, April 16, 1865, p. 1; New York *Herald*, April 16, 1865, p. 4; James G. Randall and Theodore C. Pease (eds.), *The Diary of Orville Hickman Browning* (2 vols.; Springfield, Ill.: Jefferson's Printing and Stationery, 1933), II, 20. Senator Stewart related that it was soldiers coming to the Stanton residence. See George Rothwell Brown (ed.), *Reminiscences of Senator William M. Stewart* (New York: Neale, 1908), 192. In other versions Stanton was only saved by his doorbell failing to work.

supposed to have been fired on while returning to his room and to have received a letter saying, "It is fortunate for you that my aim is not good." However, the New York *Herald* speculated that it was all a plot to make Sumner appear a martyr and to ingratiate him with Johnson, in order to secure for him the post of secretary of state, which might well have fallen vacant because of Seward's injuries. The Springfield (Mass.) *Republican* also said the guard was not needed, for the rumor of two mysterious men at the Sumner residence was caused by the social visit of two of his colleagues, Messrs. Henry L. Dawes and Daniel W. Gooch. The *Republican* concluded, "Of such stuff, undoubtedly, are made many of the anxieties and alarms and sensation incidents with which Washington and the country now naturally abound."[15]

On April 23, three men in women's clothing had supposedly made a very suspicious demonstration outside the home of Chief Justice Salmon P. Chase. No one was found, but a guard was established. Secretary of the Interior John P. Usher noted that a visitor named Fowler had told him that two men had been looking for him on the assassination night and that Attorney General James Speed had heard a man walking on his back porch. As late as April 28, after Booth had been killed, Assistant Adjutant General Adam E. King sent a message to Colonel George W. Gile, First Brigade Veteran Reserve Corps, saying that it did not appear that there were guards at the home of Secretary Usher or Judge Advocate Joseph Holt. Guards were ordered to these residences as well as to that of the president and the entire cabinet, and Gile was reminded that the guard outside the president's home must be rigidly inspected and its condition reported upon. The precautions taken to guard the president were hardly an extraordinary procedure, as letters poured in warning Johnson or threatening him with assassination. One written in an apparently friendly manner warned Johnson, "It would be well for you to take warning from the end of your predecessor and not follow in his footsteps for a like fate may be your own."[16]

15. New York *Times*, April 22, p. 8, April 29, 1865, p. 1; New York *Herald*, quoted in Philadelphia *Evening Bulletin*, May 4, 1865, p. 1; Springfield (Mass.) *Republican*, quoted in Gettysburg *Compiler*, May 22, 1865, p. 1.
16. Chicago *Tribune*, April 24, 1865, p. 1; Thomas R. Henry, in Boston *Globe*, February 12, 1931; New York *Tribune*, April 24, 1865, p. 4; *OR* Ser. I, Vol. XLVI, Pt. 3, p. 1002. For threatening letters, see Letters Received, File A 301, 308, 461, all in JAO, 1865, RG 153,

Many people became convinced that assassination was about to become a common American phenomenon. The New York *Times*, reporting rumors of Grant's demise on April 27, said that the remarkable thing was that no one deemed it impossible or even unlikely. It also called for a strict guarding of Johnson, echoing an earlier editorial that warned Johnson that he was not taking sufficient measures for his safety. In some cases, action was taken when the perpetrators of threats were discovered. One Charles Lee Armour said he had heard a man named "Jeems," at a public house called the Ruby, state that he hoped General Butler would be the next person assassinated. The endorsement in the case reads, "Commit this man (W. P.) James to Old Capitol arrested by Colonel H. H. Wells to be used before the Military Commission."[17]

The genuine fear experienced by many government officials is evident. The telegram Stanton dispatched to General Winfield S. Hancock was apparently sent in all sincerity. "In holding an interview with Mosby it may be needless to caution an old soldier like you to guard against surprise and danger to yourself, but the recent murders show such astounding wickedness that too much precaution cannot be taken." Congressman George Julian, sometimes charged with almost rejoicing at the assassination, stated that "Mr. Woods entered and told me Lincoln was murdered, and Seward and son probably, and that assassins were about to take the town. I was still half asleep and in my fright grew suddenly cold, heartsick, and almost helpless." Similarly Chief Justice Chase overcame his first impulse to go to the dying president and remained in his home that night with the heavy tramping of the guard being heard under his window. He said, "It was a night of horrors."[18]

NA. DeWitt, *Assassination of Abraham Lincoln*, 57, called the placing of guards around the homes of cabinet members an inflammatory act.

17. New York *Times*, April 27, p. 2, April 24, 1865, p. 4; Charles Lee Armour, April 20, 1865, Statement, in Evidence Book, File A, p. 5, JAO, RG 153, NA.

18. *OR*, Ser. I, Vol. XLVI, Pt. 3, p. 799. Stanton also warned General Sherman that assassins were after him, based on a report he had received from Consul F. H. Morse in England that both Seward and Sherman were marked for death. Sherman replied, "I received your dispatch describing the man Clark detailed to assassinate me. He had better be in a hurry or he will be too late." *OR*, Ser. I, Vol. XLVII, Pt. 3, p. 245. George Julian, "Journal—The Assassination of Lincoln," *Indiana Magazine of History*, XI (1915), 334; David Donald (ed.), *Inside Lincoln's Cabinet: The Civil War Diaries of Salmon P. Chase* (New York: Longmans, Green, 1954), 267.

One of the other major charges leveled at Stanton is that he almost singlehandedly set on foot a campaign to involve Jefferson Davis and other southern leaders in guilt for the assassination when in fact he knew they were innocent. As noted, this ignores the fact that at the end of a very bloody war many people were naturally going to believe that the enemy was involved. Many factors led people to reach the conclusion that the South was behind the murder.[19] While it has not generally been recognized, newspapers, particularly the sensational dime press, probably had as much influence in producing a belief in southern complicity as Stanton did. Several pamphlets appeared at the time of the assassination, recounting in lurid detail Booth's involvement with the Knights of the Golden Circle and rebel leaders. Such works are either sneeringly dismissed by historians as loaded with inaccuracies, as indeed they are, or not even considered. Yet, the fairly wide preservation in libraries of such pamphlets gives some indication of the popularity they once enjoyed. These works certainly appealed to the preconceived notions people held about the assassination.

One work, entitled *The Great Conspiracy*, details Booth's joining of the Knights of the Golden Circle and a meeting at Montreal where Booth, to the delight of all present, agreed to kill Lincoln. Meetings between Booth, Herold, Mudd, and Mrs. Surratt are described, with Mrs. Surratt being portrayed as extremely vicious. She told Booth that if she could not find a man to kill Seward, she would be glad to do the job herself. Booth was also pictured as receiving approval of the assassination plot from Davis' cabinet member, Judah P. Benjamin, through the Knights of the Golden Circle and then notifying Davis through the same source of his plans, so that proper arrangements might be made.[20]

Other similar works were *John Wilkes Booth* by Dion Haco and the spurious *Confession de John Wilkes Booth*, in both its original French and later English versions. This latter, a diary allegedly written by Booth,

19. Among those charging Stanton with stirring up antisouthern sentiment is DeWitt, *Assassination of Abraham Lincoln*, 61. Helen J. Campbell, *The Case for Mrs. Surratt* (New York: G. P. Putman's Sons, 1943), 115, goes so far as to charge that the slowing of the funeral train as it made its way to Springfield was a carefully arranged show calculated to have the desired effect on the people who viewed it.

20. *The Great Conspiracy, A Book of Absorbing Interest! Startling Developments . . . and the Life and Extraordinary Adventures of John H. Surratt, the Conspirator* (Philadelphia: Barclay, 1866), 36–37, 70, 111–13.

does not directly implicate Confederate leaders; but it does attempt to show that Booth's actions were motivated by southern loyalties, because after Bull Run, Federal soldiers had committed atrocities against some of Booth's friends. That such pamphlets were known and read is revealed by the London *Times'* criticism of the English government in 1867 for allowing the English version of Booth's confessions to be published.[21]

John Surratt received similar treatment. The *Great Conspiracy*, for example, contains a section wherein Surratt is pictured as whipping a small Negro boy and as shooting his teacher in the leg for disciplining him. Haco also produced a companion piece to his work on Booth, *The Journal and Diary of John H. Surratt*, which portrays Surratt also as a member of the Knights of the Golden Circle.[22]

Under the circumstances, it is not likely that Stanton could have changed public opinion if he had wished to, and admittedly he had no such desire. His fascination with the letter signed by Sam and found in Booth's trunk, which called for going to see how Richmond would feel about some mysterious affair, indicates his belief in southern complicity, as does the following announcement of the assassination to the United States minister to England, Charles Francis Adams: "The murderer of the President has been discovered and evidence obtained that these horrible crimes were committed in execution of a conspiracy deliberately planned and set on foot by rebels under pretense of avenging the South and aiding the rebel cause." The idea that the assassination was a southern conspiracy was too congenial to people's beliefs to have been challenged by mere assertions to the contrary, especially when

21. Dion J. Haco, *John Wilkes Booth: The Assassinator of President Lincoln* (New York: T. R. Dawley, 1865), 15–21, 30–31, 34–35. Haco is apparently a pseudonym, and there are internal evidences, both in phraseology and scenes depicted, that *The Great Conspiracy* borrowed liberally from Haco, or else he was the author of both works. *Confession de John Wilkes Booth, Assassin du Président Abraham Lincoln* (Paris: Chez Tous Les Libraires, 1865); *Wilkes Booth's Private Confession of the Murder of Abraham Lincoln and His Terrible Oath of Vengeance Furnished by an Escaped Confederate* (London: Newsagent's, 1865). London *Times*, June 6, 1867, quoted in New York *Herald*, June 21, 1867, p. 7.

22. *The Great Conspiracy*, 181–84; Dion Haco, *The Private Journal and Diary of John H. Surratt, the Conspirator, Edited and Arranged* (New York: Frederic A. Brady, 1866). Of similar nature was the *Life, Trial and Adventures of John H. Surratt, The Conspirator: A Correct Account and Highly Interesting Narrative of His Doings and Adventures from Childhood to the Present Time* (Philadelphia: Barclay, 1867), which was probably published in order to take advantage of the expected interest in the John Surratt trial in 1867.

proof seemed abundant at every turn. Had Stanton immediately asserted that the South was not involved, many people would undoubtedly have wondered what was the matter with the government.[23]

Finally, if Stanton was involved in any manner in betraying Lincoln, it would appear that he was indeed an ingenious dissimulator, for his grief seems to have been all too genuine. When Surgeon General Joseph Barnes informed him that the wounds were mortal, he is reported to have sobbed out, "Oh, no, General; no-no," and then to have sat down on a chair by the bedside and wept like a child. Corporal Tanner also recorded his impression. "I knew it was only by a powerful effort that he restrained himself and that he was near a break." When the Reverend Phineas Gurley finished his prayer on Lincoln's death, Stanton had tears streaming down his cheeks as he uttered his immortal assessment, "Now he belongs to the Ages." Even for a period after the assassination Stanton's grief was apparently uncontrollable.[24]

Stanton has often been portrayed as being extremely cold and brutal to Mrs. Lincoln in her hour of grief. Yet in the Stanton papers, dated April 28, 1865, is the following from Robert Lincoln to Stanton: "Would you, if convenient, be kind enough to call this evening to see mother?" Evidently Mrs. Lincoln felt that she could still rely on the war secretary. On Stanton's death, Robert wrote very touchingly to his son, "I know that it is useless to say anything . . . and yet when I recall the kindness of your father to me, when my father was lying dead and I felt utterly desperate, hardly able to realize the truth, I am as little able to keep my eyes from filling with tears as he was then."[25]

---

23. *OR*, Ser. I, Vol. XLVI, Pt. 3, p. 781. The Warren Report's conclusion about the John F. Kennedy assassination as well as a recent Congressional investigation have certainly not put to rest rumors and theories concerning that event. It is not apparent why the performance of government officials in 1865 should be judged by any higher standards.

24. Abott, *Assassination and Death of Abraham Lincoln*, 6; Henry L. Burnett, "Assassination of President Lincoln and the Trials of the Assassins," in James H. Kennedy (ed.), *History of the Ohio Society of New York, 1885–1905* (New York: Grafton Press, 1906), 592; James Tanner, in New York *Sun*, April 16, 1905, p. 7; Horace Porter, "Campaigning with Grant," *Century Magazine*, LIV (1897), 893. Interestingly, Eisenschiml, *Why Was Lincoln Murdered?*, 482–85, questions whether Stanton ever said "Now he belongs to the Ages," when the evidence is overwhelming that he did. See, for example, Charles Sabin Taft, "Abraham Lincoln's Last Hours," *Century Magazine*, XLV (1893), 635.

25. Robert Lincoln to Edwin Stanton, April 28, 1865, in Stanton Papers; Benjamin Thomas and Harold Hyman, *Stanton: The Life and Times of Lincoln's Secretary of War* (New York: Alfred A. Knopf, 1962), 638.

If Stanton did overreact, and few can deny a certain overzealousness, clues to it can be found very readily in his personality, without the necessity of resorting to a conspiracy theory. Gideon Welles was not friendly to Stanton, and his judgments must therefore be used with caution; however, his portrait of an August 18 cabinet meeting seems to have captured very well the impact that the assassination had on Stanton.

> Stanton is full of apprehension and stories of plots and conspiracies. I am inclined to believe he has fears, and he evidently wishes to have the President . . . alarmed. He had quite a story today, and read quite a long affidavit from someone whom I do not recall, stating he had been in communication with C. C. Clay and others in Canada, that they wanted him to be one of a party to assassinate President Lincoln and his whole cabinet. . . . I think it likely . . . Stanton believes me stupid that . . . I give so little heed to his sensational communications; but really a large portion of them seem to me ludicrous and puerile. He still keeps up a guard around his house and never ventures out without a stout man to accompany him . . . (He urges a similar guard for me and others).[26]

Stanton's attempt to hire Edwards Pierrepont, future prosecution lawyer in the John Surratt trial, to bring charges against Horace Greeley and the New York *Tribune* for allegedly urging his assassination suggests a similar overreaction. Stanton, like Judge Advocate Holt, who prosecuted the conspirators, could readily envision vast plots behind the simplest situation, but it is not unusual that under the circumstances his imagination ran away with him.[27]

While Stanton made some mistakes, when judged both by his contemporaries and in the light of other assassinations, his performance was above average. Charges of failing to protect Lincoln, inciting needless grief and apprehension, and arousing the nation to a frenzied pitch appear patently absurd. His trying experience and great responsibility during four years of Civil War, and what appeared at the time to be ample evidence, led the war secretary in one direction, and he followed it with energy—as did the majority of the American people.

26. Howard K. Beale (ed.), *Diary of Gideon Welles* (3 vols.; New York: W. W. Norton, 1960), II, 362–63.
27. *OR*, Ser. I, Vol. XLVI, Pt. 3, pp. 1141, 1149.

5.

Assassination Foreknowledge and the Kidnapping Plot

After the assassination, large numbers of people recalled previous occurrences as forewarnings of the event. This has led to further charges that, with assassination so widely anticipated, it was criminal for the government not to provide the president with better protection. Yet on the eve of the assassination, with the war almost over, people had in fact apparently assumed that the president was no longer in danger.[1]

The assassination also evoked the memory of previous assassination attempts in American history. The Albany *Atlas and Argus* reminded its readers of a plot to assassinate George Washington in 1776, when one of the privates in his bodyguard was hanged. Other journals recalled the attempt of Richard Lawrence to take the life of Andrew Jackson.[2]

Rumors rapidly arose that other presidents who had died in office had come to their end not by the ravages of disease or old age but by the secret hand of southern poisoners. This was an especially common assumption from the pulpit, where it was positively asserted that Whig presidents William Henry Harrison and Zachary Taylor had met such a fate. Others added Stephen Douglas and President James Buchanan, who was still living, to the list of those who had been the object of southern poison attempts.[3]

Johnson's unfortunate behavior on inauguration day was now ex-

1. The fact that this was the first presidential assassination in American history must have further increased the traumatic shock caused by the event. Before the assassination of John F. Kennedy, Americans of this generation had pretty much assumed that assassination was a phenomenon of the past, and again it shocked them. See Robert J. Donovan, *The Assassins* (New York: Harper Bros., 1955), for a view that Secret Service protection was so good that assassination was no longer conceivable.

2. Albany *Atlas and Argus*, April 26, 1865, p. 2; Washington *Daily National Intelligencer*, April 25, 1865, p. 1.

3. George Duffield, *The Nation's Wail . . . Brutal Murder of President Abraham Lincoln by a Brutal Assassin* (Detroit: *Advertiser* and *Tribune*, 1865), 11; William Goodwin, *Death of Abraham Lincoln: A Discourse . . . Delivered at North Colebrook, Conn., April 23, 1865* (Hartford: David B. Moselet, 1865), 9.

plained as being the result of a poison plot rather than alcohol. An anonymous writer informed Secretary Stanton that the poison administered to the vice-president was hashish and said he hoped the government might take steps to ascertain General George B. McClellan's connection in the matter.[4]

The discovery of a pane of glass at the McHenry House hotel in Meadville, Pennsylvania, with its message, supposedly written by Booth, that Lincoln died by poison on August 13, 1864, also seemed to indicate previous poison plots against Lincoln. Clerk James F. Duncan said that Booth had occupied this room June 4, 1864, and several times since, with friends. F. F. Munson of Franklin, Pennsylvania, became so incensed that the pane was being shown as a tourist attraction that he wrote the government that it should confiscate this piece of evidence. A later investigation determined that Booth had indeed stayed at the hotel, though not in the room containing the pane.[5]

News of Lincoln's assassination was also supposedly known beforehand in numerous locations. From Manchester, New Hampshire, Assistant Provost Marshal William Silvey informed Provost Marshal General James Fry that the assassination reportedly was known at 1 P.M. on the day of the murder and he was investigating the circumstances. He later enclosed reports of Captain Hosea Eaton and affidavits of people who had sworn to the story. While stating that he was still not fully convinced of the validity of the rumor, he assured Fry that it was very generally credited in that part of the country.[6]

Information also began to come into the government's possession making it appear that copperheads and rebels were generally aware of the plot. H. A. Pierce, employed in the Department of the Interior, said he had spoken to eight rebel generals in the Baltimore Depot on the day of the assassination and that one of them, General Hunton,

4. New York *Ledger*, quoted in New York *Times*, May 7, 1865, p. 1; [?] to Stanton, N.d., in Letters Received, File A 276, JAO, 1865, RG 153, NA.

5. New York *Herald*, April 26, 1865, p. 4; J. Heron Foster, April 27, Forwards Affidavit of James F. Duncan, Letters Received, File F 200, and F. F. Munson to James B. Fry, May 8, Letters Received, File M 263, both in JAO, 1865, RG 153, NA; Ernest Miller, *John Wilkes Booth, Oilman* (New York: Exposition Press, 1947), 46, 46n74.

6. William Silvey to James Fry, April 24, 1865, in RG 110, Records of the Provost Marshal General's Bureau, Correspondence and Reports Re: Disloyal and Suspects in the Lincoln Assassination Plot (1863–1865), Entry 38, and May 9, 1865, in Letters Received, File S 515, JAO, RG 153, both in NA.

had said, "I tell you, Sir, there are agencies at work which you Northern people know not of, and at the proper time they will strike, and the Confederacy will yet raise its head in some work and win for itself a name among the nations."[7]

Similarly, Susannah Hann, who had lived in Richmond three years with Samuel Murray's family, informed the government that Booth and Surratt had been there about three weeks before the fall of Richmond. She heard Murray tell his wife they were planning to kill Lincoln and that Jefferson Davis, Fitzhugh Lee, and Robert E. Lee and his wife had all contributed money to the cause.[8]

Of course, an obvious explanation for most of these reports is that people misinterpreted what had been said to them. For example, the *Whig Press* of Middleton, New York, reported on Wednesday, April 19, that in the village of Pine Bush, town of Crawford, the assassination of the president had been reported before noon on April 14. However, when General Fry investigated, he concluded that the report had evidently occurred because of a political discussion between a Miss Decker and a Mr. Taylor, and he could not find in the area any organization hostile to the government. One John Harrison, who found himself in Old Capitol Prison for wagering that Lincoln would be assassinated, explained to the authorities that he had indeed wagered that Lincoln would not hold the presidential chair for the next four years because he had a strong conviction that the president would not be reelected. He added that he believed that Amos Day had had him arrested because of a family quarrel.[9]

The important point is not that the majority of such evidence was based on erroneous notions and misinterpretations, but that in 1865 the substantial number of communications received by the government made it appear there was something behind it. While historians have generally dismissed this material out of hand, much of it was not merely crank mail but came from apparently substantial citizens. In a note Mrs. J. M. Hayes stated that E. Louis O'Donnel, employed on the Baltimore and Ohio Railroad, came to her house one evening the previous De-

---

7. H. A. Pierce, April 26, 1865, Statement, in Record Book, File P, p. 14, JAO, *ibid.*
8. Susannah Hann, May, 1865, in Letters Received, File Evidence H 418, *ibid.*
9. *Ibid.*: *Whig Press*, April 19, 1865, in File Folder 3; James B. Fry, May 12, in Letters Received, File F 388, John Harrison, May 18, Statement, in Letters Received, File H 394, both in JAO, 1865.

cember and said in the course of conversation that Lincoln would never see Illinois again whether the South succeeded or not. The interesting point is that she had written under the urging of General William Morris of Fort McHenry. Such evidence, sent at the request of a general, could hardly be ignored by the government; and most information came from sources that appeared to be equally reliable.[10]

Although no historian has considered it, the investigation conducted was rather methodical, and the files maintained coincided with the normal record-keeping procedures of this period. National Archives RG 153 contains the letters and telegrams sent by Colonel H. L. Burnett, who was in charge of the investigation; a register of letters received, along with copies; the record or evidence book set up to record material for possible use in a trial; and an endorsement book. While there are some mistakes in filing and a few missing documents, and it is not always apparent why some things were considered evidence and others were not, the files show a rather systematic gathering of evidence.

Historians, pointing to the obviously tainted evidence given at the conspiracy trials by convicted perjurers Sanford Conover, James Merritt, and Richard Montgomery, have questioned whether the entire investigation was not merely an effort to acquire evidence to convict. It is true that Judge Advocate Holt and others were at best badly deceived and at worst involved in a plot to suborn perjured testimony, but most of the evidence received came unsolicited by the government. Taking away all the testimony that was obviously perjured, there was still a volume of apparently untainted testimony that led to the same conclusion of southern involvement and foreknowledge of the plot. Amazing as it now seems, even Conover's testimony, which was rumored to be perjured before the close of the conspiracy trials because of his contradictory statements and incredible conduct in Canada, hardly aroused a ripple. People just could not conceive that his tales of rebel involvement could be untrue.

Certainly rumors of kidnapping and assassination plots against Lincoln were not new. The Civil War had engendered great hatreds against Lincoln just as it did against Davis, and constant rumors of assassination and kidnapping plots dated all the way back to the Baltimore plot

10. Mrs. J. M. Hayes to Stanton, April 23, 1865, in Letters Received, File H 38, JAO, *ibid*.

to kill the president on the way to his first inauguration. Newspapers were filled with suggestions for violence against the president. On one occasion the Baltimore *South* carried the following poem:

Two posts standant;
One beam crossant;
One rope pendent;
Abram on the end on't,
Glorious! Splendent.

The New York *Copperhead* had its own suggestions of Lincoln's fate if he did not perform his duties more to their liking. "Behave yourself in future, boss, or we shall be obliged to make an island of your head and stick it on the end of a pole. Then, for the first time, Lincoln's cocoanut will be well posted." The infamous advertisement that appeared in the Selma, Alabama, *Dispatch* several times, offering for one million dollars to take the lives of Lincoln, Seward, and Johnson before March 1, became very well known after the assassination and also seemed to indicate a concerted effort in the South to murder Lincoln.[11]

This, of course, has led to the additional charge that if plots against the president were so widely known, word of them must have come to the ears of the government. Lafayette Baker recalled that when he reported to Stanton to begin the pursuit of the conspirators, the secretary greeted him with the following words: "Well, Baker, they have now performed what they have long threatened to do; they have killed the President."[12] The question raised is why, if Stanton knew so much about these assassination plots, he did so little about them.

More specifically, it has been charged that the government possessed knowledge of the Booth plot. Kidnapping knowledge seems to have been so widespread in southern Maryland that it would appear that the

---

11. Baltimore *South*, June 7, 1861, and New York *Copperhead*, July 11, 1863, in George S. Bryan, *The Great American Myth* (New York: Carrick and Evans, 1940), 39. Bryan suggests that the climate of opinion is very important in regard to the frequency of assassinations. While no study has been made to validate these conclusions, the recent wave of assassination and corresponding levels of violence in America are suggestive of some correlation. Osborn H. Oldroyd, *The Assassination of Abraham Lincoln, Flight, Pursuit, Capture, and Punishment of the Conspirators* (Washington: O. H. Oldroyd, 1901), 218.

12. Lafayette C. Baker, *History of the United States Secret Service* (Philadelphia: King and Baird, 1867), 525. Eisenschiml believes that this reveals knowledge of assassination plots. See Otto Eisenschiml, *Why Was Lincoln Murdered?* (Boston: Little Brown, 1937), 148.

government must have been aware of the danger to the president. Thomas A. Jones, who aided Booth across the Potomac, claimed that in December, 1864, he had heard of a plot to kidnap Lincoln and carry him South. Such reports were even seen in the press from time to time. The New York *Tribune*, after the assassination, reprinted a letter of March 19, 1864, from its correspondent, relating details of a plot to kidnap Lincoln. The *Tribune* mused whether this was the Booth plot and, if so, whether the Confederate leaders had been aware of it.[13]

There was even another plot existing at the same time as Booth's, set underway by Confederate soldier Thomas Nelson Conrad. He and an accomplice named Mountjoy had secured a pass from James A. Seddon, Confederate secretary of war, to facilitate their movements, though he stoutly maintained that the Confederate authorities had no knowledge of his actual plans. However, when they went to carry out their plan of seizing Lincoln on the way to the Soldier's Home, an idea quite similar to one of Booth's schemes, they discovered that Lincoln's carriage was now surrounded by a squad of cavalry. Fearing that the authorities had discovered their intentions, they abandoned the plot.[14]

Yet there is more than just a suspicion that the government was aware of Booth's plot. Even the conspirators, according to John Surratt, were afraid either that the government had discovered them or was about to. Although the exact circumstances have remained unclear, Louis Weichmann informed D. H. L. Gleason, a fellow clerk in the Commissary General of Prisoners Office, of his suspicions of the activities going on at the house of Mrs. Surratt about February 20. Gleason supposedly passed on this information to Lieutenant Joshua W. Sharp, an assistant provost marshal on General Augur's staff. In a little-known newspaper clipping, John C. Martin, who had worked with Gleason, presents evidence that the knowledge reached all the way to Stanton. Martin says Gleason told him that Stanton said: "Thank you, Major. . . . I do not think they will be successful on February 20 or any other day, for that matter."[15] The fact that the government was able so rapidly to get on

---

13. Thomas A. Jones, *J. Wilkes Booth: An Account of His Sojourn in Southern Maryland After the Assassination of Abraham Lincoln, His Passage Across the Potomac, and His Death in Virginia* (Chicago: Laird and Lee, 1893), 39; New York *Tribune*, April 26, 1865, p. 4.
14. Thomas N. Conrad, *The Rebel Scout* (Washington: National, 1904), 118–19, 124.
15. Clara E. Laughlin, *The Death of Lincoln, the Story of Booth's Plot, His Deed and the Penalty* (New York: Doubleday, Page, 1909), 227, 229; D. H. L. Gleason, "Conspiracy

the track of the main conspirators indicates that this was a group it had under surveillance.

However, to admit that there was an atmosphere of hatred and many plots, some of which were known to the government, still does not mean that Stanton was guilty of gross negligence. Lincoln had been provided with a cavalry escort only over his objections, and Ohio Congressman John A. Bingham recalled that Lincoln had fully expected to be assassinated on the day he was inaugurated for his second term. On that occasion Stanton had offered to appoint a select body of officers to keep watch over him day and night, especially when he went out. However on this occasion, as on others, Lincoln merely replied: "Stanton, it is useless. If it is the will of Providence that I should die by the hand of an assassin, it must be so."[16]

There is some evidence that Stanton was correct in his concern and that Booth attempted to get near Lincoln at the second inauguration, perhaps for the purpose of assassination. Officer John W. Westfall detailed the story of preventing a man from bursting through police lines to reach the platform during the inauguration—a man who was identified after the assassination by Westfall and Commissioner Benjamin B. French as Booth. However, from photographs of the inauguration it appears that Booth was present on the stand, so that the man who attempted to breach the police lines must have been someone else. The fact that Booth was present is also verified by his statement to actor Samuel Knapp Chester: "What a splendid chance I had to kill the President on the 4th of March."[17]

On several other occasions precautions were taken for Lincoln's life

---

Against Lincoln," *Magazine of History*, XIII (February, 1911), 59; Lowell Ames Morris, in Boston *Herald*, Dec. 1, 1929, in Stone Collection, Boston University.

16. John A. Bingham, "Recollections of Lincoln and Stanton, by Honorable John A. Bingham of Ohio, the Judge Advocate That Tried the Assassins" (Typescript of the originals, compiled by J. L. Conwell and in the possession of Milton Ronsheim, in John A. Bingham Papers, Ohio Historical Society), Microcopy, Roll 1.

17. Ward H. Lamon, *Recollections of Abraham Lincoln, 1847–1865* (Chicago: A. C. McClung, 1895), 267–68; New York *Tribune*, February 15, 1884, p. 3. See Dorothy M. Kunhardt and Phillip B. Kunhardt, Jr., *Twenty Days* (New York: Harper and Row, 1965), 31ff, on identification of Booth. Their claim that all the rest of the conspirators are visible in the photograph of the second inauguration, especially Spangler, is dubious. Contemporaries believed Westfall's story that he had grappled with Booth. For this action he was appointed to the special office of lieutenant of police, a post he held until 1876. Samuel Chester, Statement, N.d., in Evidence Book, File B, p. 8, JAO, 1865, RG 153, NA.

when plots were uncovered, but as John Nicolay and John Hay, Lincoln's secretaries and biographers say: "In cases where there seemed a ground for inquiry it was made, as carefully as possible, by the President's private secretary and by the War Department, but always without substantial result. Warnings that appeared to be most definite, when they came to be examined proved too vague and confused for further attention."[18]

Lincoln, then, like most presidents, was a difficult person to guard even when precautions were taken, and arrangements in 1865 were certainly far more primitive than today. Protection provided was hardly systematic, and Lincoln often went unattended to places where it was obviously unsafe for him to go. Even in 1865, the president felt the need not to have the appearance of being isolated from the people.

Lincoln's fatalistic reply to Stanton about assassination was echoed in a similar discussion with William Crook, his chief of security. And one of the president's closest friends, Marshal Ward Hill Lamon, said that Lincoln once told him that Adam Gurowski, a Polish count who served as a State Department translator, might be out to take his life but that if he feared anyone else, it certainly did not interfere with his daily routine.[19]

The major reason, however, why concern for Lincoln was beginning to lessen at the end of the war was that people apparently felt that assassination was no longer possible. Even Marshal Lamon, who recounted an attempt against Lincoln on his way to the Soldier's Home (he was fired upon and his hat was knocked off) and who was probably the most anxious of all Lincoln's friends for his safety, expressed the belief that assassination was not really an American phenomenon. "But the truth is, the crime of assassination was so abhorrent to the genius of Anglo-Saxon civilization, so foreign to the practice of our republican institutions, that little danger was apprehended of an outrage against society at large, the recollection of which even now suffices to tinge

18. John G. Nicolay and John Hay, "Abraham Lincoln: A History of the Fourteenth of April—The Fate of the Assassins—The Mourning Pageant," *Century Magazine*, XXXIX (1890), 431.
19. Margarita S. Gerry (ed.), *Through Five Administrations: Reminiscences of Colonel William H. Crook, Body-Guard to President Lincoln* (New York: Harper and Bros., 1910), 66; Lamon, *Recollections*, 269.

with a blush of shame the cheek of every true American, whether of Northern or Southern birth."[20]

Others shared this view. On the night of the assassination Senator Orville Browning wrote in his diary: "The Marshal W. H. Lamon has several times within the last two months told me that he believed the President would be assassinated, but I had no fear whatever that such an event would occur. . . . It seemed to me that the people in rebellion had many reasons for desiring the continuance of his life—none to wish his death—and I did not think any of the disaffected among us could be insane and fiendish enough to perpetrate the deed." Diarist George T. Strong also wrote, "I predicted an attempt would be made on Lincoln's life when he went to Richmond; but just now, I should have said the danger was past."[21]

It appears, then, that the government may have been aware of Booth's plot to kidnap the president in hopes of exchanging him for rebel prisoners. However, many rumors of such plots, and probably several real plots, existed, and Stanton could not take them all seriously or go public with them. Thus when the unexpected occurred, and one of these plots that seemed to have no chance of success led to murder, Stanton probably tried to keep any prior knowledge as quiet as possible, so as to avoid embarrassing questions.

As part of this coverup, historians have often argued that the reason Booth's diary was suppressed during the conspiracy trial was to keep knowledge of just such a kidnapping plot from the public and to make it appear that murder had been contemplated from the beginning. This would screen the government's negligence and allow for the hanging and imprisonment of legally innocent people who had been involved only in the abortive kidnap plot.[22]

20. Lamon, *Recollections*, 262, 272.
21. James G. Randall and Theodore C. Pease (eds.), *Diary of Orville Hickman Browning* (2 vols.; Springfield, Ill.: Jefferson's Printing and Stationery, 1933), II, 18; Allan Nevins and Milton Thomas (eds.), *Diary of George T. Strong* (4 vols.; New York: MacMillan, 1952), IV, 582. Benjamin Thomas and Harold Hyman, *Stanton: The Life and Times of Lincoln's Secretary of War* (New York: Alfred A. Knopf, 1962), 393, argue with justification that Stanton shared these feelings.
22. David M. DeWitt, *The Assassination of Abraham Lincoln and Its Expiation* (New York: MacMillan, 1909), 36, 96–97; Victor L. Mason, "Four Lincoln Conspirators, Including New Particulars of the Flight and Capture of the Assassins," *Century Magazine*,

Others hint darkly that Booth's statement, "I have a greater desire and almost a mind to return to Washington and clear my name which I feel I can do," refers to the involvement of high-ranking northern officials. Again this is misleading, for while the diary was technically suppressed or simply not introduced during the trial, many people were aware that the plot had originally been one to kidnap. The pamphlet *Terrible Tragedy at Washington* clearly stated that the letter Booth left with his brother-in-law John Sleeper Clarke revealed that abduction, not assassination, was planned. The New York *World*, citing the same letter, made the following comment: "It is tolerably plain, from the text of this letter, that so long ago as last November Booth had planned, not indeed the assassination, but the capture of President Lincoln, with the object of surrendering him as a prisoner to the rebel government."[23]

The diary was not *suppressed* in the sense historians have used the term, for its existence was rumored at the time. The New York *Times* of April 28 told its readers that Booth had a diary in which he had jotted down events since the assassination. The Albany *Atlas and Argus* commented that it doubted reports that the diary connected the rebel government to the plot.[24] That the government would willfully suppress this document when its existence was so widely mentioned is inconceivable. A chance reading about the diary in the newspapers and subsequent investigation could have caused the government no end of embarrassment. Why defense lawyers were not aware of the diary and did not attempt to have it introduced is puzzling, but the fact remains that they did not.

The diary also became controversial later on during the impeachment investigation, when Lafayette Baker charged that some pages had been removed. Before the House Judiciary Committee, Baker testified that he or Colonel Everton Conger had handed the diary to Stanton and

---

LI (1896), 897; George F. Milton, *The Age of Hate* (New York: Coward-McCann, 1930), 32; E. W. Coggeshall, *The Assassination of Lincoln* (Chicago: Walter M. Hill, 1920), 15; Francis X. Busch, *Enemies of the State* (Indianapolis: Bobbs-Merrill, 1954), 79.

23. John Wilkes Booth Diary (Xerox copy in LC); *The Terrible Tragedy at Washington: Assassination of President Lincoln* (Philadelphia: Barclay, 1865), 91; New York *World*, April 20, 1865, p. 4.

24. New York *Times*, April 28, 1865, p. 1; Albany *Atlas and Argus* May 1, 1865, p. 2. For further mention of the diary, see George A. Townsend, *The Life, Crime, and Capture of John Wilkes Booth with a Full Sketch of the Conspiracy of Which He Was the Leader, and the Pursuit, Trial, and Execution of His Accomplices* (New York: Dick and Fitzgerald, 1865), 37.

that after looking at it, Stanton handed it back to him. He was then asked about the condition of the diary. "Q. Do you mean to say that at the time you gave the book to the Secretary of War there were no leaves gone? A. I do."[25]

Without exception, those who had the diary in their possession or had seen it testified that the leaves were missing from the time it first came into possession of the government. Baker was even caught in a direct lie by a man usually considered to be one of his trusted subordinates, for he had claimed that there was in the diary a sheet with a house on it and that he and Colonel Conger had examined it to determine if it might be Mrs. Surratt's house. Yet Conger testified not only that Baker had not examined the book before it was given to Stanton, but that Baker did not even know that Conger had it in his possession. It is interesting that historians who would hardly believe Baker under oath if he swore to his own name are so willing to believe this testimony, especially when it was so widely contradicted.[26]

Stanton himself testified that the diary was brought to him by Baker and another officer. He did not retain it after examining it but returned it to either Baker or Major Eckert, who delivered it to the judge advocate, and he had not seen it since. Eckert verified that it had been given to him and placed in his safe, where it had remained until given to Judge Holt.[27]

Judge Holt, when examined before the committee, gave the following reason why the diary had not been introduced: "There was nothing in the Diary which I could conceive would be testimony against any human being, or for anyone except Booth himself, and he being dead, I did not offer it to the Commission." Stanton had testified the day before that although he had examined it with great care, he could find

25. Lafayette C. Baker, May 20, 1867, in U.S. Congress, House, Committee on the Judiciary, *Impeachment Investigation: Testimony Taken Before the Judiciary Committee of the House of Representatives in the Investigation of the Charges Against Andrew Johnson*, 39th Cong., 2nd Sess, 40th Cong., 1st Sess, (Washington: Government Printing Office, 1867), 827, hereinafter cited as *Impeachment Investigation*. Eisenschiml, *Why Was Lincoln Murdered?*, 142–44.

26. Joseph Holt, February 7, April 7, 1867, Everton J. Conger, May 13 and 14, 1867, Luther B. Baker, May 22, 1867, Thomas T. Eckert, May 30, 1867, *Impeachment Investigation*, 282, 285, 324, 330, 332, 485, 672.

27. Edwin M. Stanton, April 1, 1867, Thomas T. Eckert, May 30, 1867, *Impeachment Investigation*, 280–82, 672. See also Thomas T. Eckert, Statement, April 2, 1867, in Edwin M. Stanton Papers, LC.

no trace of any other person being connected with Booth in an assassination conspiracy.[28]

Stanton and Holt's statements in this case would seem to have merit, for the point is that a large portion of the public was aware of the original nature of the plot but did not care to quibble over fine distinctions. If abduction had led to murder, then so much the worse for those who had been involved in any manner. It is inconceivable that the uncontested statement of Booth in his diary that murder was contemplated only on April 14 would have made one bit of difference to people in 1865. There has also been some attempt to seize on John Surratt's Rockville speech, wherein he called the kidnap plot noble and said any youth in the North with one spark of patriotism would have done the same thing in the case of Jefferson Davis. Such a statement in 1865, however, would have placed the speaker in imminent bodily danger, and even in 1870, there was sentiment against Surratt being allowed to present his lecture.[29]

In any case, people looked back after the assassination and thought they saw many events that foreshadowed the deed. The hatred of Lincoln and the numerous plots that had been rumored throughout the war all seemed to point to southern complicity. The cries for vengeance grew increasingly louder.

28. Edwin M. Stanton, April 1, 1867, Joseph Holt, April 2, 1867, *Impeachment Investigation*, 281, 285. Even Dr. Mudd was later puzzled as to why the diary had not been introduced during the trial, for he felt it would show the guilt of Booth's associates and his own innocence (although what he bases this on is unclear). Samuel Mudd, June 3, 1867, in Nettie Mudd, *The Life of Dr. Samuel A. Mudd, Containing His Letters from Fort Jefferson, Dry Tortugas, Where He Was Imprisoned Four Years for Alleged Complicity in the Assassination of Abraham Lincoln* (Marietta, Ga.: Continental Book, 1955), 238. Of course, if David Balsiger and Charles E. Sellier, Jr., *The Lincoln Conspiracy* (Los Angeles: Schick Sunn Classic Books, 1977), were correct in stating that incriminating pages were indeed removed as Lafayette Baker charged, then the authorities would have had ample reason to suppress the diary.

29. Laughlin, *Death of Lincoln*, 226–27.

6.

Voices from the Pulpit

Sermons preached after the assassination are an excellent means of gauging public reaction, yet they have been virtually unexamined by historians. Thousands of people flocked to churches after the assassination to hear ministers attempt to express their grief in words. A sermon preached by the Reverend R. J. Keeling drew 1,500 persons to a building that would only seat 1,200. Often the publication of the sermons was precipitated by the request of parishioners who petitioned the minister because they felt that his views so well mirrored their own and ought to be preserved for posterity. However, there is evidence that interest did wane to a degree, for the Reverend Mr. Keeling lamented that if his sermon had been printed right after the assassination, several more editions might have been sold.[1]

Very little emotional restraint was shown in sermons preached between April 16 and June 1. This is evident even in the texts chosen for sermons, for the majority were selected from the Old Testament, whose vengeful God was apparently more congenial to the hatreds raised by the assassination. Such views extended outside the churches and revealed themselves in harsh plans for reconstruction and reconciliation, and a speedy return to peace became extremely unpopular.[2]

Ministers usually began sermons by noting the happiness produced by the end of the war and then the contrast in public feeling that oc-

---

1. R. J. Keeling, *The Death of Moses* (Washington: W. H. and O. H. Morrison, 1865), Frontpiece. J. Monaghan, "An Analysis of Lincoln's Funeral Sermons," *Indiana Magazine of History*, XLI (1945), 31–44; Lloyd Lewis, *Myths After Lincoln* (New York: Harcourt Brace, 1929); Charles J. Stewart, "Lincoln's Assassination and the Protestant Clergy of the North," *Journal of the Illinois State Historical Society*, LIV (1961), 268–93, "The Pulpit and the Assassination of Lincoln," *Quarterly Journal of Speech*, L (1964), 299–307, and "A Rhetorical Study of the Reaction of the Protestant Pulpit in the North to Lincoln's Assassination" (Ph.D. dissertation, University of Illinois, 1963). Several of these individuals are speech experts who analyzed the sermons more for rhetorical patterns than for what they might reveal historically.

2. Stewart, "Rhetorical Study of the Reaction," 25, 79, 96.

curred after Lincoln's death. The belief was also frequently expressed that the murder was carried out by the South. If the Radicals have been criticized for vindictiveness, the clergy in sheer weight of numbers, influence, and level of harshness, "out-radicaled" the Radicals. Ministers were quick to brand the assassination as the legitimate offspring of the rebellion. The Reverend W. H. Benade told his congregation, "And, thus, did the rebellion prove itself, by its own last act, to have been all a murder, clothed in the dark and filthy rags of a lie, the very child and image of him who was a 'murderer and a liar from the beginning.'"[3]

However, bitterness was directed not only against the South but even more against what many considered to be behind the southern treason—that is, the system of slavery. Therefore, the Reverend T. H. Robinson told his listeners that whereas the assassin had shouted "So perish the tyrant evermore," intending it to be the verdict of mankind and history against Lincoln, in fact it had become the verdict not only of mankind and history but also of God, against the murderer, "that in one foul deed, they might see the whole nature and disposition of slavery."[4]

In several cases the assassination had apparently changed the minds of those who had been moderate to a more vindictive position. The Reverend Morgan Dix said that before April 14 he had held the view that the South was still a Christian area and that the moral level of the people was not below that of other areas. "But now the thing is to be determined—the truth is to be made plain—in the red and bloody light of this cruel and diabolical outrage." He also called on the people of the South to say loudly and clearly that they abhorred the deed.[5]

This calling on the South to express disapproval of the assassination was a very common sentiment, along with some charges that the South had not yet done so. The Reverend Pliny White said that if the murder was not devised by the rebellion leaders, nor sanctioned by them in advance, they would now sanction it by failing to disavow it. And the

3. *Ibid.*, 6–7; W. H. Benade, *The Death of Abraham Lincoln; What It Represents* (Pittsburgh: W. G. Johnston, 1865), 5.

4. T. H. Robinson, *The Unvailing of Divine Justice in the Great Rebellion* (Harrisburg: Ambrose Taylor, 1865), 30.

5. Morgan Dix, *The Death of Abraham Lincoln* (Cambridge, Mass.: Riverside Press, 1865), 11.

Reverend C. H. Edgar assumed that at that very moment there were miserable wretches in the South laughing over this calamity.[6]

Some ministers took a slightly more liberal view, believing that the murder could not be directly traced to southern leaders like John C. Breckenridge and Lee, even though it was still the legitimate offspring of slavery and rebellion. The Reverend Herrick Johnson was one minister willing to admit this, although he noted, "It puts an eternal stigma upon their cause and sends it down to posterity loaded with infamy."[7]

Other ministers were ready to denounce the southern leaders in very specific terms, not in mere generalities. William Binney, delivering a eulogy before the City Council of Providence, Rhode Island, reminded his hearers that Lincoln's election had been announced to the Senate and House of Representatives by Vice-President Breckenridge, "his rival at the time, his assassin since." The Reverend George H. Hepworth told his congregation that there was no doubt whatever that Lee's officers had a carousal in Richmond on the night after the president's assassination, and that it might even have been held in the same house where the assassination was planned months ago. The fact that the assassination of Lincoln and attempted assassination of Seward occurred at the same time unavoidably suggested to clergymen, as it did to the general public, that there was a widespread conspiracy. As the Reverend O. E. Daggett said, "We first thought, this is the insanity of fanaticism; but since two murders were attempted at the same hour, we must reckon it the work of bribed conspirators."[8]

Trial testimony brought out during the conspirators' trials also influenced ministers. The Reverend R. H. Steele told his listeners that "the miserable wretch whose grave no one wants to know, and his aids and accomplices now on trial, did not stand alone. We are told by the Government that the plan was known by the authorities in rebellion, and

6. Pliny H. White, *A Sermon Occasioned by the Assassination of Abraham Lincoln* (Brattleboro: Vermont *Record* Office, 1865), 13–14; C. H. Edgar, *Three Sermons Occasioned by the Assassination of President Lincoln*, (Easton, Pa.: *Free Press* Office, 1865), 7.

7. Herrick Johnson, *God's Ways Unsearchable* (Pittsburgh: W. G. Johnston, 1865), 9. For a similar view, see Newman Hall, *A Sermon on the Assassination of Abraham Lincoln Preached at Surrey Chapel London* (Boston: James P. Magee, 1865), 24.

8. *Proceedings of the City Council of Providence on the Death of Abraham Lincoln with the Oration Delivered Before the Municipal Authorities and Citizens* (Providence: Knowles, Anthony, 1865), 30; George H. Hepworth, *Two Sermons Preached in the Church of the Unity* (Boston: John Wilson and Son, 1865), 23; O. E. Daggett, *A Sermon on the Death of Abraham Lincoln* (Canandaigua, N.J.: Milliken Printer, 1865), 12.

approved by them. And I for my part believe that the Southern Chivalry are capable of the deed." He also went on to quote Jefferson Davis' alleged statement about the deed being well done, which was revealed during the trials. The Reverend J. B. Wentworth reminded his flock of the papers found in the rebel archives since the fall of Richmond, showing the organization of a Secret Service Bureau and its new methods of espionage and irregular warfare. Many believed that Booth was part of the bureau and that it was responsible for Lincoln's death. Of course, many held such views long before they had them reinforced by the conspiracy trial. The Reverend William Murray preached a sermon claiming that there had been a plot to murder Lincoln on March 4. When his address was finally published, he added in a footnote, "It should be remembered that this was written before any of the facts of the conspiracy since ascertained were published."[9]

The effect of such sermons on people is revealed in the comment of George T. Strong, "What would we have said four years ago of Vinton earnestly enforcing on us the duty of hewing the (Southern) Agag in pieces before the Lord, not from personal animosity, but as a sacred obligation to be neglected only at peril of divine punishment, public and private."[10]

One striking fact, which indicates clearly that ministers blamed the Confederacy and slavery for the assassination even more than Booth, was the relative infrequency with which the assassin's name was mentioned in sermons. There were some choice epithets hurled at Booth, such as "accursed devil," "fiend," "poor, miserable, wicked assassin," "demon in human form," "wretch," and "Drunken debased assassin," but with a few insignificant exceptions, these were very general terms, almost as if Booth did not exist as an individual. The lack of urgency that most pastors felt about the apprehension of Booth also shows that they believed he was merely a tool. The Reverend Morgan Dix told his congregation that even should Booth flee abroad, "He shall not long

9. Richard H. Steele, *Victory and Mourning* (New Brunswick: Terhune and Van Anglen's Press, 1865), 15; J. B. Wentworth, *A Discourse on the Death of President Lincoln* (Buffalo: Matthews and Warren, 1865), 22; William H. H. Murray, *Address Delivered on the Sabbath Following the Assassination of President Lincoln* (New York: John F. Trow, 1865), 8.

10. Allan Nevins and Milton Thomas (eds.), *Diary of George T. Strong* (4 vols.; New York: MacMillan, 1952), IV, 586.

have shelter there; the years at last shall bring him into our hands, if the months and the days do not do it sooner."[11]

The thought that Booth might be insane did cross the minds of some ministers, but it was usually rather quickly rejected. The Reverend H. Dunning said that it would be comforting to think the assassin had been mentally unbalanced but no such excuse could be made. The real causes, added Dunning, were his disloyalty to the government, the bad company he kept, and a certain desire for notoriety. The Reverend Henry C. Badger, who admitted that Booth was probably insane, pointed out that Seward's assailant and Preston Brooks, who had attacked Senator Sumner with a cane, were not insane.[12]

Despite the fact that they often viewed Booth as an anonymous agent, many did call for harsh treatment for the assassin. The Reverend Sidney Dean lumped Davis, Lee, and Booth together indiscriminately and called for their rapid trial and execution. The Reverend P. B. Day reveled in Booth's death. "Before the victim at which he aimed his deadly blows was in the tomb, he died in agony and was ingloriously buried in an unknown grave. Millions of curses roll over his head, and the execrations of posterity will sink him deeper and deeper in infamy."[13]

If southern leaders were an obvious target for the pulpit, so were northern copperheads. The Reverend Marvin Vincent expressed his belief that there was nothing in the letter and spirit of the Constitution that would prevent the silencing of traitors such as ex-Congressman Clement Vallandigham and putting them beyond the possibility of doing further mischief. The Reverend S. L. Yourtee charged that the

---

11. Stewart, "The Pulpit and the Assassination," 303. There were some exceptions to the view that the Confederate government was to blame. See Daniel Clark, *Eulogy on the Life and Character of Abraham Lincoln* (Manchester, N.H.: *Mirror* Steam Job Printing Establishment, 1865), 9, who presented a very detailed description of the assassination scene, and J. G. Butler, *The Martyr President, Our Grief, and Our Duty* (Washington: McGill and Witherow, 1865), 7. Dix, *Death of Abraham Lincoln*, 10. T. M. Eddy, *Abraham Lincoln: A Memorial Discourse* (Chicago: Methodist Book Depository, 1865), 20, who called for hunting Booth down wherever he might be, had a very atypical attitude.

12. H. Dunning, *Address Delivered on the Occasion of the Funeral Solemnities of the Late President of the United States* (Baltimore: John Woods, 1865), 3; Henry C. Badger, *The Humble Conqueror* (Boston: Printed for the Cambridge Parish, 1865), 12–13.

13. Sidney Dean, *Eulogy on the Occasion of the Burial of Abraham Lincoln* (Providence: H. H. Thomas, 1865), 4; P. B. Day, *A Memorial Discourse on the Character of Abraham Lincoln* (Concord, N.H.: McFarland and Jenks, 1865), 5.

plot had originated in the councils of the Knights of the Golden Circle, while others claimed that all those who had spoken ill of Lincoln, both North and South, were responsible for the murder.[14]

In a few cases, the Radical Republicans also came in for a share of the blame. The Reverend A. G. Hibbard charged that the Radicals held views similar to those of the southern leaders and northern copperheads that had helped bring about Lincoln's death. Former Attorney General Bates, after hearing Dr. Post preach a particularly harsh and vindictive sermon that was out of keeping with his usual bland and amiable character, could only wonder if the doctor had not fallen under Radical influence.[15]

Criticism of the Radicals was rather minor, however, because after Lincoln's death the view was half-expressed that Lincoln had actually brought assassination upon himself by being too tender toward the rebellion. Nevertheless, assassination placed Lincoln in the ranks of true martyrs. Previously controversial and despised by many groups, he became instantaneously the savior of his country. The Reverend C. E. Everett expressed the view that now that Lincoln was removed from controversy in death, the true worth of his life could be gauged.[16]

The Baltimore plot and the attempt to assassinate Lincoln on his way to Washington was another theme constantly elaborated upon. His statement at Philadelphia, "But if this country cannot be saved without giving up that principle, I was about to say I would rather be assassinated on this spot than surrender to it," seemed to make Lincoln a prophet of his martyrdom.[17]

Because Lincoln was assassinated on Good Friday, many religious parallels were drawn. Several ministers echoed the *Alta Californian*'s statement that the assassination was the blackest crime, save one, that

14. Marvin Vincent, *A Sermon on the Assassination of Abraham Lincoln* (Troy, N.Y.: A. W. Scribner, 1865), 38; S. L. Yourtee, *A Sermon Delivered in the Central M. E. Church, Springfield* (Springfield, Ohio: *News* and *Republic* Job Printing Rooms, 1865), 14.

15. A. G. Hibbard, *In Memory of Abraham Lincoln* (Detroit: O. S. Gulley's Steam Book and Job Printing Office, 1865), 10; Howard K. Beale (ed.), *The Diary of Edward Bates, 1859–1866*, Vol. IV of the Annual Report of the American Historical Association, 1930 (Washington: Government Printing Office, 1933), 474–75.

16. Charles E. Everett, *Eulogy on Abraham Lincoln, Late President of the United States* (Bangor, Me.: Samuel S. Smith, 1865), 6.

17. Joseph P. Thompson, *Abraham Lincoln, His Life, and Its Lessons* (New York: Loyal Publication Society, 1865), 24; Robert Norton, *Maple Leaves from Canada for the Grave of Abraham Lincoln* (St. Catherine's: E. S. Leavenworth, 1865), 10.

had ever been committed in the world. That exception was the Cruci-
fixion upon Calvary. Lincoln's death also vaulted him into the ranks of
the true Christians. Many ministers felt an uneasiness for the state of
his soul at the time of his death and eagerly repeated the story of the
president's conversion to Christianity. Most commonly repeated were
stories of his early morning prayer and Bible reading or his revelation
to some ministers that when he left Springfield and even after his son
had died, he was not a Christian, but that after Gettysburg he became
a Christian and did love Jesus.[18]

Since his death occurred before the rebellion was completely sub-
dued, there was also some comparison with Moses and Joshua. In retrospect it seemed that Lincoln had been the proper type of figure to
lead the nation through four years of bitter warfare, but now a sterner
leader like Joshua was needed, and Johnson appeared ready to fill the
void.[19]

The idea was also expressed, as it had been by many people, that
Lincoln's words "with malice toward none," were no longer proper
policy. A reporter was present when the Reverend George B. Loring
delivered his sermon and noted the reaction of the congregation. "My
friends, clemency was his danger. And now that he has laid down his
life, let us remember that danger and be warned by it. (Great applause)." A minor few did not agree with this criticism. The Reverend
Thomas Laurie said he was aware that some were saying that Lincoln
would have been unfit for punishing evildoers, but he was not so sure,
since Lincoln had never been found wanting either in appreciating the
duties of the hour or meeting its demands.[20]

Many contemporaries seemed to feel as if God in his wisdom had
allowed Lincoln's death to occur, because the people had placed more
reliance on generals, force of arms, and even the benevolent president
than they had on Him. On Good Friday, men were rejoicing in victory
but forgetting the one who had given them the victory. Therefore God

---

18. San Francisco *Alta Californian*, April 16, 1865, p. 2; Herrick Johnson, *God's Ways Unsearchable*, 7; Stewart, "Rhetorical Study of the Reaction," 85.

19. Stewart, "Rhetorical Study of the Reaction," 41.

20. George B. Loring, *The Present Crisis* (South Danvers, Mass.: *Wizard* Office, by Charles D. Howard, 1865), 4; Thomas Laurie, *Three Discourses Preached in the South Evangelical Church, West Roxbury, Mass., April 13th, 19th, and 23d, 1865* (Dedham, Mass.: John Cox, Jr., 1865), 24.

removed Lincoln to demonstrate that people should rely only upon Him, not upon any man, no matter how good he was. Hope for the future, however, was still a commonly expressed theme; although God had removed Lincoln, he had not destroyed the government as he might have done. The Reverend S. F. Johnson said, "He falls, the Nation's chief; but the Nation dies not. It shows its mighty self-command. The wheels of State move on!"[21]

The initially favorable response to Johnson and the pleas to support him were sometimes accompanied by misgivings. This was largely the result of Johnson's drinking episode at the second inauguration. The Reverend H. L. Edwards admitted that had people known that Lincoln might have to be replaced, Johnson probably would not have been their choice for vice-president. And the Reverend Henry Badger said the people waited in trembling hope to see if any successor could manifest the desirable qualities that Lincoln had.[22]

Of course, what recommended Johnson to ministers, and to the general public, was his reported sternness. Daniel Rice revealed with admiration how the new president had confronted the rebels at the start of the rebellion. Pliny White, taking an obvious satisfaction in Johnson's words, "But the leaders I would hang," called upon him to translate these noble sentiments into action.[23]

Johnson was also seen as a much better man to carry out a harsh reconstruction policy, particularly one that included hanging large numbers of southerners, both in the army and the government. Those that were not black enough criminals to be hanged were to be exiled and shot if they ever showed their faces on American soil again. Other clergymen wished to enfranchise the Negro, divide the southern land and give it to them, and send missionaries to the South. Some views appear extreme, yet when the Reverend Maxwell Gaddis remarked that for every drop of blood that flowed from Lincoln's veins a leading rebel must die or be exiled, "hundreds rose to their feet; thousands of hand-

21. John Chester, *The Lessons of the Hour, Justice as Well as Mercy* (Washington: Washington *Chronicle* Print, 1865), 6; B. Hawley, *Truth and Righteousness Triumphant* (Albany: J. M. Munsell, 1865), 5; Samuel Johnson, *A Discourse Preached on the Day of the National Funeral of President Lincoln* (N.p., n.d.), 9.
22. Henry L. Edwards, *Discourse Commemorative of Our Illustrious Martyr* (Boston: Wright and Potter, 1865), 12; Badger, *The Humble Conqueror*, 14.
23. Daniel Rice, *The President's Death—Its Import* (Privately published, n.d.), 6; White, *Sermon Occasioned by the Assassination*, 17.

kerchiefs waved all over the hall and it was many seconds ere the eloquent preacher could proceed."[24]

The language used by many ministers was not always in keeping with what one might expect from a man of the cloth. Orville H. Browning described a sermon by a Mr. Chester as "an inflammatory stump speech—the first one I ever heard in an old school Presbyterian Church." Ministers themselves sometimes saw the paradox in extolling the gentleness of Lincoln and the mercy of Jesus while at the same time calling for the harshest of reconstruction policies, but under the circumstances they apparently could not control their emotions.[25]

In the midst of this turmoil, a minority of ministers urged moderation. Samuel Crocker told his congregation, "Let us not in our just indignation, read in it a lesson at variance alike with every principle of our religion, and with those qualities of his character which have especially endeared him to the memory of mankind." The Reverend Herrick Johnson felt, very perceptively, that too much retribution would only serve to make martyrs of those against whom it was leveled. Others believed that the best way to guard against future treason and rancor between the sections was to avoid persecution, and some feared that once the mob spirit was unleashed there was no telling against whom it might ultimately be directed.[26]

Throughout most sermons was an undeniable belief in the sanctity of the law and a rather congratulatory tone when mention was made that the violence which had occurred had been kept within narrow bounds. Few ministers called for direct and unlawful action even against the worst offenders. The ideal expressed was a trial and then

24. Stewart, "Rhetorical Study of the Reaction," 137; "Lincoln's Assassination and the Protestant Clergy of the North," 272ff; Maxwell P. Gaddis, *Sermon upon the Assassination of Abraham Lincoln, Delivered in Pike's Opera House, April 16, 1865* (Cincinnati: *Times* Steam Book and Job Office, 1865), 10.

25. James G. Randall and Theodore C. Pease (eds.), *Diary of Orville Hickman Browning*, (2 vols.; Springfield, Ill.: Jefferson's Printing and Stationery, 1933), II, 21; Charles Lowe, *Death of President Lincoln* (Boston: American Unitarian Association, 1865), 23. Even two years later, just before the trial of John Surratt, Justin D. Fulton preached a sermon in Tremont Temple, Boston, Mass., recommending that Jefferson Davis be hanged. Memphis *Daily Appeal*, June 20, 1867, p. 2.

26. Samuel L. Crocker, *Eulogy upon the Character and Services of Abraham Lincoln* (Boston: John Wilson and Son, 1865), 27; H. Johnson, *God's Ways Unsearchable*, 11; Thompson, *Abraham Lincoln, His Life, and Its Lessons*, 33; John McClintock, *Discourse Delivered on the Day of the Funeral of President Lincoln* (New York: J. M. Bradstreet and Son, 1865), 27.

punishment for those found guilty. The Reverend Newman Hall, although slightly exaggerating the lack of violence, cataloged the riot and massacre that might have occurred. The Reverend Charles Backman proudly called on the world to "look on and see whether we have borne this wonderful trial manfully or not. It has produced no revolution, only here and there have there been cases of personal violence, and those seemed to be cases of righteous retribution."[27]

Despite ministers calling for action within the law, their violent language probably incited some to take the law into their own hands. Most ministers seemed to assume that a trial for those involved in the assassination would inevitably lead to a verdict of guilty and immediate execution. Many ministers apparently tried to establish a distinction between vengeance and justice in order to support their demands for the death penalty. Richard Eddy told his congregation: "I clamor not for blood, nor would I countenance a resting in torture. I would have no unlawful executions, no mere vengeance; but the justice which comes from judicial trial, the execution of the penalty which the law has provided for treason." C. H. Edgar thundered, "Make a distinction between holy wrath and sinful hatred." It is obvious that this was, and is, a very fine distinction, especially difficult to make in practice.[28]

Ministers were also quick to castigate the South for a whole list of atrocities committed on the battlefield and not even connected with the assassination. Peter Russell, who on April 19 had preached a rather moderate sermon, on June 1 enumerated southern atrocities such as the burning of northern cities, the Saint Albans raid, and the yellow fever plot. The Reverend Treadwell Walden included nearly all the charges made.

> The spirit that could take pride in holding four millions of human beings in bondage forever; the spirit that could strike down a helpless Senator in the national halls, and applaud the act; the spirit that could so wantonly rebel against rightful and constituted authority . . . that could rejoice in firing upon its flag and in trampling the holy symbol under foot; the spirit that could mutilate the dead, massacre garrisons, mine prisons and set fire

27. Hall, *Sermon on the Assassination*, 11; Charles Backman, *Abraham Lincoln, The World's Great Martyr* (Jamaica, N.Y.: Charles Weiling, 1865), 12. See also Chicago *Tribune*, April 19, 1865, p. 2.

28. Richard Eddy, *The Martyr to Liberty* (Philadelphia: Horace W. Smith, 1865), 23; Edgar, *Three Sermons*, 7.

to cities in the night; the spirit that could starve to death uncounted thousands of prisoners of war,—is the self-same spirit that stole into the heaven of our peace, and struck the unsuspecting, confiding President from behind.

The Reverend C. E. Everett went so far as to argue that the death of Lincoln, as bad as that was, was not to be compared for infamy of crime with the death of one of those northern soldiers, tortured in a Confederate prison camp.[29]

Ministers also used the assassination to preach some of their own personal themes. One of these was the evil of theaters. Many felt uncomfortable that the president of the United States had been murdered in a theater, doubly so because it had been Good Friday. Some criticized Lincoln mildly for being there, while others pointed out that he went merely because he did not wish to disappoint the people who were expecting him. In any case, most who mentioned it expressed the hope that henceforth the theater might be made odious in America.[30]

There was also an opportunity to criticize those who held liberal feelings toward capital punishment. Ministers argued that if sentimentality about capital punishment had not existed, there would have been fewer deaths by violence and Lincoln's life might have been saved.[31]

Newspapers also became embroiled in controversies about sermons, which is another indication of the impact that sermons had. Normally, journals that were progovernment tended to agree with the sermons that expressed vindictive sentiments. Thus the Hartford *Courant* praised the Reverend N. J. Burton of the Fourth Church for placing guilt for the assassination where it belonged, on the slave power and northerners who had criticized the president. The Easton (Pa.) *Free Press* chided the Democratic Easton (Pa.) *Argus* for its criticism of overzealous ministers and went on to say that "the preacher or the editor

29. Peter Russell, *Our Great National Reproach and the Counsel of Ahitopel Turned into Foolishness: Two Sermons Preached in St. James Church, Eckley, Penna.* (Philadelphia: King and Baird Printers, 1865), 25; Treadwell Walden, *The National Sacrifice* (Philadelphia: Sherman, 1865), 25; Everett, *Eulogy on Abraham Lincoln*, 19. See Stewart, "The Pulpit and the Assassination," 304.

30. Laurie, *Three Discourses*, 34; W. R. Gordon, *The Sin of Reviling and Its Works* (New York: John A. Gray and Green Printers, 1865), 13.

31. Edgar, *Three Sermons*, 16; John L. Dudley, *Slavery's Last Word* (Middletown, Conn.: D. Barres, 1865),19.

that counsels leniency towards such infamous assassins as Booth and all his accomplices, is secretly rejoicing at the death of Mr. Lincoln, and that such a man is no better than Booth himself." The opposition press, like the Easton (Pa.) *Argus* and Columbus (Ohio) *Crisis*, generally supported a more moderate view. The Easton (Pa.) *Sentinel* remarked editorially, "We have a class of preachers in this country who have been not inappropriately termed 'Bloodhounds of Zion,' in consequence of their persistent cry for blood."[32]

Many ministers called for, or else realized, that the country was so aroused that only some sort of symbolic punishment could quiet it down again. Leonard Swain told his listeners, "Let the leaders of the rebellion, or a suitable number of them, be tried, sentenced and executed for treason . . . then justice having had its place, and the majesty of the law having been honored, mercy may have its exercise, and the people of the rebellious states be forgiven." Wheelock Craig also sensed that this was the mood of the people when he said, "The Public heart is irritated. The land is vexed. A mighty nation is enraged, and each several community clamors for a victim; not merely the real culprit, for the whole earth would rejoice to see him punished; but, in lieu of him, for any scapegoat on whom the stroke due to him may be inflicted."[33]

It might be argued that this symbolic punishment is exactly what happened, although the accused were kept within much narrower bounds than they might have been. With the exception of Mrs. Surratt, there is little doubt that those executed were guilty of the charges lodged against them. Of those sentenced to the Dry Tortugas, again with the exception of Mudd and Spangler, they were certainly involved in the abortive kidnapping plot and could hardly expect more mercy to be shown. This symbolic execution under form of trial and law, despite what may have been in some instances a miscarriage of justice, may have prevented a more serious outbreak from occurring.

Lincoln's assassination raised as much animosity and vindictive feeling among the clergy as among other classes of society. In many cases,

32. Hartford *Daily Courant*, April 24, 1865, p. 1; Easton (Pa.) *Free Press*, May 11, 1865, p. 2; Easton (Pa.) *Argus*, May 4, 1865, p. 2; Stewart, "Rhetorical Study of the Reaction," 171; Easton (Pa.) *Sentinel*, June 29, 1865, p. 2.

33. Leonard Swain, *A Nation's Sorrow* (Providence: Privately printed, 1865), 8; Wheelock Craig, *A Sermon on the Fruits of Our Bereavement* (New Bedford, Mass.: E. Anthony and Sons, 1865), 10.

ministers were even more vindictive than the people or the extreme Radical Republicans. If one grants to ministers the influence that some feel they had in the nineteenth century, it is again logical to maintain that sermons recounting southern atrocities and involvement in the assassination had a much more important influence in arousing people than Stanton ever thought of having. However, Stanton is heaped with blame, and most historians ignore sermons almost completely. There is little wonder that people felt that the South was involved, and the worst was yet to come.

7.

Southern Reaction to Lincoln's Assassination

Northerners in 1865 felt that they knew
what the reaction of the South was to Lincoln's assassination, but historians have generally censured northerners for an erroneous assumption, arguing that southern reaction and northern were quite similar.
On the surface, there exists a great deal of evidence to bolster this view.

Members of the Confederate army, especially prisoners of war, were
quick to express their abhorrence of the assassination. General R. S.
Ewell, expressing the sentiments of several other Confederate generals,
wrote from Fort Warren to General Grant of his disapproval and said
he would be ashamed of the southern people if they did not express
similar sentiments. Twenty-two thousand prisoners at Point Lookout
sent resolutions to the War Department expressing their warm sympathy with the distressed family. Even the officers and men of John
Singleton Mosby's command, from whom one might expect to find
some sympathy for the assassin if it existed at all, were reported to have
expressed their regret.[1]

In Richmond, the effect of the news was apparently profound. The
Richmond *Whig* of April 17 commented, "The heaviest blow which has
ever fallen upon the people of the south has descended." Local citizens
were moved, like their counterparts elsewhere, to call a public meeting,
but permission was denied by the authorities for fear of what might
happen. On April 25, the *Whig* remarked that Lincoln had walked the
streets of Richmond on his recent visit and remained unharmed—clear
proof that southerners had not wished any physical violence against the
president. Newspaperman J. W. Forney, who was in Richmond, wrote,

---

1. *The War of the Rebellion: A Compilation of the Official Records of the Union and Confederate Armies* (130 vols., Washington: Government Printing Office, 1880–1901), Ser. I,
Vol. XLVI, Pt. 3, pp. 787, 839, hereinafter cited as *OR*; New York *Times*, April 21, 1865, p.
1; Richmond *Whig*, quoted in New Orleans *Times-Picayune*, May 12, 1865, p. 4.

"It is equally right to say that in what I saw of the people of Richmond I saw little but grief and despondency."[2]

In an interview General Lee said he considered the event one of the most deplorable that could have occurred. Not only had the scheme not been known in the South, but if it had been it would have received the most severe condemnation. The Washington *Evening Star*, which reprinted the interview, expressed the opinion that Lee's candid expressions had done him much honor personally and that he and Richmond were out of the danger of mob violence.[3]

In other areas of the South the reaction seemed to be the same. From Charleston, South Carolina, word was received that people of both Union and Confederate sentiments had joined in denouncing the deed. One or two unprincipled creatures had expressed joy at the assassination, but they were immediately arrested and given proper military punishment.[4]

The Raleigh *Standard* broke the news to the people of North Carolina with the statement, "We announce with profound grief the assassination of the President of the United States." When the news was released by the government to the troops at Raleigh, it was pointed out that the vast majority of Confederate troops would scorn such acts. General Sherman received word at Durham Station and informed General Joseph E. Johnston, with whom he was conducting surrender negotiations. Johnston remarked that this news was "the greatest possible calamity to the South."[5]

The reaction was similar at New Orleans. H. E. Rhoades, who was there on April 15, recounts that within less than an hour of receipt of the news, one-third of all public and private buildings were draped in mourning. In other cities like Savannah, there were great mass meetings and demonstrations, though centered more among Unionists and

---

2. Richmond *Whig*, April 17, April 18, 1865, p. 4. See also New York *Times*, April 30, 1865, p. 2; Richmond *Whig*, April 25, 1865, p. 4; Baltimore *Sun*, April 28, 1865, p. 1.

3. Richmond *Whig*, May 2, 1865, p. 2; Washington *Evening Star*, April 21, 1865, p. 1.

4. New York *Times*, April 27, p. 1, May 12, 1865, p. 5.

5. Raleigh *Standard*, April 18, 1865, quoted in Richmond *Whig*, May 1, 1865, p. 2; *OR*, Ser. I, Vol. XLVII, Pt. 3, pp. 238–39; Joseph E. Johnston, *Narrative of Military Operations Directed During the Late War Between the States* (Bloomington: Indiana University Press, 1959), 402.

northern residents in the city. Even in Port Tobacco, Maryland, the home of arrested conspirator George Atzerodt and a reported hotbed of secession sentiment, Edwin Middleton observed, "No one there seemed to rejoice over it—never heard of any intimations of delight from anyone."[6]

Southern sympathizers in California also denounced Lincoln's murder. One man who had been an extremely violent secessionist now said: "Damned to the bottomless pit of hell [are] the men who plotted and carried it out—we have come to look on the restoration of the Union as a foregone conclusion and the whole South was on the eve of accepting the fact. We should have been friends and brothers once more, within six months, but for this. Now, God help us all!" The *Alta Californian* also expressed satisfaction that with one insignificant exception, all men, no matter their origin, had denounced the murder, some southerners doing so in terms as bitter as any ultra-Unionist.[7]

Even Assistant Judge Advocate H. L. Burnett later felt that Booth's reception in the South proved that southerners had no sympathy with his actions. Those who aided Booth's escape attempted to make it clear that despite their actions, they did not sanction the assassination. Lieutenant Ruggles, who had aided Booth in reaching Garrett's barn, in an 1890 issue of *Century Magazine* detailed his involvement, saying, "I believe that had the war been going on, Booth, instead of finding an asylum in the South, would have been taken and surrendered to the United States by the Confederate Government." Samuel Cox, Jr., said that his father and Thomas A. Jones, who had also sheltered Booth, later denounced the assassination as being fraught with dire consequences for the South.[8]

Private sources such as diaries also reveal that many southerners were

6. New Orleans *Times-Picayune*, April 20, 1865, p. 4; H. E. Rhoades, Unidentified newspaper clipping, in Truman H. Bartlett Collection, Boston University; Martin Abbott, "Southern Reaction to Lincoln's Assassination," *Abraham Lincoln Quarterly*, VII (1952), 121; Edwin Middleton, May 12, 1865, Statement, in RG 110, NA.

7. Katie Van Winden, "The Assassination of Abraham Lincoln: Its Effect in California," *Journal of the West*, IV (1965), 217; San Francisco *Alta Californian*, April 16, 1865, p. 1.

8. Henry L. Burnett, "Assassination of President Lincoln and the Trials of the Assassins," in James H. Kennedy (ed.), *History of the Ohio Society of New York, 1885–1905* (New York: Grafton Press, 1906), 605; Prentiss Ingraham, "Pursuit and Death of John Wilkes Booth," *Century Magazine*, XXXIX (1890), 444.

genuinely touched by Lincoln's death. Susanna Waddell belived that it was the worst calamity that could have befallen the South; and a Tennessee businessman wrote, "Great God what are we coming to. Instead of peace I now fear anarchy without law." Sarah Dawson wrote: "Charlotte Corday killed Marat in his bath, and is held up in history as one of Liberty's martyrs, and one of the heroines of her country. To me, it is all murder. Let historians extol blood-shedding; it is woman's place to abhor it."[9]

There is little wonder that on May 3 the New York *Times* could produce an editorial saying that "the assassination of President Lincoln evoked at every point the strongest expressions, not only of abhorrence for the act, but of sorrow for the public loss."[10] However, in almost all southern expressions, one fact stands out. While no one would deny that there was a genuine degree of sympathy for Lincoln's death, there was an equal amount of fear for the southern position. Since the war was clearly lost, southerners feared the horrible retribution that might be delivered upon them should they be charged with the deed. Most of the areas where protests were the loudest were already in the hands of northern troops, and under these circumstances no other response was possible. The slightest sympathy for the assassin would have met with even sterner treatment than it did in the North. Many undoubtedly felt that the better part of political wisdom was to make at least a proper outward show.

The belief that Lincoln would have treated the South more fairly than President Johnson and the Radical Republicans was expressed by many. The Reverend J. Lansing Burrows told his congregation in the First Baptist Church at Richmond, "No harsh or vengeful or malignant thoughts toward our people seemed to find place in his heart, in arranging for the settlement of the great controversy." Madame Loreta Velazquez, a Confederate agent, said the news startled her greatly because "I felt it could work nothing but harm to the South." Mr. T. Bailey Meyers told the New York Athenaeum Club that he felt there would be many to exult in Lincoln's death "and would be more if he

9. Abbott, "Southern Reaction," 114; Sarah Morgan Dawson, *A Confederate Girl's Diary* (Boston: Houghton Mifflin, 1913), 36–37.

10. New York *Times*, May 3, 1865, p. 4.

had not lived to inaugurate measures which they fear his successor may not carry out."[11]

Many southerners were very much afraid of Andrew Johnson. Former judge Beverley Tucker, replying to charges that he was involved in the assassination, said that the South would have no interest in Lincoln's murder for this very reason. An unknown author in Alabama wrote of Johnson: "The Southerners here seem to dread him, and look upon the affair as a still deeper humiliation and misfortune to them." Eliza Andrews of Georgia wrote, "It is a terrible blow to the South, for it places that vulgar renegade, Andy Johnson, in power."[12]

Jefferson Davis himself expressed similar views: "For an enemy so relentless in the war for our subjugation, we could not be expected to mourn; yet, in view of its political consequences, it could not be regarded otherwise than as a great misfortune to the South." At the time, of course, Davis was charged with exulting over the assassination. Lewis F. Bates of Charlotte, North Carolina, at whose house Davis was stopping when he received the news of the assassination, testified that Davis had said, "If it were to be done, it were better it were well done." Secretary Burton Harrison recalled an interesting episode in which he and Davis had attended church after the assassination and the minister had preached strongly against the murder, causing Davis to say, "I think the preacher directed his remarks at me; and he really seems to fancy I had something to do with the assassination."[13]

Other evidence poured into government offices, leading many to the conclusion that Davis was involved. Solomon Landis, a respectable citizen of Atlanta, offered to testify to hearing Davis say he would lead his

11. J. Lansing Burrows, *Palliative and Prejudiced Judgements Condemned* (Richmond: *Commercial Bulletin* Office, 1865), 5; C. J. Worthington (ed.), *The Woman in Battle: A Narrative of the Exploits, Adventures and Travels of Madame Loreta Janeta Velazquez* (Hartford: T. Belknap, 1876), 510; *Commemorative Proceedings of the Athenaeum Club* (New York: C. S. Wescott, 1865), 12.

12. James H. Young (ed.), *Address of Beverley Tucker, Esq., to the People of the United States* (Atlanta: Emory University Library, 1948), 16; "Death of a President," *Abraham Lincoln Quarterly*, III (1945), 303; Abbott, "Southern Reaction," 114.

13. Jefferson Davis, *The Rise and Fall of the Confederate Government* (2 vols.; New York: D. Appleton, 1912), II, 683; Benn Pitman, *The Assassination of President Lincoln and the Trial of the Conspirators* (New York: Funk and Wagnalls, 1954), 46; Fairfax Harrison (ed.), *Aris Sonis Focisque, Being a Memoir of an American Family, the Harrisons of Skimino and Particularly of Jesse Burton Harrison and Burton Norvell Harrison* (New York: DeVinne Press, 1910), 243.

troops to assassinate the whole vandal Congress and burn New York and Philadelphia. Letters in the rebel archives, such as the one to the secretary of war from Lieutenant W. Alston and endorsed by Burton Harrison, which offered to rid the Confederacy of some of its deadliest enemies, also seemed to indicate Davis' acquiescence in assassination.[14]

Of course, it has long been apparent that much of the evidence against Davis was perjured or dubious, and many people recalled that he had expressed regret over the assassination. There is also evidence that he discouraged kidnapping schemes or at least did not wish violence against Lincoln. It seems certain that Davis was innocent of all such charges, yet his reaction was hardly all that sympathetic, for as he told Secretary of the Navy Stephen Russell Mallory, "I certainly have no special regard for Mr. Lincoln; but there are a great many men of whose end I would much rather have heard than his."[15]

Whereas Davis could only give this grudging assessment, many others could not conceal their joy. Thomas A. Jones, who had been so instrumental in aiding Booth's escape, recalled in 1893 that at the time of Lincoln's death he regarded him only as the enemy of his country. As Booth lay hidden in the woods, he was anxious to read newspapers and questioned Jones as to what people thought about the murder. Jones informed him that it was gratifying news to most men of southern sentiments.[16]

In Texas, where military control was not yet as stringent as in other parts of the Confederacy, newspaper comment was especially vicious. The Texas *Republican* of April 28 said, "From now until God's judgment day the minds of men will not cease to thrill at the killing of Abraham Lincoln, by the hand of Booth, the actor." The Galveston *Daily News* spoke of martyrdom for Booth: "Inspired by patriotic impulse and be-

14. John J. Oliver to James A. Wilcox, May 18, 1865, in RG 110, NA; Pitman, *The Assassination of President Lincoln*, 52.

15. Harrison (ed.), *Aris Sonis Focisque*, 241; Stephen Russell Mallory, "Last Days of the Confederate Government," *McClure's Magazine*, XVI (1901), 244. See Thomas N. Conrad, *The Rebel Scout* (Washington: National, 1904), 131–32.

16. Thomas A. Jones, *J. Wilkes Booth: An Account of His Sojourn in Southern Maryland After the Assassination of Abraham Lincoln, His Passage Across the Potomac, and His Death in Virginia* (Chicago: Laird and Lee, 1893), 7–8; George A. Townsend, "How Wilkes Booth Crossed the Potomac," *Century Magazine*, XXVII (1884), 828. For a discussion of how Lincoln was transformed by the South from hated enemy to an authentic American and even southern hero, see Michael Davis, *The Image of Lincoln in the South* (Knoxville: University of Tennessee Press, 1971).

lieving he was ridding the world of a monster, his name will be inscribed on the roll of true-hearted patriots along with Brutus and Charlotte Corday."[17]

The following from the Chattanooga (Tenn.) *Daily Rebel* shows that such expressions might have been more widespread had the opportunity presented itself: "If it was right for Brutus to slay the despotic Caesar, who shall say that the man who slit the throat of this arch plotter [Seward] against the lives and liberties of this people is not worthy of the laurel leaf." And of Lincoln, "Abe has gone to answer before the bar of God for the innocent blood which he has permitted to be shed, and his efforts to enslave a free people." Even newspapers that tried to be moderate could hardly restrain their bitter feelings. The Shreveport (La.) *Sentinel*, for example, said that two weeks before his death it had called Lincoln a despicable despot and its feeling had not changed.[18]

Some people did record in their diaries what was apparently their true feeling about the assassination. Charles Hardee of Georgia wrote that when the news was received at a nearby store, everyone hurrahed and threw his hat in the air. Mrs. Cornelia McDonald said that when she first heard of Lincoln's death, she felt it was just what he deserved; and Robert Park, who personally opposed the assassination, said that one of his comrades had expressed a willingness to share his last crust of bread with Booth. Sarah Dawson, in Baton Rouge, said that one of the houses decorated most profusely with outward mourning belonged to people that had been most hateful against Lincoln: "For the more violently 'Secesh' the inmates, the more thankful they are for Lincoln's death, the more profusely the houses are decked with emblems of woe. They all look to me like 'Not sorry for him, but dreadfully grieved to be forced to this demonstration.'"[19]

17. Robert S. Harper, *Lincoln and the Press* (New York: McGraw Hill, 1951), 360; Abbott, "Southern Reaction," 126–27.

18. Chattanooga (Tenn.) *Daily Rebel*, April 20, 1865, quoted in Philadelphia *Evening Bulletin*, May 10, 1865, p. 1; Shreveport (La.) *Sentinel*, April 27, 1865, quoted in Richmond *Whig*, May 18, 1865, p. 1. See also Roy P. Basler (ed.), *The Assassination and History of the Conspiracy: A One-Hundred-Year-Old Chronicle of the Assassination of President Abraham Lincoln, from the Early Plotting to the Execution of the Conspirators* (New York: Hobbs, Dorman, 1965), 30.

19. Martha G. Waring (ed.), "Reminiscences of Charles Seton Henry Hardee," *Georgia Historical Quarterly*, XII (1928), 264; Cornelia McDonald, *A Diary with Reminiscences of*

Much later, many southerners honestly recalled their true feelings as Thomas Jones had done. John S. Wise wrote: "Perhaps I ought to chronicle that the announcement was received with sentiments of sorrow. If I did, I should be lying for sentiments sake. Among the higher officers and the intelligent and conservative men, the assassination caused a shudder of horror at the heinousness of the act and at the thought of its possible consequences; but among the thoughtless, the desperate, and the ignorant, it was hailed as a sort of retributive justice. In maturer years I have been ashamed of what I felt and said of that awful calamity."[20]

Booth also became somewhat of a hero in the South, both at the time and afterwards. On May 27, 1865, the Charleston *Courier* carried the following advertisement: "Persons desiring photographs of J. Wilkes Booth, the assassin, should call at the store No. 234 King Street, where a large supply has been recently received." The poem "Our Brutus," a eulogy to Booth, also had quite a long and honored career in the South. Although Judge A. W. Tyrrell is generally credited with being the author, a handwritten copy in the papers of John A. Bingham, assistant judge advocate in the conspiracy trails, claims this honor for Judge Arrington of Chicago. According to this version Arrington gave it to J. P. Southworth, United States district attorney, upon his promise that it would not be published, and he presented a copy to Bingham on the same conditions. Whatever its origins a portion of it set to music as a vocal solo by E. B. Armand was published in New Orleans in 1868, and a version of it appeared in the *Confederate Veteran's Magazine* as late as 1913. Another memorial to Booth was a stone erected in Troy, Alabama, by Pink Parker, with the following inscription: ERECTED BY / PINK PARKER / IN HONOR OF JOHN WILKS [*sic*] / BOOTH / FOR KILLING OLD / ABE LINCOLN APRIL 15, 1906. Although causing some controversy it remained standing until 1921, when it blew down in a windstorm.[21]

---

the War and Refugee Life in the Shenandoah Valley, 1860–1865 (Nashville: Cullom and Charter, 1934), 260; Robert E. Park, "Diary of Captain Robert E. Park, Twelfth Alabama Regiment," *Southern Historical Society Papers*, III (1877), 245; Dawson, *Confederate Girl's Diary*, 437–38.

20. George S. Bryan, *The Great American Myth* (New York: Carrick and Evans, 1940), 384.

21. Charleston *Courier*, May 27, 1865, p. 2; "Our Brutus" (Microfilm copy of the originals in the possession of Milton Ronsheim, in John A. Bingham Papers, Ohio Historical

The reaction to the activities of Willie Jett and ferryboat operator William Rollins, who were perceived by some of their neighbors as having given information that led to Booth's capture, indirectly indicates some southern feelings. Victor Louis Mason in the *Century Magazine* of April, 1896, claimed that Jett, who told authorities he had left Booth at Garrett's barn, had been jilted by his sweetheart, ostracized by his friends, outlawed by his family, and forced to leave the neighborhood, and that he had died in a Baltimore insane asylum. Rollins was also reported to have been an outcast among his neighbors for the previous thirty years, because they believed he had received money for betraying Booth. When newspaperman George Townsend traced Booth's escape route in 1881, he made remarks about John Garrett in Port Royal, and a woman said, "I reckon John Garrett has been ashamed of himself ever since that time; he ought to be and Jett was no better." When asked to explain what she meant, she replied, "Why they got a lot of the reward, of course, for giving Booth up." Townsend discovered that this view was rather common in the vicinity.[22]

The interesting thing is that there apparently is not a great deal of truth to the story of Jett's ostracism. John L. Mayre, a near relative denied it completely. Jett traveled to Baltimore a year after the assassination; engaged in business, constantly traveling in Virginia; and married the daughter of a prominent Baltimore physician. He remained friendly with his ex-sweetheart and her family despite the fact he did not marry her, and very few people blamed him in the least for piloting the troops where Booth was. Paresis, not remorse, caused his insanity, and he died at Williamsburg, Virginia, respected by everyone who knew him. The significant point is not that the story of Jett's ostracism was exaggerated but rather that many people felt such punishment was due to those who had betrayed Booth.[23]

Similarly Thomas A. Jones felt that ostracism would also have been in store for him had he informed on Booth. Years later, when he met

Society), Roll 1; Bryan, *Great American Myth*, 384–85; Stewart W. McClelland, *A Monument to the Memory of John Wilkes Booth* (Indianapolis: N.p., 1951).

22. Victor L. Mason, "Four Lincoln Conspiracies, Including New Particulars of the Flight and Capture of the Assassin," *Century Magazine*, LI (1896), 910; Cincinnati *Enquirer*, October or November, 1881, in George A. Townsend Papers, LC.

23. John L. Mayre, "Mr. Jett and the Capture of Booth," *Century Magazine*, LII (1896), 637–38.

Captain Williams, one of the officers engaged in Booth's pursuit, and was reminded that by turning in the assassin he could have been the biggest hero in America and had much more money, Jones replied, "Yes, and a conscience as black as purgatory . . . and the everlasting hatred of the people I loved."[24]

Historians, then, have generally assumed that the South abhorred Lincoln's assassination and treated Booth with scorn and contempt. At a superficial level this was the reaction of many southerners. However, there is much evidence that many acted because of fear of their own helpless position and the belief that Johnson could only be much worse than Lincoln had been. Still others secretly applauded the deed where circumstances permitted. When northerners assumed that the South would exult over the murder and that it might pump new life into the dying Confederacy, they would not have been so far wrong as historians have assumed, if only conditions had been slightly different.

24. John E. Buckingham, *Reminiscences and Souvenirs of the Assassination of Abraham Lincoln* (Washington: Press of R. H. Darby, 1894), 79.

8.

Pursuit

While controversy persists concerning
what was done and was not done in the pursuit and capture of the
assassins, the numerous dispatches sent on the night of the assassination and the following days show that the government was hardly in-
active. The first person alerted was Colonel John Leverett Thompson,
commanding at Darnestown, who was informed that the assassins were
supposed to have escaped toward Maryland. He was ordered to scout
north of Washington. Thompson replied on April 15 that he had received the dispatch at 11:30 P.M. on April 14 and by midnight had sent
out three cavalry squadrons.[1]

Next, General John P. Slough at Alexandria was ordered to prevent
all persons from leaving the city until further notice, although he was
informed that it was not known in what direction the assassin had escaped. At 12:35 A.M. General Augur wired Slough to use cavalry to the
best advantage to carry out his orders. At 4 A.M. he identified the assassin as Booth and said it might be well to have a squadron of cavalry
sent down toward the Occoquan. At 5 A.M. Slough notified Augur that
he had the river and shore between Alexandria and Washington suffi-
ciently patrolled and would send out the cavalry when he could gather
sufficient numbers.

General James A. Hardie had also notified the agent of the military
railroad at Alexandria that the assassins had gone to Alexandria and
then on to Fairfax, and ordered him to have all unknown persons on
the road or train arrested. General William Gamble at Fairfax Courthouse was also alerted at 1 A.M., and at 3 A.M. General William W. Morris, commanding the District of Baltimore, was told to make arrangements for guarding thoroughly every avenue leading into Baltimore

---

1. *The War of the Rebellion: A Compilation of the Official Records of the Union and Confederate Armies* (130 vols., Washington: Government Printing Office, 1880–1901), Ser. I,
Vol. XLVI, Pt. 3, pp. 752, 768, hereinafter cited as *OR*.

and, if possible, to arrest Booth. Colonel G. W. Gile, commanding 1st Brigade, Veteran Reserve Corps, was directed to detail an officer and ten enlisted men to accompany a train that left Washington for Baltimore on April 15. They were to search every car and attempt to arrest Booth.[2]

At an early hour, Commander Foxhall A. Parker at Saint Inigoes, Maryland, was informed that the assassins might attempt to escape across the Potomac River. Colonel Frederick D. Sewall at Annapolis was ordered to permit no boats to leave until further orders. General James Barnes received a similar dispatch and wired back at 11:20 A.M., April 15, "Your dispatch was received and communicated at once to the gunboats, and the river and bay are closely watched. The District of Saint Mary's is being thoroughly patrolled by mounted men."[3]

Sunday, April 16, Montgomery Meigs ordered Colonel Reece Marshall Newport, the chief quartermaster at Baltimore, to patrol the west shore of the Chesapeake as far as Point Lookout, explaining, "The murderers of the President and Secretary of State have, it is believed, gone southeast, and will attempt to escape by water to the Eastern Shore, or to board some vessel waiting for them, or some vessel going to sea." The following day Gideon Welles ordered Parker to search all vessels on the river and guard against all boats and vessels touching the Virginia shore.

In some cases, the orders issued were enforced too stringently, for on April 15 at 2:50 P.M. General Halleck telegraphed General Hancock at Winchester reminding him that orders in the previous evening's telegram were not to include women, children, or well-known loyal men, nor persons coming from a direction that would clearly indicate they had not been in Washington that night.[4]

General Augur pretty well summed up the actions the government had taken on the assassination night when he questioned a General Nichols as to what further measures might be pursued: "I have sent to arrest all persons attempting to leave the city by all approaches. Have telegraphed to troops on the upper Potomac to arrest all suspicious persons.—also to Genl. Slough at Alexandria and Genl. Morris at Bal-

2. *Ibid.*, 751, 752, 770, 772, 773, 775.
3. *Ibid.*, 754, 756, 769.
4. *Ibid.*, 765, 806, 816.

timore. All our own police and detectives are out. No clue has yet been found by which I can judge what further steps be taken. Can you suggest any?"[5]

Preparations were also made for detention of the assassins once they were apprehended. General Halleck wired General Augur that if the assassins were caught, they were to be placed in double irons and escorted under guard to Commodore J. B. Montgomery, the commander of the Navy Yard. Secretary Welles had ordered Montgomery to put the assassins on a monitor and anchor it in the Potomac with strong guards.[6]

Given the number of people involved in the assassin's pursuit and the very confused circumstances, some sort of centralized direction of the pursuit would have been desirable, and yet Secretary Stanton, who attempted to bring order out of chaos, has been unfairly charged with seizing dictatorial power. Stanton attempted to consolidate the investigation in the War Department under Judge Advocate Holt. A confidential order in the Stanton papers ordered all military and police officers and magistrates to place themselves under Holt's instructions.[7]

Such instructions were reinforced on several different occasions. In one instance, Stanton received a request from Provost Marshal John Cuthbertson for permission to furnish an additional five hundred dollars to detective C. W. Taylor in Canada, who guaranteed the arrest of some of the conspirators. The endorsement to General Fry ordered him to tell Cuthbertson that his actions were not approved, as no arrests would be made without the express authority of the War Department. H. L. Burnett also wrote to Police Chief Almarin Cooley Richards on May 3, "The Sec. of War directs that any testimony in your hands in regard to the late assassination be at once sent to this office." On April 21 newspapers informed the general public that the secretary had forbidden the divulging of any information except to the War Department

5. Christopher C. Augur to General Nichols, April 14, 1865, in File Folder 36, RG 153, NA.

6. *OR*, Ser. I, Vol. XLVI, Pt. 3, pp. 766, 768. Vaughan Shelton, *Mask For Treason* (Harrisburg: Stackpole Books, 1965), 94, claims that mention of possible suicide of prisoners was made only so that they might be put out of the way if necessary. See Gideon Welles, April 15, 1865, in Letterbook, Gideon Welles Papers, LC, for a copy of Welles' order to Montgomery.

7. Edwin Stanton, April 20, 1865, Confidential Order, in Edwin M. Stanton Papers, LC.

and its headquarters. "All parties violating this order will be looked upon as obstructing the prompt arrest of the conspirators, and will be punished accordingly."[8]

Stanton also acquired the finest detectives possible for the pursuit. At 1 A.M. on April 15, he telegraphed New York City Chief of Police John Kennedy to send three or four of his best detectives to Washington. Forty-five minutes later Colonel H. S. Olcott offered the services of Colonel Richard C. Morgan or any of his employees, and Stanton ordered him to come on with his force of detectives. At 3:20 P.M. Stanton sent a wire to Lafayette Baker: "Come here immediately and see if you can find the murderers of the President." On April 16, he sent an order to Major James O'Beirne saying, "You are relieved from all other duty at this time and directed to employ yourself and your detective force in the detection and arrest of the murderers of the President and the assassin who attempted to murder Mr. Seward, and make report from time to time."[9]

From all accounts the investigation and pursuit were conducted with zeal. Abner Hard, a member of the 8th Illinois Cavalry, which was ordered out the night of the assassination and subsequently sent to Leonardtown, wrote, "The country [was] so thoroughly picketed and searched, that a rabbit could have hardly made his escape through our lines without being discovered." George T. Strong also revealed the stringency of measures taken, for on both April 22 and April 26 he was stopped, first on a government mail boat and then on a train, and forced to show papers to prove his identity. Rather than being annoyed at the inconvenience he was glad that the government was so watchful. Such efforts were apparently not relaxed until the time of Booth's capture.[10]

Newspapers, even though forced to exercise censorship, were gen-

8. John Cuthbertson to Edwin Stanton, June 27, 1865, in RG 110, NA; Henry L. Burnett to A. C. Richards, May 3, 1865, in Letters Sent, RG 153, NA; Philadelphia *Evening Bulletin*, April 21, 1865, p. 2; New York *Times*, April 20, 1865, p. 2.

9. *OR*, Ser. I, Vol. XLVI, Pt. 3, p. 783; Edwin Stanton to Maj. O'Beirne, April 16, 1865, in RG 110, NA.

10. Abner Hard, *History of the Eighth Cavalry Regiment Illinois Volunteers During the Great Rebellion* (Aurora, Ill.: N.p., 1868), 320–21. Hard also mentioned that citizens were reluctant to provide information. Allan Nevins and Milton Thomas (eds.), *Diary of George T. Strong* (4 vols.; New York: MacMillan, 1952), IV, 591, 594; *OR*, Ser. I, Vol. XLVI, Pt. 3, pp. 900–902, 910.

erally pleased with the manner in which the government organized the pursuit. The Philadelphia *Evening Bulletin* expressed the sentiment of most journals: "Every effort that ingenuity, excited by fervor, can make, is being put forth by all the proper authorities to capture or trace the assassins of Mr. Lincoln and Mr. Seward." Shortly before the commencement of the trial, the New York *Herald* reminded its readers, "In almost every other respect equal success has crowned the efforts of the authorities; and in fact, in some instances, with much greater success as the public will see in the due course of time."[11]

Despite historians' assertions, there was actually a great deal of confusion as to where Booth had fled. One example of historians' erroneous handling of this issue is the treatment of the actions of Washington Chief of Police Richards. It has often been argued that the Washington Metropolitan Police Force soon learned the route that Booth had taken out of the District, but lack of horses prevented them from pushing the pursuit. Detective James A. McDevitt revealed in 1894 his version of how narrowly he and the other policemen had missed getting onto Booth's trail. He recalled Chief Richards rushing into headquarters after the murder and telling the telegraph operator to raise the alarm. As McDevitt recorded it:

> We traced him from the stage door of Ford's Theater up through the alley and into F street and then eastward to the Anacostia bridge. One of the bridge tenders described a horseman who had crossed the bridge at just about the time when Booth at the gait at which he was moving could have reached it from the theater. We hastened back and reported. The police board at once made a request of the military authorities for a few cavalry horses to mount a picked body of men and a cavalry escort for the party who were to strike at full speed for Charles county MD., toward which we believed Booth headed. Had the request been granted I have no doubt we should have caught up with him at his first halting place.[12]

Yet, while McDevitt's recollection is usually cited as an example of,

11. Philadelphia *Evening Bulletin*, April 17, 1865, p. 5; New York *Herald*, May 4, 1865, p. 1.

12. The fact that stableman John Fletcher turned up at police headquarters after having followed David Herold probably put the police on the track, although there is a discrepancy in his testimony as to just how quickly he reached police headquarters. See Otto Eisenschiml, *Why Was Lincoln Murdered?* (Boston: Little Brown, 1937), 109–15; A. L. Daggett, "Some Interesting Reminiscences of a Thrilling Night," Washington *Evening Star*, April 14, 1894, p. 17.

at worst, treachery, and, at best, bureaucratic red tape, in reality Richards was sending out erroneous information on the assassination night. In the papers of General Benjamin Butler is a telegram, dated April 14 but lacking the hour of dispatch, to the chiefs of police of Baltimore, Philadelphia, New York, and Alexandria: "J. Wilkes Booth the tragedian is the person who shot the President this evening at Ford's Theatre. He made off on horseback probably towards Baltimore."[13]

This confusion in pursuing the assassins led to many problems and erroneous messages. There seemed to exist as many theories as there were people to express them. This explains why one commander might be informed that Booth was fleeing to Baltimore while another was told at almost the same time that he was on a train to Fairfax. Some even felt Booth was on his way to Canada, as commanders along the border were notified to check all those trying to cross and to arrest all suspicious persons.[14]

This confusion, instead of abating, continued for some period of time. On Monday, April 17, the New York *Times* noted, "There have been a dozen rumors of Booth's capture but so far as can be learned from the authorities, not only has he not been captured but they are not even too certain in which direction he made his escape." On April 16, James W. Forsyth informed Colonel F. C. Newell, at Nottoway Courthouse, that Lincoln was dead, "stabbed" by J. Wilkes Booth, the actor. And as late as April 24, General Alfred Thomas Torbert, commanding the army of the Shenandoah, was ordering General William Hemsley Emory at Cumberland, Maryland, to notify all subordinate commanders along the Baltimore and Ohio Railroad and in West Virginia to the Kanawha not to relax their vigilance, as Booth might attempt to escape in this direction disguised as a woman.[15]

The mention of Booth being disguised as a woman highlights the fact that the government received numerous reports of suspicious strangers said to be Booth. A great deal of energy was expended in

13. A. C. Richards, April 14, 1865, in Benjamin Butler Papers, LC. This is also interesting, for it reveals that no concerted effort existed to hide the fact that Booth was the assassin and thus to facilitate his escape.

14. New York *Times*, April 16, 1865, p. 1. See J. Gregory Smith to Edwin Stanton, April 22, 1865, in Letters Received, File S 3, JAO, RG 153, NA.

15. *OR*, Ser. I, Vol. XLVI, Pt. 3, pp. 767, 795, 934–35; New York *Times*, April 17, 1865, p. 1.

tracking them down and arresting them. For example, on April 20, a report was received from Reading, Pennsylvania, that Booth had been seen there, and a train was sent out to overtake him. Other dispatches said that the individual who had identified Booth was no longer so certain it was he, but G. A. Nichols, superintendent of the Philadelphia and Reading Railroad, assured the public that the individual had been apprehended at Tamqua and was definitely Booth. It was not until April 22 that it was ascertained that the person was not Booth.[16]

At Williamsburgh, New York, a mysterious individual had come into the shop of Antemeith and Ritter, leaving a suit of clothes to be cleaned. He returned with two men of similar appearance who possessed large sums of gold. Ritter believed that they were the assassins. In Washington, Luther Davi was arrested because of his slight resemblance to Booth, while at Sheffield, Massachusetts, authorities were seeking an individual from a traveling exhibition.[17]

These arrests reached such proportions that the Albany *Atlas and Argus* humorously tallied up the score sheet. It included two conductors of the Central Railroad, arrested for their good looks; W. W. Leonard of New York, who was followed by detectives and taken to a police station to establish his identity; a man in Detroit; and James L. Chapman, son of the sheriff of Pittsfield, Massachusetts. Also arrested was one Boyd of Rochester, who "was discharged after an admonition that a man looking so much like Wilkes Booth as he did should keep as quiet as possible at present."[18]

Oftentimes, danger seemed imminent for such unfortunate individuals. When J. F. Nagle, the leading actor of McVicker's Theater in Chicago, was arrested, the soldier who had identified him as Booth said if he had been armed, he would have shot him. Mr. Scott of the police asked him why he had not. Some members of a crowd at Titusville, when informed that a Mr. Stevens was not Booth, exclaimed, "Well d——n him, he ought to be shot anyhow."[19]

Initially there were also many rumors that Booth had been captured. On April 15, the Philadelphia *Evening Bulletin* reported the arrest of

---

16. New York *Times*, April 21, p. 1, April 22, 1865, p. 8.
17. Washington *Evening Star*, April 15, p. 3, May 2, 1865, p. 2.
18. Albany *Atlas and Argus*, April 27, 1865, p. 2.
19. Gettysburg *Compiler*, May 15, 1865, p. 4.

Booth and an accomplice, William Springer of Illinois. William Daggett, who had been ready to shoot those who spoke against Lincoln, wrote a letter to his sister on April 16, repeating a rumor that Booth had been captured and placed on a monitor for safekeeping. The Washington *Intelligencer* noted these conflicting rumors and expressed fear that if news of Booth's apprehension and the location of where he was being held were not kept secret, the people might take the law into their own hands.[20]

Some evidence that reached the government could readily be dismissed as false or the work of cranks. Several letters came to Seward from individuals either expressing pleasure at Booth's escape or claiming to be the assassin and expressing regret that he had only half done the job. Of a similar nature was a letter from E. Mattocks of York, Pennsylvania, to Colonel Baker, which expressed Mattock's belief that a much stronger case could be made by the government if they could draw out of the witnesses any evidence of the plan he believed the conspirators had, to escape from the city in a balloon. Some stories seemed to have more basis. A few miles below Port Tobacco, a woman said she heard a man enter her cellar at night and depart in the morning. Major O'Beirne told her to place a light in the window the next time this occurred. She did but when the house was searched no one was found. The woman was determined to be insane.[21]

Many persons also imagined they saw Booth disguised, especially in women's clothing. Silas Jones of West Troy, New York, informed the government that he had information that the assassin was concealed in a house of ill fame in Chicago at 16 Tenth Avenue, disguised as a female.[22]

The fact that such communications were often from well-intentioned citizens is seen in Jones's assertion that he was not all that certain that his information was correct but felt no means should be untried to

20. Philadelphia *Evening Bulletin*, April 15, 1865, p. 5; *Lincoln Lore*, No. 1478 (April, 1961), Lincoln National Life Foundation, Fort Wayne, Indiana; Washington *Daily National Intelligencer*, April 18, 1865, p. 1.
21. Theodore Roscoe, *The Web of Conspiracy* (Englewood, N.J.: Prentice-Hall, 1959), 148; [?] to Edwin Stanton, in Letters Received, File A 111, 179, 202, 246, 543, 548, 551, all in JAO, 1865, RG 153, NA; Lafayette C. Baker, *History of the United States Secret Service* (Philadelphia: King and Baird, 1867), 552, 491.
22. Silas Jones to Edwin Stanton, April 20, 1865, in Letters Received, File J 11, JAO, RG 153, NA.

apprehend Booth. And when P. H. Knapp wrote to General Hancock about a clairvoyant he knew who placed Booth in Washington at 11 J Street, he added, "What I write you may prove of great value or it may prove the worst possible nonsense." Any information that appeared to have a degree of validity had to be investigated. A letter from Joseph Hill that he had seen Booth in women's clothes between E Street and Eleventh and Twelfth streets, brought about the seizure of the entire block by the military and the search of every house. Silas Jones's letter caused H. L. Burnett to wire the commanding general at Chicago to investigate and report.[23]

Strangely, perhaps, one view that strongly persisted was that the assassin was still in Washington. Britten A. Hill, who was aiding in the immediate investigation, informed Stanton that Booth had apparently fled toward Bladensburg; however, he added: "My opinion is that he is still in Washington secreted. If not, then I am wholly at fault." If Stanton was acting on such advice, and it seems that he was, it is hardly a wonder that the defenses north of Washington and towards Baltimore were among the first alerted.[24]

The view that Booth was still in Washington was so widely expressed that many must have given it credence. Joseph Hazelton, program boy at Ford's, described how the neighborhood around the Petersen House was being searched on the assassination night, because no one knew where the assassins had gone. The New York *Herald* said on April 17, "Two theories are pursued in regard to the escape of the assassins of Mr. Lincoln and the Sewards. One is that they have really gone from the city; the other that they are still concealed here." Many prominent citizens shared this view. From Pittsburgh, Sidney F. Von-Bonnhorst wrote to General Hancock of his belief that four soldiers should be detailed to every disloyal home to seize all suspicious papers and persons found. He also suggested that Postmaster S. J. Bowen be authorized to search the mail of people like John Ford—advice that Stanton took, though he directed that letters be opened in the presence of the parties themselves. Among those holding to the Booth-in-Washington

23. P. H. Knapp to Winfield S. Hancock, April 26, 1865, in Letters Received, File K 125, and Joseph Hill, April 26, 1865, in Letters Received, File H 609, *ibid.*; Henry L. Burnett to General B. J. Sweet, April 22, 1865, in Telegrams Sent, RG 153, NA; New York *World*, April 27, 1865, p. 4.
24. Britten A. Hill to Edwin Stanton, April 15, 1865, in Stanton Papers.

theory was the postmaster himself and some of his friends. Bowen suggested that a rigid search of every house be made.[25]

The *National Republican* of Washington called for a house-to-house search of the city on April 26, the day Booth was killed. The New York *Herald* of April 28 credited General Ben Butler with having been in favor of such a search. But using hindsight, the *Herald* praised the government for not wasting time searching in Washington but instead pursuing the action it did to bring Booth to justice. On April 23, even government detectives must still have had some lingering suspicions that Booth was not in lower Maryland, for William Wood found it necessary to write Colonel Levi Turner: "All the tales about Booth being in Washington, Pennsylvania, or Upper Maryland are a hoax. We are on his track rely on it."[26]

Critics will counter by saying that when Booth gave his name at the Eastern Branch Bridge and stableman John Fletcher told his story of pursuing David Herold, it should have been abundantly clear which direction the assassins had fled. Whether Booth gave his name foolishly or with an audacious insight into the effect it would have is not clear, but many contemporaries sincerely believed that the rider at the bridge was not Booth but a decoy sent to draw the detectives off the track. Several newspapers expressed this view. Even the Democratic Easton (Pa.) *Argus* agreed. "As they crossed the eastern branch at Uniontown, Booth gave his proper name to the officer at the bridge. This, which would seem to have been foolish, was, in reality, very shrewd. The officers believed that one of Booth's accomplices had given the name in order to put them out of the real Booth's track. So they made efforts elsewhere, and so Booth got a start."[27]

Among the rumors and evidence that proliferated concerning the

25. Campbell MacCulloch, "This Man Saw Lincoln Shot," *Good Housekeeping*, LXXXIV (February, 1927), 122; New York *Herald*, April 17, 1865, p. 1; Sidney Von-Bonnhorst to Winfield S. Hancock, April 24, 1865, in Letters Received, File V 124, JAO, RG 153, NA. See Files B 36, B 489, and F 681, JAO, 1865, and Endorsement Book, No. 16, April, 1865, all *ibid*. See also Albany *Atlas and Argus*, May 2, 1865, p. 1. S. J. Bowen, April 26, 1865, in Register of Letters Received, File B 76, JAO, *ibid*.

26. New York *Tribune*, April 26, 1865, p. 4; New York *Herald*, April 28, 1865, p. 1; William P. Wood to Levi C. Turner, April 23, 1865, in File Folder 72, *ibid*.

27. Philadelphia *Evening Bulletin*, April 28, 1865, p. 1; New York *Herald*, April 28, 1865, p. 1; Baltimore *Sun*, April 18, 1865, p. 1; Baker, *History of the United States Secret Service*, 486–87; Easton (Pa.) *Argus*, May 11, 1865, p. 1.

involvement of other people in the assassination, unexplained suicides were of particular interest. D. R. Keigwin felt compelled to write the Baltimore *American* denying that the suicide of hospital steward George B. Love had anything to do with the assassination. Stanton also showed much interest in the suicide of Joseph Thomas, who had stayed at the Branson Boarding House in Baltimore at the time Seward's assailant, Paine, was there. On April 27 the secretary wrote to General Lew Wallace asking why no report had been made in the case to the provost marshal and requesting that the body be disinterred and embalmed for identification. Wallace evidently referred the matter to Provost John Wooley, who replied that he was aware of the case but had no reason to suspect Thomas, a loyal citizen, whose suicide had been brought on by his recent heavy drinking.[28]

Word also came to the government of individuals such as Thomas Green and his wife, who had reportedly excavated an area under their house where a kidnap victim might be secreted. Green found himself in Old Capitol, trying to explain away a letter in his possession that was addressed to John Surratt as well as other mail that was apparently destined to be sent South.[29]

As late as June 1, people were still in an aroused state about the conspiracy's being more widespread, even though all involved were presumably on trial. B. Wills wrote Stanton that J. B. Hammars of Paris, Illinois, who had been away for some time on a mysterious errand, should be brought before the court and examined.[30]

In fact, while historians have been rather upset that the government did not apprehend Booth more quickly, many contemporaries would not have been altogether surprised had he escaped. Most people had confidence in the government, but they also appreciated the difficulties involved. Helen A. DuBarry wrote to her mother April 16, "The authorities think there is no chance for the assassins to escape but I think it is like hunting for a needle in a haystack." Former Attorney General

---

28. Baltimore *American*, April 23, 1865, quoted in Philadelphia *Evening Bulletin*, April 25, 1865, p. 1; Edwin Stanton to Lew Wallace, April 27, 1865, John Wooley to Wallace, April 28, 1865, both in Letters Received, File W 249, JAO, RG 153, NA.

29. Thomas Shankland, N.d., Statement, in Letters Received, File E 378, Thomas Green, May 10, 1865, Statement, in File G, RB, p. 103, both in JAO, RG 153, NA.

30. B. Wills to Edwin Stanton, June 1, 1865, in Letters Received, File W 477. See also H. Walsh to Stanton, June 2, 1865, File W, both in JAO, RG 153, NA.

Bates expressed his belief that "the longer the time, the greater the chance of the escape of the wretches." Some of the soldiers who had taken part in the pursuit were also reported to have commented that they were lucky to find Booth, for a man could hide in the swamps for a year, especially among a sympathetic populace.[31]

Given the unsettled circumstances after the assassination, the pursuit of the conspirators was not, and could not have been, as simple as historians have wished. The first reaction of contemporaries was to determine how widespread the conspiracy was and to safeguard the government. When pursuit was launched, authorities were rapidly alerted. It is true that officers perhaps labored under erroneous assumptions as to where Booth had gone and were deluged by rumors of Booth's being seen and confederates who were involved with him. What emerges is a climate of uncertainty and confusion, and although the government eventually did strike Booth's track, which led to Garrett's barn, another round of nagging questions about the death of John Wilkes Booth soon presented themselves.

31. San Francisco *Alta Californian*, April 22, 1865, p. 2; Helen A. DuBarry, "Letters April 16th, 1865, April 25, 1865," *Journal of the Illinois State Historical Society*, XXXIX (1946), 368; Howard K. Beale (ed.), *The Diary of Edward Bates, 1859–1866*, Vol. IV of the Annual Report of the American Historical Association, 1930 (Washington: Government Printing Office, 1933), 474; New York *Times*, April 28, 1865, p. 1.

9.

Capture

John Wilkes Booth managed to elude his pursuers until April 26, 1865, when he was tracked down and killed at Garrett's barn near Port Royal, Virginia. After leaving Washington, he and Herold stopped first at Lloyd's tavern and then proceeded to the home of Dr. Mudd, where he received medical attention for his injured leg. Leaving Dr. Mudd's, they finally made their way to Colonel Samuel Cox's, where they were put under the care of Thomas A. Jones, who sheltered them and eventually got them across the river to Virginia. After receiving less than a warm reception from Confederate sympathizers Elizabeth R. Quesenbury and Dr. Richard H. Stewart, they fell in with Jett, Ruggles, and Bainbridge. These rebel soldiers deposited Booth with farmer Richard Garrett, in whose barn Booth was surrounded by Union troops and allegedly shot and killed by Boston Corbett.

The actual killing of Booth and capture of Herold was carried out under the direction of the head of the Union secret service, Colonel Lafayette Baker. How he was able to direct the pursuers to Booth's exact location has been a mystery to many historians. When Baker reached Washington in response to Stanton's summons, he recorded the following scene: "As I entered the Secretary's office, and he recognized me, he turned away to hide his tears. He remarked . . . 'You must go to work. My whole dependence is upon you.'"[1] Baker then supposedly set out with all the forces at his command to track down the murderers.

The use of reward money, though considered the proper method of bringing Booth to justice, led to much rivalry and greatly hampered the operation. Baker expressed his willingness to cooperate with Colonels H. H. Wells, John Foster, and H. S. Olcott, who had been placed

1. Lafayette C. Baker, *History of the United States Secret Service* (Philadelphia: King and Baird, 1867), 525.

in charge of gathering all information relating to the assassination, but his professions of cooperation do not accord with the evidence. Dr. James G. Coombe made the following additional statement after informing the government of his belief that Booth had gone from the house of Dr. Mudd to that of Stoughton Dent: "I went last night to Colonel Baker but found that he was a $200,000 man, and I want the government to have the information, and to save the reward."[2]

Lafayette Baker's cousin, Luther B. Baker, also revealed that the colonel's detectives encountered difficulties because of the reward money: "The large reward offered . . . filled the whole country between Washington and Port Tobacco with detectives. They would not work with us or give us any information they may have obtained. They preferred rather to throw us off the trail, hoping to follow it successfully themselves."[3]

According to Lafayette Baker, however, the real break in Booth's pursuit occurred when some detectives he sent to lower Maryland returned with an old Negro. As newspaper correspondent George Alfred Townsend described it, "This negro, taken to Colonel Baker's office, stated so positively that he had seen Booth and another man cross the Potomac in a fishing boat, while he was looking down upon them from a bank, that the Colonel was first skeptical; but, when examined, the negro answered so readily and intelligently, recognizing the man from the photographs, that Baker knew at last that he had the true scent." According to Townsend, Baker then underwent almost a mystical experience that allowed him to dispatch his men to the exact location where Booth could be found. The story of the old Negro was corroborated by other Baker detectives, yet the whole affair has an air of untruth about it, for the time scheme of the sending of the detectives and the return of the Negro seems to have been impossible. As Congressman Albert Gallatin Riddle said of the Negro: "The old Negro informant is to be relegated to the realm of myth. . . . He was a pure creation of the genius of L. C. Baker. . . . The old negro was a necessary creation, to give color as a real informant, and to make seeming ground

2. *Ibid.*, 529; Dr. James G. Coombe, N.d., Statement, in Record Book, File C, p. 7, JAO, 1865, RG 153, NA.
3. Luther B. Baker, "An Eyewitness Account of the Death and Burial of J. Wilkes Booth," *Journal of the Illinois State Historical Society*, XXXIX (1946), 427.

on which the expedition could rest; and those who derided the invention unconsciously did homage to the genius of the inventor."[4]

Despite the fact such an informant did not exist, there is no need to place a sinister interpretation on Baker's actions. The old Negro was the perfect device through which Baker could set up his claim for the lion's share of the reward money. His avowal on July 7, 1866, when he was still attempting to collect the reward, that he had received no information from any outside source makes it very apparent where his interests lay.[5]

Since other government operatives were in the area, some sending back information to the War Department, there is little mystery as to where Baker got his information. Major O'Beirne's detectives, among others, were hot on the track and almost succeeded in capturing Booth, although some mysterious events occurred that have not been satisfactorily explained to this day.

To aid O'Beirne and provide better communication with the War Department, General Grant's telegraph operator, S. H. Beckwith, was sent to lower Maryland on April 23, 1865, where he soon found Major O'Beirne. On April 24, O'Beirne sent the following telegram to Stanton: "Since receiving your orders, myself and force have been active night and day in Maryland and Virginia and not unproductively. Detailed reports will be handed in to you." The following day Beckwith sent this dispatch to Stanton's assistant, Major Eckert: "They have been tracked as far as the swamp near Bryantown, and under one theory it is possible they may still be concealed in swamp. . . . Other evidence leads to the belief that they crossed from Swan's Point to White Point, VA., on Sunday morning, April 16, about 9:30 in a small boat, also captured by Major O'Beirne."[6]

The mystery lies in the fact that O'Beirne was operating under erroneous information, for Booth and Herold had crossed to Virginia on

<hr />

4. George A. Townsend, *The Life, Crime, and Capture of John Wilkes Booth with a Full Sketch of the Conspiracy of Which He Was the Leader, and the Pursuit, Trial, and Execution of His Accomplices* (New York: Dick and Fitzgerald, 1865), 28; L. C. Baker, *History of the United States Secret Service*, 495, 527, 533. See Otto Eisenschiml, *Why Was Lincoln Murdered?* (Boston: Little Brown, 1937), 126, for argument that Baker's story was untrue. Albert G. Riddle, *Recollections of War Times* (New York: G. P. Putnam's Sons, 1895), 334–35.

5. L. C. Baker, *History of the United States Secret Service*, 528.

6. James O'Beirne to Edwin Stanton, April 24, 1865, in File Folder 62, RG 153, NA; S. H. Beckwith, in New York *Sun*, April 27, 1913, p. 6.

April 21. Colonel Wells, on April 25, enclosed in a letter to General Augur the statement of Amelia A. Green, Negro servant, who had seen two men near Bryantown, one with a crutch and the other with a revolver. They asked her for something to eat, but she refused, as the white people were not at home. The fact that this was not the mere imagining of an old lady was verified by Wells himself. "I made personal inspection of the locality and was able to trace the course of the fugitives by the hole made by the crutch—and find that they passed almost around the clearing, and back to the swamp—where the trace is lost."[7]

O'Beirne's diary also reveals that he had suspicions of Colonel Cox, whose mill servant had said that he had been cooking provisions and carrying them into the swamp. Despite Baker's assertion, it is apparent that he was using information relayed to the War Department by Beckwith on which to base his decisions. O'Beirne reminded Stanton on December 27, 1865, of the praise he had given his efforts, "You have done your duty nobly and you have the satisfaction of knowing that if you did not succeed in capturing Booth, it was, at all events, certainly the information which you gave that led to it." Beckwith, himself, felt that his five-hundred-dollar share of the reward indicated the valuable part he had played in the pursuit.[8]

Other agents also narrowly missed capturing Booth. H. W. Smith, assistant adjutant general, wrote to Colonel Foster on May 1 that after distributing handbills on April 23, he had been informed by a man who had come from Metompkin Point that two men had crossed the river on April 21, one lame and carrying a crutch and answering Booth's description. "I at once went on board of the gunboat and all speed was used to reach Port Conway in time to intercept the two men, but we arrived too late, Booth, being shot at four o'clock on the morning of the day of my arrival. Had the Boat given me from Washington been a

7. H. H. Wells to Christopher Augur, April 26, 1865, in File Folder 6, RG 153, NA. See also S. H. Beckwith to Thomas Eckert, April 25, 1865, in File Folder 23, RG 153, NA. David Balsiger and Charles E. Sellier, Jr., *The Lincoln Conspiracy* (Los Angeles: Schick Sunn Classic Books, 1977), claim that two sets of individuals were moving through southern Maryland—Booth and Henson, and Boyd and Herold—which would account for the tracks reported by Beckwith and Wells.

8. Eisenschiml, *Why Was Lincoln Murdered?*, 120, 128; S. H. Beckwith, in New York *Sun*, April 27, 1913, p. 6.

Boat of even average speed, I feel confident that I should have captured Booth and Herold before the Cavalry came up." Colonel H. S. Olcott also confirmed that Smith had narrowly missed the capture when he wrote Judge Advocate Holt in September complaining of the preferential treatment that he felt Baker had received: "A party of twenty-five cavalry that we sent under Smith on a tug reached the scene of Booth's death eleven hours after that occurrence, and would have been there eight hours before it if the steampower of the vessel had not been inadequate. And yet we see Baker made a general and receiving all credit, while the rest of us are not even mentioned in anyway."[9]

Some contemporaries also felt that the War Department detectives had received undeserved credit for the capture, as in a letter signed "Justice" in the New York *Herald*: "I am informed from good authority that the greater part of the information which led to these arrests was given to the War Department by detectives not employed by it. Colonel Baker remained in Washington as a special agent for the department, received by telegram all the information collected by the different parties who were on the trail of Booth, and upon this acted. The matter should be thoroughly investigated and the parties who gave the information to the department should receive their full amount of credit for it."[10]

The unseemly scramble after the reward money has caused historians to be critical of the rewards offered. Many claims were put forth after the capture, some of them dubious. Lafayette Baker himself became embroiled in a controversy, trying to get more of the reward money than Congress wished to allot him. As early as May 3, the Albany *Argus* reported: "A quarrel has already sprung up among the detectives and others, about the division of the reward for the capture of Booth. Several of them who were actively engaged in the capture say there is an attempt on the part of others to crowd them out and claim the lion's share."[11]

9. H. W. Smith to Colonel Foster, May 1, 1865, in Letters Received, File S 679, JAO, RG 153, NA; H. S. Olcott to Joseph Holt, September 15, 1865, in Joseph Holt Papers, LC.
10. New York *Herald*, May 3, 1865, p. 5.
11. David M. DeWitt, *The Assassination of Abraham Lincoln and Its Expiation* (New York: MacMillan, 1909), 58, 276–80; Eisenschiml, *Why Was Lincoln Murdered?*, 122; Lafayette C. Baker to Joseph Holt, June 2, 1865, in Letters Received, File B 745, JAO, RG 153, NA. Baker requested affidavits of Luther Baker and Everton Conger for the purpose of reward claims. Albany *Atlas and Argus*, May 3, 1865, p. 2.

Reward claims poured in. Special Officer George Cottingham claimed to have seen Paine in the woods near Mrs. Surratt's tavern after the assassination. James P. Stabler, who had led a party in pursuit of a man who had stolen a horse in Montgomery County, claimed his share of the reward money for information leading to Atzerodt's capture. Claims persisted, for in March, 1866, T. B. Robey was still attempting to obtain money for Dr. Mudd's capture, and as late as 1867 Henry Ste. Marie was inquiring of Judge Holt whether it was true, as he had seen in the papers, that Congress was going to deny him any share in the reward.[12]

Despite the excesses that occurred, contemporaries felt that the method of offering rewards would have infallible results, rousing the entire country to a pitch where even friends of the assassin would not hesitate to deliver him to the authorities. The Washington *Evening Star* stated editorially, "It is a matter of surprise that rewards have not been offered in every state, city and town in the land. . . . Put a million of dollars on the head of the criminal, and earth has not a hiding place that would conceal him." Lincoln's 1860 campaign manager, David Davis, also wrote to Governor Richard James Oglesby of Illinois on Stanton's behalf, "The Secretary of War thinks there is a very great propriety in your offering a reward for the arrest of Booth." That people really did believe in the efficacy of reward money is shown by the fact that many also recommended it as a means of apprehending Jefferson Davis.[13]

The actual killing of Booth has raised many questions, including his possible suicide, deliberate murder by government detectives to silence him, and even whether it actually was John Wilkes Booth who died in Garrett's barn. Detective Everton Conger initially believed that Booth

---

12. George Cottingham to Edwin Stanton, July 18, 1865, in RG 110, NA. Such a claim was apparently erroneous. James P. Stabler to Edwin Stanton, May 2, 1865, in Letters Received, File S 684, JAO, RG 153, NA. W. B. Evans to Joseph Holt, March 12, 1866, Henry B. Ste. Marie to Joseph Holt, December 26, 1867, in Holt Papers. The Hartford *Daily Courant*, June 10, 1867, p. 4, carried news of the equity court of Washington attempting to decide the controversy over the twenty-thousand-dollar reward offered by the District of Columbia City Council.

13. Washington *Evening Star*, April 21, 1865, p. 2; *The War of the Rebellion: A Compilation of the Official Records of the Union and Confederate Armies* (130 vols.; Washington: Government Printing Office, 1880–1901), Ser. I, Vol. XLVI, Pt. 3, p. 906; New York *Herald*, April 28, p. 4, April 29, 1865, p. 1.

had committed suicide, while his colleague Luther Baker thought that Conger, who had been around the other side of the barn, might have shot him.[14]

Many people who knew Booth or had talked with him after the assassination felt that he would never be taken alive. Confederate soldier Willie Jett, in a statement dated May 6, 1865, said that Booth had told him he did not intend to be taken alive: "If they don't kill me I'll kill myself." Actor Edwin Adams, who knew Booth, also felt he would not be taken alive—a feeling that coincided with the statement in the Gettysburg *Compiler*: "Those who know him best, feel confident that he has committed suicide." Actor W. J. Ferguson claimed to have talked with the sergeant of the cavalry squadron about two weeks after Booth's death. "He gave me the impression that Booth shot himself with the carbine he held in his hand, and was not shot by Boston Corbett from outside the barn where Booth was brought to bay."[15]

Although charges have been raised that Colonel Conger, acting under secret orders, killed Booth to silence him, there is certainly no direct proof for them. Luther Baker, who himself harbored such suspicions, testified that there were strict orders against shooting and that Conger had made these known to the men a number of times. Conger himself verified that the orders from Stanton had been to take Booth alive if possible and recounted that Stanton, when he had heard of a man alleged to be Booth being strung up by a mob, issued a proclamation that any person who harmed a prisoner without authority should be tried by a military court. The initial reaction of the authorities was not

14. Benn Pitman, *The Assassination of President Lincoln and the Trial of the Conspirators* (New York: Funk and Wagnalls, 1954), 91–93; Everton J. Conger, May 14, 1867, Luther B. Baker, May 22, 1867, in U.S., Congress, House, Committee on the Judiciary, *Impeachment Investigation, Testimony Taken Before the Judiciary Committee of the House of Representatives in the Investigation of the Charges Against Andrew Johnson*, 39th Cong., 2nd Sess., 40th Cong., 1st Sess. (Washington: Government Printing Office, 1867), 325–30, 479–82; hereinafter cited as *Impeachment Investigation*.

15. Willie Jett, May 6, 1865, Statement, in Record Book, File J, p. 55, JAO, RG 153, NA; E. Wallace, April 21, 1865, in Letters Received, File W, RB, p. 30, JAO, RG 153, NA; Gettysburg *Compiler*, April 24, 1865, p. 2; William J. Ferguson, "Lincoln's Death," *Saturday Evening Post* (February 12, 1927), 49. Some historians who have argued that Booth committed suicide are DeWitt, *Assassination of Lincoln*, 91, 275–79; Stanley Kimmel, *The Mad Booths of Maryland* (Indianapolis: Bobbs Merrill, 1940), 257; and Eleanor Ruggles, *Prince of Players, Edwin Booth* (New York: W. W. Norton, 1953), 194.

to make a hero out of Corbett but to send him back to Washington under arrest.[16]

Sergeant Boston Corbett stepped forward and laid claim to Booth's killing. A letter dated May 11 to "Brother" Broughton presents clearly his part in the shooting. Thus, while there was some contemporary belief and evidence that Booth might have committed suicide—and many historians have held to this view—it is still not inconceivable that Corbett actually killed Booth. He was a devout religious fanatic, and it could easily have appeared to him that he was carrying out the will of God in bringing the murderer to justice.[17]

One thing is clear. While it might be assumed that the killing of Booth was a universally popular act, such was, in fact, not the case. The number of newspapers that expressed this view is astonishing. Of course, this was not due to any sympathy for Booth but went back to the often expressed idea that it would have been better to handle the assassin in a legal manner. The *National Intelligencer* greeted the news of Booth's death with the statement, "It was hoped that he had been taken alive, and that offended justice would be avenged by his summary execution in due course of law; but he has paid in a less public manner the penalty of his great crime." There was also a feeling that Booth's death had robbed the American public of a chance to fathom the true nature of the conspiracy.[18]

Obviously, too, there was something of an ambivalent feeling, for many people, despite misgivings, could not help but feel some satisfaction at Booth's death. Some regretted his not being taken alive because they were deprived of the pleasure of seeing him hang. Others reveled in his death agony and the manner in which he met his fate, comparing it to a dog's death.[19]

---

16. Luther B. Baker, May 22, 1867, *Impeachment Investigation*, 481; William L. Reuter, *The King Can Do No Wrong* (New York: Pageant Press, 1958), 49–50.

17. New York *Times*, May 15, 1865, p. 2; New York *Tribune*, April 28, 1865, p. 1. See Kimmel, *Mad Booths of Maryland*, 257, and George S. Bryan, *The Great American Myth* (New York: Carrick and Evans, 1940), 267.

18. Washington *Daily National Intelligencer*, April 28, 1865, p. 2; New York *World*, April 28, 1865, p. 2; New York *Times*, April 28, 1865, p. 1; New York *Tribune*, April 28, 1865, p. 4.

19. Chicago *Tribune*, April 28, 1865, p. 2; Washington *Evening Star*, April 27, 1865, p. 2; New York *Times*, April 28, 1865, p. 4.

There was also some mixed feeling as to whether the nature of his death had not really been more heroic than hanging would have been. However, the Philadelphia *Evening Bulletin* felt a trial would have allowed Booth to indulge his theatrical passion; and the Reverend Joseph Thompson told his congregation that such a trial might have drawn for Booth the sympathy and pity that even the greatest criminals seem to gain after the first hideousness of their crime has passed.[20]

Many people were also glad that the furor which taking Booth alive and trying him would have caused, could now be avoided. As the Albany *Atlas and Argus* said, "Had he been brought to the Washington Navy Yard alive nothing could have withstood the fury of the excited congregated thousands." H. S. Foote, writing in 1873, in the Washington *Daily Morning Chronicle*, gave credit to the people of Washington for not bringing the other conspirators to the scaffold in a manner reflecting the excited circumstances at the time.[21]

That Booth's death was not altogether approved is also shown by the criticism of Corbett for disobeying orders. However, most of this, though not all, came from antiadministration newspapers. The Toronto *Leader* charged that "the shooting of Booth was a cold-blooded murder—nothing more or less." The Albany *Atlas and Argus* added, "The attempt to make a hero of 'Boston Corbett' shows a perversity of taste on the part of those engaged in it." This criticism had some effect on loyal Union people, for the New York *Tribune* correspondent felt compelled to wire his paper that despite attempts to censure Corbett, his action was justified and approved by the entire party at the time, and now received the approbation of his superior officer.[22]

Rumors circulating that Corbett had been shot caused some excitement until they were proven to be untrue. Also, Corbett received threatening letters from cranks, one of whom signed himself "Booth's Avenger" and told Corbett he would end up the same way Booth had.[23]

20. New York *Herald*, April 28, 1865, p. 1; New York *Times*, April 28, 1865, p. 4; Philadelphia *Evening Bulletin*, April 27, 1865, p. 4; Joseph P. Thompson, *Abraham Lincoln, His Life and Its Lessons* (New York: Loyal Publication Society, 1865), 33–34.

21. Albany *Atlas and Argus*, April 29, 1865, p. 1; Washington *Daily Morning Chronicle*, August 14, 1873, p. 6.

22. Toronto *Leader*, quoted in New York *Times*, May 2, 1865, p. 4; Albany *Atlas and Argus*, May 6, 1865, p. 2; New York *Tribune*, May 9, 1865, p. 5.

23. Philadelphia *Evening Bulletin*, May 1, 1865, p. 5; New York *Times*, May 2, p. 1, May

To the majority of loyal northerners Corbett did become something of a celebrity. Although Luther Baker had threatened to send him back to Washington in chains, he went back a hero. Stanton is reported to have said, "The rebel is dead—the patriot lives . . . he has saved us continued excitement—delay and expense—the patriot is released." Corbett's testimony at the conspiracy trial also pretty effectively succeeded in removing the stigma from the minds of many.[24]

The secrecy surrounding the disposal of Booth's body was widely applauded in 1865, although historians have again been supplied with much fuel for controversy. The public wished the body to go to an unknown grave or else to be displayed in a way to bring shame upon it. In Dayton, Ohio, a public meeting resolved that Booth's body should be taken to mid-ocean and buried there. Others suggested dissecting it and putting it on display, hanging the body in chains, or fixing it in iron as an eternal warning to all assassins.[25]

One of the primary reasons for confusion as to the fate of Booth's body was a sketch that appeared in *Leslie's Illustrated* with the caption: "The sketch below was furnished by one of the two officers employed in the duty of sinking the body of Booth in the middle of the Potomac. Although not authorized to divulge his name, I am able to vouch for the truth of the representation." Lafayette Baker, who was not always known for a scrupulous fostering of the truth, apparently was not backward in promoting this version of disposal.[26]

Among all the conflicting rumors, the Washington *Evening Star* correctly reported that the body had been buried under the floor of the arsenal in an ammunition box. The reason the government acted as it did was that in the heated circumstances it was determined that Booth's body was not to become a relic and an object of Confederate venera-

---

3, 1865, p. 5; Albert T. Reid, "Boston Corbett, the Man of Mystery of the Lincoln Drama," *Scribner's Magazine*, LXXXVI (1929), 13.

24. DeWitt, *Assassination of Abraham Lincoln*, 89; Lloyd Lewis, *Myths After Lincoln* (New York: Harcourt Brace, 1929), 292; Eisenschiml, *Why Was Lincoln Murdered?*, 37, 38. Of course, Eisenschiml muses about the sinister meaning behind Stanton's reference to continued excitement when most logically it referred to the aroused condition of the country.

25. New York *Tribune*, April 29, 1865, p. 5; L. C. Baker, *History of the United States Secret Service*, 552–53; A. Lathrop to Edwin Stanton, April 27, 1865, in Edwin M. Stanton Papers, LC.

26. *Frank Leslie's Illustrated Newspaper*, May 20, 1865, p. 129; Lafayette C. Baker, May 20, 1867, *Impeachment Investigation*, 453; Townsend, *Life, Crime and Capture*, 38–39.

tion. Baker reported that this was the motive Stanton gave him when ordering him to take charge of burying the body. He also claimed that he found unauthorized people on board the monitor, and a woman snipping off a lock of the assassin's hair, though this may not have occurred. Stanton also testified to a similar intention before the House committee investigating the impeachment and said that not only had he not had anything to do with the story of Booth's burial at sea but that, in fact, it disgusted him.[27]

There was an occasional call for Booth's body to be delivered up to his family. Junius Henri Browne suggested that it be given to Booth's mother or brother so that the family might have the consolation of mourning at his grave. Edward Stimson wrote from Canada, also deploring the withholding of the body.[28]

The secrecy has proven historically, however, to be unfortunate and unwise in at least one respect, for it has made it much easier to charge that the government acted as it did because it had something to hide. Such charges began with the moment Baker informed Stanton of Booth's capture and described a reaction uncharacteristic of the normally emotional Stanton. "Secretary Stanton was distinguished during the whole war for his coolness, but I have never seen such an exhibition of it in my life as at that time. He put his hands over his eyes, and lay for nearly a moment without saying a word. Then he got up and put on his coat very coolly." However, once he received the body, it is also darkly hinted that he discovered that it was not Booth who had been killed. This belief was shared by some contemporaries. Dr. J. Frederick May, who identified the remains, later claimed that the reason the government took so many pains to identify Booth was the rumors that it was not his body. The Baltimore *Sun* surmised that the reason May was put on the stand at the John Surratt trial was to set at rest rumors that Booth had not been captured with Herold.[29]

27. Washington *Evening Star*, July 7, 1865, p. 2; L. C. Baker, *History of the United States Secret Service*, 507–508; Edwin M. Stanton, May 18, 1867, *Impeachment Investigation*, 408–409.

28. New York *Tribune*, May 11, 1865, p. 1; Edward Stimson, May 1, 1865, in Letters Received, File S 172, JAO, RG 153, NA.

29. L. C. Baker, *History of the United States Secret Service*, 540. See Theodore Roscoe, *The Web of Conspiracy* (Englewood, N.J.: Prentice-Hall, 1959), 425; John F. May, *The Mark of the Scalpel* (Washington: Columbia Historical Society, 1910), 54; Baltimore *Sun*, June 25, 1867, p. 4.

On April 27, Stanton issued the following order countersigned by Gideon Welles: "You will permit Surgeon General Barnes and his assistant accompanied by Judge Advocate General Holt, Hon. John A. Bingham, Special Judge Advocate Major Eckert, William G. Moore, Clerk of the War Department, Colonel L. C. Baker, Lieutenant Baker, Lieutenant Colonel Conger, J. L. Smith, Gardiner [photographer] and his assistant, and Chas. Dawson to go on board the 'Montauk', and see the body of John Wilkes Booth." The results of this inquest would seem to leave little question in the mind of the unbiased observer that J. Wilkes Booth was killed, for a host of witnesses who were acquainted with Booth testified it was his body that lay on the deck of the *Montauk*.[30]

However, immediately after the shooting there were rumors that the corpse was not Booth.[31] Men who had some resemblance to Booth were also later rumored to be the culprit. One was the Reverend Dr. James Glasgow Armstrong, who preached for many years in Richmond, Virginia, and did nothing to dissuade people's beliefs that he was Booth.[32]

The surrendering of the assassin's body to his family and its reburial, instead of settling the controversy, has actually raised more questions as to whether it was Booth. That Booth was still extremely controversial as late as 1869 is shown by the fact that the Reverend Fleming James of New York, who presided at the burial, was dismissed by his northern congregation. He felt compelled to send a letter to the New York *Times*, June 30, 1869, justifying his actions. Again, many reputable people identified the corpse, including a dentist who had filled Booth's teeth,

---

30. Edwin Stanton and Gideon Welles to Commandant of Navy Yard, April 27, 1868 [1865], in Stanton Papers; William W. Crowninshield, Charles M. Collins, Charles Dawson, Dr. J. Frederick May, Seaton Monroe, April 27, 1865, Testimony on the *Montauk*, File M, RB, p. 20, JAO, RG 153, NA. Otto Eisenschiml notes some discrepancies in the testimony but concludes that the body was probably Booth's, in *In the Shadow of Lincoln's Death* (New York: Wilfrid Funk, 1940), Chap. III. Balsiger and Sellier, *Lincoln Conspiracy*, believe the body was J. W. Boyd.

31. New York *Times*, Jan. 12, 1867, p. 8; Louisville *Journal*, quoted in Charleston *Courier*, August 21, 1867, p. 2; Saint Louis (Mo.) *Republican*, September 7, 1873, p. 8.

32. New York *Herald*, April 26, 1903, Literary Sec., p. 1; New York *Tribune*, March 13, 1885, p. 1. Rufus Woods compiled a pamphlet in which he reiterated and gave credit to all the stories he could find of Booth's survival, *The Weirdest Story in American History: The Escape of John Wilkes Booth* (Wenatchee, Wash.: World, 1944).

but because of discrepancies and uncertainty on the part of others who were present, grave doubts have again been raised.[33]

A possible explanation for the persistent belief that Booth survived Garrett's barn may have to do with folklore, which is, at best, difficult to define but which sometimes can provide great insights. In traditional folklore, the slayer of a hero was never allowed to rest in peace in his grave but was believed to be wandering the world, friendless and branded with infamy. Lincoln, of course, became the American folk hero, and Booth, the American folk-story slayer, soon took the role of the traditional mythological betrayer. If this interpretation is correct, it may be difficult to ever completely put to rest the rumor that Booth survived Garrett's barn.[34]

Booth's capture, while bringing the assassin to a rough sort of justice, has created numerous historical problems. The scramble for the reward raised questions as to how Booth was captured, or whether in fact it was even Booth that died in Garrett's barn. Yet, it is clear that most of these occurrences have a much more logical explanation than the majority of historians has been willing to give them.

33. New York *Times*, July 2, 1869, p. 5, and William Pegram, "An Historical Identification: John Wilkes Booth—What Became of Him?" *Maryland Historical Magazine*, VIII (1913), 328, verified that the remains were Booth. However, Basil Moxley, doorkeeper at Ford's Baltimore theater, in the Baltimore *American*, June 3, 1903, p. 14, raised doubts. See George S. Bryan, *The Great American Myth* (New York: Carrick and Evans, 1940), 308–18, for a thorough discussion of this incident.

34. For a stimulating discussion on folk myth and assassination, see Lewis, *Myths After Lincoln*, 347–56. Among writers who have perpetuated this "myth" of Booth's escape, see Finis L. Bates, *Escape and Suicide of John Wilkes Booth, Assassin of President Lincoln* (Memphis: Pilcher Printing, 1907), and Izola Forrester, *This One Mad Act: The Unknown Story of John Wilkes Booth and His Family by His Granddaughter* (Boston: Hale, Cushman and Flint, 1937). For a thorough refutation of the story of Booth's escape, see Bryan, *Great American Myth*, 347–54; F. L. Black, "Identification of John Wilkes Booth," *Dearborn Independent*, XXV (May 2, 1925), 19, 27, 28, 31.

10

Implication of Southern Leaders
in the Assassination

The public assumed that the Confederates both in the South and in Canada shared responsibility for the assassination. Lincoln's policy had been to allow Confederates to escape if they wished, but now that he was dead, the government moved to apprehend those whom it felt were involved. The Confederates accused of complicity in the murder were either official or unofficial agents in Canada. Since they had been involved with illegal acts of violence that violated Canadian neutrality, it was only natural at the time to believe that from their sanctuary on Canadian soil they were involved in plotting the president's murder.

At 4:40 A.M. on April 15, 1865, shortly after Booth had been identified as the president's assailant, Charles A. Dana, by order of the secretary of war, wired the United States marshal of Portland, Maine, "Arrest Jacob Thompson and his companion . . . who are either in Portland or on the way to Portland from Montreal en route to Europe." On the 27th, Stanton informed the provost marshal at Portland that Confederate agents George Sanders, Beverley Tucker, and Jacob Thompson either were or would be in the vicinity, attempting to escape to Europe; and he ordered every train and vessel searched and no effort spared to apprehend them. William Hunter, acting secretary of state, also wired Robert Murray, United States marshal of the Southern District of New York, to proceed to Canada with proper assistants to determine the involvement of insurgents there and arrange possible extradition. On May 10, an American official informed Stanton from Montreal that Sanders, Tucker, and W. C. Cleary were still there, and asked if he wished them arrested to await the demand for extradition. However, Stanton wired back, "The government is taking measures upon the subject of your telegram of yesterday, of which you will be advised when action is required."[1]

In many cases, more contempt was held for the rebels in Canada than for any other class of traitors, since they were considered to be cowards operating clandestinely from a privileged sanctuary. *Harper's Weekly* said on May 13, "Infinitely the most contemptible class is composed of those who sneaked into Canada too far to be reached by the military conscriptions of the Rebel despotism at Richmond but near enough to the loyal part of the country to plot thefts, raids, railway slaughters, the burning alive of innocent women and children in theatres and hotels and to instigate assassination."[2]

Those whose names were mentioned as being involved rushed into print to defend themselves, even before an official proclamation was released by the government. On April 20, George Sanders criticized the editor of the New York *Times* for making inflammatory statements against him and offered to come to New York and let him attempt to prove his charges. The *Times* responded: "It is rather late for George to try to pass for a meek apostle of peace and brotherly love . . . we advise Mr. Sanders not to come to this city just yet. He would not find the atmosphere congenial to his bodily health. . . . He had better tarry a while longer where he can take cowardly 'advantage' of his neutral protection, and concoct expeditions for plunder, robbery and murder against peaceable citizens of the United States."[3]

On April 25, Stanton sent an order to General Dix in New York which was to be released to the public, stating that there was now evidence that the plot was organized in Canada and approved at Rich-

---

1. *The War of the Rebellion: A Compilation of the Official Records of the Union and Confederate Armies*, (130 vols., Washington: Government Printing Office, 1880–1901), Ser. II, Vol. VIII, pp. 493, 517, 549; William Hunter to Robert Murray, April 29, 1865, in Letters Received, File H 132, JAO, RG 153, NA. Among the accused Confederate agents in Canada was Jacob Thompson, the chief Confederate commissioner, who was a former Mississippi senator and secretary of the interior in the Buchanan administration. Clement Clay had been a senator from Alabama, and Beverley Tucker had been a judge in Virginia and also served as consul to Liverpool under Buchanan. George Sanders had served as consul to London in the administration of Franklin Pierce. William Cleary, of Kentucky, was secretary of the Confederate Commission. These and other individuals were involved with the Lake Erie raid, the Saint Albans raid, and other schemes to bring the war to the North.
2. *Harper's Weekly*, May 13, 1865, p. 290. See also New York *Times*, April 19, 1865, p. 4.
3. New York *Times*, April 23, 1865, pp. 1, 4.

mond. The New York *Herald* added that there was no doubt that Jefferson Davis was implicated as well as former Secretary of the Interior Thompson and his Canadian clique.[4]

However, the action that served dramatically to demonstrate the government's belief in the involvement of Confederate officials was the proclamation issued on May 2, 1865, that "the atrocious murder of the Late Pres. Abraham Lincoln and the attempted assassination of Hon. W. H. Seward Secretary of State, were incited, concerted and procured by and between Jefferson Davis, Clement C. Clay, Beverley Tucker, George Sanders, W. C. Cleary, and other rebels and traitors."[5] Although people were generally inclined to this view anyway, the proclamation caused a profound sensation.

On May 2, 1865, Judge Advocate Holt received a memorandum from Stanton saying that President Johnson desired to be furnished a list of those in Canada and Richmond against whom there was proof of complicity in Lincoln's murder. While the question arises as to whether Stanton used Holt as a shield to cover his own operations, it appears that on this and other occasions, Stanton relied on the Bureau of Military Justice to gather information on which he might make decisions. Joseph Holt was far more than a mere puppet in Stanton's hands. Stanton took the information he received from Holt, together with the proposed proclamation, which he fully endorsed, to a cabinet meeting on the same day. Cabinet members Hugh McCulloch and William Hunter, who was acting for the injured Seward, strongly supported Stanton, and even the cautious Welles had this reaction, "I . . . remarked if there was proof of the complicity of those men, (as stated there was,) they certainly ought to be arrested, and that reward was proper, but I had no facts." Apparently some time later, he added a note to his diary entry of April 25 which indicates the influence Stanton had upon the cabinet. "No one, except perhaps Speed, fully sympathized with Stanton. Yet all were in a degree influenced by him. At the time we had been made to believe . . . that he and Judge Advocate General Holt had positive evidence that Jeff Davis, Clay, Thompson, and others had conspired to assassinate Mr. Lincoln, Mr. Johnson, and most of the cabinet. Strange stories were told us and it was under these representations, to which

4. New York *Herald*, April 25, 1865, p. 4.
5. *Ibid.*, May 4, 1865, p. 1.

we then gave credit, that we were less inclined to justify Sherman [in his leniency toward the South]."[6]

Most Union supporters received the proclamation warmly, believing that the government would never issue a document without sufficient proof to support it. Former Attorney General Bates expressed the view that there must be pretty good evidence to implicate Davis, as Andrew Johnson was not a petty man who would make politics out of the assassination.[7]

Newspapers also expressed their opinions, although in this case there was a differentiation in opinion between those favoring the administration and those opposed. The New York *Times* greeted the news with the headlines: IMPORTANT PROCLAMATION BY PRESIDENT JOHNSON, MR. LINCOLN'S MURDER PLANNED BY LEADING TRAITORS, MOST OF THESE TRAITORS ARE HARBORED IN CANADA, and JEFFERSON DAVIS IS THE HEAD OF THE ASSASSINS. It also gloated that it had been proven correct about its original statements of George Sanders' involvement. The New York *Herald* said that many might be doubtful in spite of Mr. Johnson's proclamation but that if they would only recall that for four years Davis and his associates had attempted to ruin the government, they would see that this was fitting training for any crime. The Gettysburg *Adams Sentinel*, expressing one of the most extreme views, said that it would be better if tools of the archconspirator, like Herold and Atzerodt, escaped than that any of those named in the proclamation should go unpunished.[8]

Foreign journals were not so convinced by the president's unsupported word. The Montreal *Gazette* said it seemed no government could issue such a document without proof, yet the charges made were all at odds with Davis' life and character: "If Mr. Davis could be proved to be guilty of such a crime as that imputed to him, then no term of infamy would be too strong with which to brand him; but if he cannot be so proved, it must be said that no civilized government was ever

6. Edwin Stanton to Joseph Holt, May 2, 1865, in Edwin M. Stanton Papers, LC; Howard K. Beale (ed.), *Diary of Gideon Welles* (3 vols.; New York: W. W. Norton, 1960), II, 296, 299.

7. Howard K. Beale (ed.), *The Diary of Edward Bates, 1859–1866*, Vol. IV of the Annual Report of the American Historical Association, 1930 (Washington: Government Printing Office, 1933), 477.

8. New York *Times*, May 4, 1865, pp. 1, 4; New York *Herald*, May 5, 1865, p. 4; Gettysburg *Adams Sentinel*, May 9, 1865, p. 2.

before guilty of so infamous a libel." Even the more friendly Montreal *Herald*, which was calling for John Surratt's surrender to the United States government if he was in Canada, said of southern complicity, "They will have to see proof before they believe it." Loyal papers often chided foreign papers on their incredulity; for example, the *Alta Californian* said that English papers had attributed unworthy motives to Stanton in publishing the proclamation, but any one who had read the conspiracy trial's suppressed testimony could see that he was justified.[9]

Generally, antiadministration newspapers could not bring themselves to believe that Davis was involved in any way. The Utica *Daily Observer* clearly demonstrated its bias against Stanton, who, it said, "has been noted for years past for his readiness to arrest men on 'evidence in his possession,' who, after long suffering and persecution, have been pronounced innocent even by his own packed tribunals." The Easton (Pa.) *Sentinel* felt that Stanton had been caught in a web of contradiction. "First we are told the conspiracy was hatched in Baltimore, then some place in Tennessee, and now in Canada. We are inclined to think that the worthy Secretary does not know much more about this terrible business than any other man." The Albany *Atlas and Argus* reflected the views of many when it said, "We want the proofs."[10]

Even most loyal papers were keenly aware that the government must be prepared to make good its charges. The New York *Times*, which had so exuberantly greeted the proclamation, warned the judge advocate against exaggeration. The *Tribune* also advised, "Let us candidly scrutinize the forthcoming facts before passing judgment," for while there was no doubt proof in the Bureau of Military Justice, its weight could not be determined until after it had been revealed.[11]

The assassination and proclamation also caused some apprehension as to the direction relations between Canada and the United States might take. The Montreal *Herald* said it was dangerous to follow the recent opinion of Justice Smith that belligerent rights cloak any crime, for if Booth came to Canada and was acting for the South, the Cana-

---

9. Montreal *Gazette* and Montreal *Herald*, quoted in New York *Times*, May 7, 1865, p. 2; San Francisco *Alta Californian*, July 6, 1865, p. 2.

10. Utica *Daily Observer*, May 4, 1865, in RG 110, NA; Easton (Pa.) *Sentinel*, April 27, 1865, p. 3; Albany *Atlas and Argus*, May 18, 1865, p. 2. See also New York *World*, May 4, 1865, p. 4.

11. New York *Times*, May 5, 1865, p. 4; New York *Tribune*, May 5, 1865, p. 4.

dian government would be forced to shield him. Americans were also afraid that the Canadian government might shield guilty parties, but on May 9, the New York *Herald* said that the government's evidence was so complete that no foreign government with which the fugitives might take refuge would hesitate for a moment in giving them up. The fact that government authorities were aware of this problem is shown in Congressman George Boutwell's letter to General Butler on April 20: "If there be evidence connecting any of the rebel leaders with the plot to assassinate the President indictments should be found that we may follow them to other countries."[12]

On the other hand, the New York *World* feared that the proclamation was hastily drawn and might well induce detectives to violate the sovereignty of Canadian territory to apprehend the assassin. The *World* felt this would have been avoided if Secretary Seward had been well enough to aid in drafting the proclamation.[13]

On May 4, 1865, two of the accused, George Sanders and Beverley Tucker, wrote to Johnson, "Your proclamation is a living, burning lie, known to be such, by yourself and all your surroundings, and all the hired perjurers in Christendom, shall not defer us from exhibiting to the civilized world, your hellish plot to murder our Christian President." On May 6, there was a report that Tucker and Sanders had agreed to go to Rouses Point to be tried and that they accused Johnson of the plot. The *Times* also carried a letter from William Cleary dated May 5, denying all knowledge of the assassination. Many seized rumors of the flight of Sanders and Tucker as proof of their guilt, although the Montreal *Gazette* on May 10 denied that they had fled.[14]

Jacob Thompson, taking up the theme introduced by Tucker and Sanders, addressed the following letter to the New York *Tribune*: "The proof, whatever it is, is a tissue of falsehoods, and its publication cannot

12. Montreal *Herald*, quoted in New York *Times*, April 23, 1865, p. 1; New York *Herald*, May 9, 1865, p. 5; George S. Boutwell to Benjamin Butler, April 20, 1865, in Benjamin Butler Papers, LC.

13. New York *World*, May 5, 1865, p. 4.

14. George M. Sanders and Beverley Tucker to Andrew Johnson, May 4, 1865, in Andrew Johnson Papers, LC, Microcopy, Roll 14. See also New York *Herald*, May 7, 1865, p. 1. For an account of Tucker's reaction, see Jane Ellis Tucker: *Beverley Tucker; A Memoir by His Wife* (Richmond: N.p., 1893). New York *Times*, May 6, p. 8, May 7, p. 1, May 8, 1865, p. 4; Montreal *Gazette*, quoted in New York *Times*, May 14, 1865, p. 1.

be made without exposing its rottenness. I know that there is not half the ground to suspect me that there is to suspect President Johnson himself." The charges of Johnson's complicity angered the New York *Times* and caused it to question the *Tribune*'s motive in printing the letter.[15]

In light of the shrill controversy concerning the charges in the proclamation and the protestations of innocence from those accused, the New York *World* advised the government: "Secretary Stanton should bring forth from the dark portals of the 'Bureau of Military Justice' the proofs on which his representations to the President were founded. These proofs ought to be strong; but whether they are strong or weak, the government will appear to better advantage by their exhibition than by their further concealment." Equal interest was expressed in bringing Jefferson Davis to justice. Some Southerners felt that the proclamation was just one more evidence of the vindictive spirit in Washington that was operating against the southern people.[16]

Davis, according to his secretary, Burton Harrison, received the news of the proclamation with a composure unruffled by any feeling other than scorn. However, Harrison speculated on Stanton and Holt's motivation, concluding that they "well knew that Mr. Davis could never be convicted upon an indictment for treason, but were determined to hang him anyhow, and were in search of a pretext for doing so." Mrs. Clement Clay felt that Holt's motive was personal hatred for Clay and Davis because they knew Holt's heart was with the Confederacy but he had gone with the Union because he received a higher office.[17]

Once Davis was captured, the question arose what should be done to him. Many would have agreed with the sentiment of the New York *Times*: "If before the atrocious murder of the President, the life of the

---

15. New York *Tribune*, May 22, 1865, p. 4; New York *Times*, May 23, 1865, p. 4.

16. New York *World*, May 9, 1865, p. 4; New York *Times*, May 9, p. 1, May 14, 1865, p. 4; W. D. Chadwick, "Civil War Days in Huntsville," *Alabama Historical Quarterly*, IX (1947), 330.

17. Fairfax Harrison (ed.), *Aris Sonis Focisque, Being a Memoir of an American Family, the Harrisons of Skimino and Particularly of Jesse Burton Harrison and Burton Norwell Harrison* (New York: DeVinne Press, 1910), 256; Ada Sterling (ed.), *A Belle of the Fifties: Memoirs of Mrs. Clay of Alabama, Concerning Social and Political Life in Washington and the South, 1853–1866* (New York: Doubleday, 1904), 339.

rebel chieftain was not worth a pin's fee, of what value is it now?"[18] Despite a wish for his execution, it was realized he must be brought to trial and that it would have to be determined whether it would be in a military tribunal or a civil court. This problem was further complicated by Constitutional provisions that a trial for treason must be in civil courts.

Opinion was greatly divided on this issue. On May 15, the *Times*, while admitting that Davis might be properly tried before a military commission for assassination complicity, said he would probably be tried first by a civil jury for the greater offense of treason. On stationery from the Union League Club of New York, an anonymous writer advised the government, "The fact that the war is over is no reason why Jeff should not be tried before a court martial."[19]

Sentiment was also divided in the cabinet. Welles noted that Seward and Stanton were for a military trial, while he favored a civil trial for treason only, not for involvement in the assassination. Finally, on July 21, Stanton agreed that Davis should be tried in the civil courts for treason but arraigned before a military commission on all other charges. Attorney General Speed also came around to this position, and when a vote was taken on the issue, all were in favor except Seward and Harlan.[20]

Davis, however, was never to be brought to trial on either charge. Edwards Pierrepont, who was special prosecutor for the John Surratt trial, had warned Stanton on May 14, "Forthwith springs up a party against his immediate trial; the plan being to postpone, in order to get up public sympathy in his favor and to oppose his conviction and execution; placing the act on the ground of public policy." To some extent, this is what happened. The Judiciary Committee of Congress sought testimony over the next two years to determine why, if there was so much evidence to implicate Davis, he was not being brought to trial. The House of Representatives adopted a resolution in April, 1866, calling on the Judiciary Committee to inquire whether people included in

18. New York *Times*, May 12, 1865, p. 4

19. New York *Times*, May 15, 1865, p. 4; Anonymous, June 10, 1865, in Letters Received, File A 519, JAO, RG 153, NA.

20. Beale (ed.), *Diary of Gideon Welles*, II, 335–40.

the proclamation of May, 1865, were guilty as alleged. The majority report of the committee concluded that they were guilty as charged, although the minority report of Congressman A. J. Rogers did much to destroy the evidence of Sanford Conover and his group of perjurers. Conover, whose real name was Charles Dunham, coached witnesses in perjury and manufactured evidence that led Holt to believe that Davis, Thompson, and other southerners were involved in the assassination.[21]

In the midst of this investigation in June, 1866, Chief Justice Chase was still informing Horace Greeley that Davis could be tried before Judge Underwood, and that while the court would be quasi military, there could be no question of the trial's regularity. As late as May, 1867, the Judiciary Committee, during the impeachment investigation, was still trying to determine the charge on which Davis was being held. Attorney General Henry Stanbery said that while Davis had originally been arrested for complicity in the assassination, it was his understanding that he was presently being held as a prisoner of war. The previous month, Secretary Seward had testified that he and President Johnson had interviewed some witnesses on the subject but the testimony was discredited and they had failed to get enough evidence.[22]

The most important factor in the change of feeling was the growth over a two-year period of a renewed "era of good feeling" on the part of a substantial segment of the population. The almost complete reversal in opinion that had occurred during Andrew Johnson's term of office was evident by 1869. An article in *Blackwood's Magazine* assessed the potential of the outgoing and incoming presidents and said of Mr. Johnson, "The cruel murder of Mr. Lincoln excited so violent a rage against the defeated South, whose chiefs and leaders were stupidly accused by the War Secretary, Mr. Stanton, of having abetted and instigated it . . . that he [Mr. Johnson] . . . without the slightest warrant accused seven high-minded gentlemen, as innocent of murder as him-

---

21. Edwards Pierrepont to Edwin Stanton, May 14, 1865, in Stanton Papers. *House Reports*, 39th Cong., 1st Sess., No. 104.

22. Salmon P. Chase to Horace Greeley, June 5, 1866, in Salmon P. Chase Papers, LC; Henry Stanbery, May 20, William Seward, May 16, 1867, in U.S. Congress, House, Committee on the Judiciary, *Impeachment Investigation, Testimony Taken Before the Judiciary Committee of the House of Representatives in the Investigation of the Charges Against Andrew Johnson*, 39th Cong., 2nd Sess., 40th Cong., 1st Sess. (Washington: Government Printing Office, 1867), 379–80, 422.

self, of complicity in the foulest crime of the age." Most Americans who had considered Johnson to be the Joshua to lead the country in 1865 would probably now have agreed with these sentiments.[23]

As early as August, 1865, former Alabama Senator Clay, who was imprisoned with Davis at Fortress Monroe, had seen very incisively that he and the others were still being held because once the government had made the charge it could hardly admit that it had been wrong and let them go. By October he was writing to Thomas Withers, "Indeed I now think the reward for me, Mr. Davis, Tucker, et al was a mere political trick to serve party or sectional ends. I have no expectation of ever being tried for murder of Mr. L. or, indeed, for any other crime." By the spring and summer of 1866, this shift in public sentiment was quite evident. Mrs. Clay said it was manifest in the press in early February, 1866, and Burton Harrison wrote to his mother in June of the same year, "As to the charge about complicity in the plot to assassinate Lincoln, some of them still clamor about that occasionally for party purposes, but the people generally, and the most respected of the party leaders, particularly, have long ago abandoned the use of such a reproach to them rather than to the great man against whom it was directed."[24]

The Clay case is almost as interesting as that of Jefferson Davis himself. He protested his innocence, like the others, but he was the only one to surrender to the government in an effort to clear his name. Both Mrs. Clay and Mrs. Davis attempted to intercede with the president on their husbands' behalf. Mrs. Clay claimed that Johnson expressed his disbelief of Clement Clay's involvement in the assassination and by December, 1865, he promised her that neither Davis nor Clay would be tried by a military commission. Friends also urged her to appeal to

---

23. Roy F. Nichols, "United States vs. Jefferson Davis, 1865–1869," *American Historical Review*, XXXI (1926), 274; "The Out-going and the In-coming President," *Blackwood's Magazine*, April, 1869, p. 451. However, it is true that many people were still convinced even years later that Davis had been involved in the murder. See Thomas M. Harris, *Assassination of Lincoln: A History of the Great Conspiracy Trial of the Conspirators by a Military Commission and a Review of the Trial of John H. Surratt* (Boston: American Citizen, 1892), 310.

24. Sterling (ed.), *Belle of the Fifties*, 355; Clement C. Clay to his wife, August 11, and to Thomas Withers, October 25, 1865, in Clement Clay Papers, Duke University Library; James Elliot Walmsley, "Some Unpublished Letters of Burton N. Harrison," *Publications of the Mississippi Historical Society*, VIII (1904), 81–85.

Judge Holt on the basis of past friendships, but Holt was apparently unmoved in the matter.[25]

Two facets of Clay's case were especially interesting. One was the effort of some of his friends to create a favorable climate of opinion for him in the press, a maneuver Judge Holt was also fond of using, though on a much larger scale. The second was the offer of many northerners, including some Radicals, to aid in his defense. Robert Barnwell Rhett wrote Mrs. Clay on December 19, 1865, that he had been to see James Gordon Bennett, editor of the New York *Herald*, about taking up her husband's case. Bennett was at first unenthusiastic because he felt Clay had been involved in town burning, though Rhett felt he had finally reached an agreement with Bennett. However, in February, 1866, Rhett wrote that he was disappointed with Bennett's efforts and thought Mrs. Clay might contact Mrs. Bennett, who said she sympathized with the South and might have some influence with her husband.[26]

On July 24, 1865, Mrs. Clay was informed by R. J. Haldeman that Radical Congressman Thaddeus Stevens did not believe in her husband's guilt or that of prominent rebels in Canada. On July 3, George Shea wrote to Mrs. Clay that Horace Greeley also did not believe in such a charge. Frederick Aiken, one of Mrs. Surratt's defense counsel, sent her a copy of Judge Advocate John A. Bingham's argument at the conspiracy trial, underlining the passages dealing with her husband and offering to assist if she so desired. On January 8, 1866, she also received a certified copy of a letter from Stevens to Haldeman, which stated: "In answer to your question about Mr. Clay, I say that, having acknowledged him as a belligerent, I should treat him as such, and in no other light, unless he was in conspiracy to assassinate Mr. Lincoln, of which I have seen no evidence, and do not believe. But I would confiscate his property and that of most of the others and let them go." Mrs. Clay

25. For the favorable impression Clay's voluntary surrender made, see New York *Times*, May 25, 1865, p. 4; Sterling (ed.), *Belle of the Fifties*, 318–19, 328; William Seward to Joseph Holt transmitting letters from Mrs. Clement Clay and Mrs. Jefferson Davis, June 4, 1865, in Record Book, File S, p. 54, JAO, RG 153, NA; James Lawrence Orr to Mrs. Clay, December 14, 1865, in Clay Papers; Mrs. Clay to Joseph Holt, May 22, 1865, in Joseph Holt Papers, LC. See Clement C. Clay Memorandum regarding his return from Canada, May, 1865, Clay to Andrew Johnson, November 22, 1865, in Clay Papers.

26. Robert Barnwell Rhett to Mrs. Clay, December 19, 1865, February 14, 1866, in Clay Papers.

herself expressed amazement when Senator Henry Wilson appeared and offered to do all he could to aid her or Mr. Clay. He followed up his promise by requesting Johnson for a parole for Clay so that he might visit his father, who was near death. Clay was finally released in April, 1866.[27]

Others that came in for a great deal of criticism were subversive groups in the North and the copperhead press, who were believed linked with Davis and the Canadian rebels. The journals that had opposed Lincoln were now as effusive in their praise of him as were the most loyal, but many doubted this last-minute conversion. The Chicago *Tribune* asked, "Did the Copperhead Party Assassinate Lincoln?" and went on to print one paragraph each from a letter written by Booth and an editorial from the Chicago *Times*, which it said expressed remarkably similar sentiments. Many others saw a connection between expressions in disloyal newspapers and the assassination, and the Provost Marshal General's Bureau investigated certain newspapers to see if any action could be taken.[28]

The Knights of the Golden Circle, a secret subversive group in the North, were also considered to have been conspiratorially involved with the Canadian rebels. Friends wrote to Judge Holt warning him of their fears that the Circle was after him, and Stanton requested Judge Advocate Burnett to summarize the history of the Circle, to which he replied, "There is reason to believe that many if not all the persons connected with the late assassination of the President were members of the resuscitated order of Knights of the Golden Circle."[29]

27. Richard J. Haldeman to Mrs. Clement C. Clay, June 28, July 24, George Shea to Mrs. Clay, July 3, Frederick Aiken to Mrs. Clay, November 25, 1865, Thaddeus Stevens to Richard J. Haldeman, June 8, 1866, Mrs. Clement C. Clay Diary, February 14, 1866, Henry Wilson to Andrew Johnson, March 30, 1866, all in Clay Papers. Once again the position of Eisenschiml and others, that the Radicals were all alike in their views and policies, is proved to have no foundation. See Otto Eisenschiml, *Why Was Lincoln Murdered?* (Boston: Little Brown, 1937), 174, 315–23, 368, 370.

28. New York *Times*, April 21, 1865, p. 4; Robert S. Harper, *Lincoln and the Press* (New York: McGraw Hill, 1951), 453; Chicago *Tribune*, April 24, p. 2, June 21, 1865, p. 2. See also Uriah Gane to James B. Fry, April 19, 1865, William James to Fry, July 29, 1865, both in RG 110, NA.

29. New York *Herald*, April 27, 1865, p. 1; New York *Times*, April 26, 1865, p. 2; J. R. Gilmore to Joseph Holt, April 22, Mary Stevens to Holt, April 20, 1865, both in Holt Papers; Henry L. Burnett to Edwin Stanton, May 2, 1865, in File Folder 49, RG 153, NA.

In short, the people were ready to believe that Davis and his Confederates in Canada were involved in Lincoln's assassination, and this view was strongly reinforced when President Johnson issued a proclamation declaring their guilt. While none of those accused ever came to trial, during the conspiracy trial much evidence was introduced regarding their involvement. This evidence, although at first suppressed and later shown to be largely perjured, was extremely important in keeping opinion inflamed during the trials and had at least as much influence as the specific testimony directed against individual conspirators.

II.

What Type of
Trial?

With the apprehension of the alleged conspirators, hard decisions had to be made about the method of trial. The fact that a military tribunal was finally decided upon has been one of the major reasons that critics have condemned the trials as among the most biased in American jurisprudence. Even those people thought to be clearly involved have thereby gained a degree of sympathy. Since a civil jury failed to find John H. Surratt guilty in 1867, this view has been strongly reinforced. However, to make the claim that basically the same evidence was brought out in both trials and then use this to criticize the military trial is untenable, for given the inflamed conditions in 1865 it appears that a civil trial would have dealt with the conspirators in a similar manner.

President Johnson, after consulting with Attorney General Speed, issued an order on May 6 detailing General Hunter as president, and Generals Lew Wallace, James A. Ekin, August V. Kautz, Allison P. Howe, Robert Sanford Foster, Thomas M. Harris, and Cyrus B. Comstock, and Colonel Horace Porter as members, of the tribunal. The latter two were eventually replaced by Colonel Charles H. Tompkins and Lieutenant Colonel David R. Clendenin. Holt, assigned as judge advocate, had as his special assistants John A. Bingham and Henry L. Burnett. Attorney General Speed, in an opinion given to Johnson prior to the trial but not produced formally in writing until sometime afterward, said, "My conclusion, therefore, is that if the persons who are charged with the assassination of the President committed the deed as public enemies . . . they not only can, but ought to be tried before a military tribunal."[1]

The trying of civilians by military tribunal as well as incarcerating

---

1. Benn Pitman, *The Assassination of President Lincoln and the Trial of the Conspirators* (New York: Funk and Wagnalls, 1954), 17–18. See also James Speed, April 28, 1865, in Letters Received, File S 144, JAO, 1865, RG 153, NA.

them in prison for long periods without trial, was, of course, a fairly common practice during the Civil War. At that very moment Lambdin P. Milligan and several other people were under sentence of execution, although Milligan's conviction was to be reversed in the famous Supreme Court decision, *ex parte Milligan*.[2] Both contemporaries and historians have attempted to apply this decision to the conspiracy trials in an effort to demonstrate their illegality.

Simultaneous with the conspiracy trials, several other military trials of civilians were in process, one of them involving a woman. One case was that of B. S. Osbon of the New York *Sun*, who was accused of furnishing information to the enemy. His defense counsel, General Calvin Pratt, used the familiar technique of arguing against the jurisdiction of the court over civilians. The judge advocate, Major John A. Bolles, however, said this was a plea with no validity, although it had been used in a number of cases; and the court rejected it. The New York *World* did criticize Osbon's trial and called for a return to more normal proceedings.[3]

Another case was that of the Honorable Benjamin Harris, representative in Congress from southern Maryland, who was convicted of violating the fifty-sixth article of war in harboring two paroled soldiers of Lee's army and urging them to violate their pardons by returning South to fight. Harris was convicted, and his pardon by Johnson caused some dissatisfaction.[4]

Undoubtedly the most interesting case, however, was that of Mrs. Bessie Perrine. She was charged with helping to break open trunks and give goods to the rebels during their raid on the Baltimore and Philadelphia Railroad the previous July. Her lawyers also tried to contest the jurisdiction of the court but with no success. She was ultimately convicted, with the case shifting between the president and judge advocate in an attempt to determine what should be done about her ninety-day sentence. On July 17, 1865, the New York *Tribune* reported that this nominal sentence would probably be remitted, as she was witty and pretty and pleaded her case before the president most adroitly. On June

2. Henry L. Burnett to A. P. Hovey, May 2, 1865, in Letters Sent, RG 153, NA.
3. New York *Times*, May 9, 1865, p. 8; Joseph Beach to Joseph Holt, June 20, 1865, John A. Bolles to Holt, June 27, 1865, all in Joseph Holt Papers, LC; New York *World*, May 11, 1865, p. 4.
4. Gettysburg *Compiler*, June 12, 1865, p. 2.

18, Stanton signed the following order: "The proceedings finding and sentence are approved . . . execution of the sentence is suspended during her good behavior." On July 3, President Johnson received a letter from Mrs. Perrine thanking him for his kindness.[5]

The interesting thing is that in the light of the other trial proceedings, including Bessie Perrine's, the military tribunal does not appear to have been so extraordinary. The plea for jurisdiction was used before virtually every military court, and it was no indication of extraordinary viciousness on the part of the conspiracy commission to reject it, any more than it was when rejected by countless other tribunals.

However, to say that military tribunals were common is not to imply that there was no opposition to them. Even the New York *Times*, which was generally staunchly behind the administration, bitterly complained that the conspirators were to be tried before a military commission. The New York *Tribune* reminded its readers that there was in existence a curious old document, the Constitution of the United States, but that "under the rule of our present cabinet, it seems to have gone out of fashion." Other papers generally followed the same tone. Newspapers in opposition to the administration, like the New York *World*, were generally the most vehement in their opposition to military trials. On May 12, the *World* printed an editorial entitled "The Military Star Chamber at Washington."[6]

Naturally, comment was not universally against military trials. In fact, the New York *Times*, obviously feeling that some of the criticism of the government was becoming too vehement and feeling uncomfortable at being too closely associated with it, reversed its original position and said that the government had sufficient reasons to justify the course it had adopted. Former Attorney General Bates noted this in his diary, saying the editor of the *Times* had retracted its position "scared, perhaps, at his own boldness, in daring to assert a principle contrary to the dictatorship of the war office." Horace Greeley also criticized the

5. Washington *Evening Star*, May 9, 1865, p. 2; New York *Tribune*, June 17, 1865, p. 4; Edwin M. Stanton, June 18, 1865, Approval of Sentence, Bessie Perrine to Andrew Johnson, July 3, 1865, both in Andrew Johnson Papers, LC, Microcopy, Roll 15.

6. New York *Times*, May 11, 1865, p. 4; New York *Tribune*, May 11, 1865, p. 4; Easton (Pa.) *Sentinel*, June 8, 1865, p. 2; New York *World*, May 12, p. 4, May 13, 1865, p. 4. However, it will be seen in examining the trials that opposition to military tribunals did not necessarily mean belief in the innocence of Mrs. Surratt, as many historians have stated.

Times for its about-face. The New York *Herald*, however, attacked the New York *Daily News* for criticizing the court and threatening the members of the court with "the legal consequences of their illegal action." The *Herald* added, "Its assault on the court is merely its defense of these murderers, to defend them openly would be to go too far even for the *News*."[7]

Private citizens also expressed their doubts as to the wisdom of a military trial. Again, former Attorney General Bates said that he found it hard to believe that his successor, Speed, could have given an opinion favorable to the military court. He blamed Stanton for the military trial but expressed the hope that Johnson was now aware of the dangers. Secretary of the Navy Gideon Welles also expressed his doubts about military trials, while former Congressman Henry W. Davis was reported to have scathingly characterized the commission as being composed of "officers too worthless for field service, ordered to try, and organized to convict."[8]

Oftentimes, even very vindictive Radicals were still against military tribunals. Britten A. Hill was reported by Orville H. Browning to have said "that the entire South must be depopulated, and repeopled with another race, and that all of the 'Copperheads' among us must be dragged from their houses and disposed of." But Andrew Johnson's papers contain a letter from Hill stating that while he favored the assassins' punishment, he doubted the legality of the commission.[9]

In his address to the people of the United States, Beverley Tucker, who had been accused of plotting the assassination, clearly did not relish the thought of standing trial himself before such a body. "A Bureau of Military Justice . . . has been constituted with all the damnable features of the 'Star Chamber,' before which are to be tried, men whose lineage is not tainted with murder, and whose antecedents justify no

---

7. New York *Times*, May 13, 1865, p. 4; Howard K. Beale (ed.), *The Diary of Edward Bates, 1859–1866*, Vol. IV of the Annual Report of the American Historical Association, 1930 (Washington: Government Printing Office, 1933), 481; New York *Tribune*, May 13, 1865, p. 4; New York *Herald*, June 23, 1865, p. 4.

8. Beale (ed.), *Diary of Edward Bates*, 483; Howard K. Beale (ed.), *Diary of Gideon Welles* (3 vols.; New York: W. W. Norton, 1960), II, 303; Albany *Argus*, June 24, 1865, p. 2.

9. James G. Randall and Theodore C. Pease (eds.), *Diary of Orville Hickman Browning* (2 vols.; Springfield, Ill.: Jefferson's Printing and Stationery, 1933), II, 21; Britten A. Hill to Andrew Johnson, June 19, 1865, in Johnson Papers, Microcopy, Roll 14.

suspicion of guilt, save what an unholy revenge and gold-bought testimony furnishes."[10]

Many sensed instinctively what might, and in fact did, happen—that regardless of the guilt or innocence of those involved, the military trial would make them martyrs. It is interesting to speculate that even Booth might have lost a degree of his villainy had he lived to face a military trial. Again Bates wrote, "If the offenders be done to death by that tribunal, however truly guilty, they will pass for martyrs with half the world." The New York *World* had also said that in advising against a military trial, it, too, had been thinking of the honor and dignity of the government. Former Congressman Henry Davis, who had spoken so vehemently against military trials, was also somewhat of a prophet in the following note to Johnson: "But I cannot refrain from expressing to you my conviction that the trial of the persons charged with the conspiracy against President Lincoln and Secretary Seward by Military Commission will prove disastrous to yourself your administration and your supporters who may attempt to apologize for it."[11]

It was also reported on occasion that some sort of judicial action might be taken against members of military commissions. Judge Peckham of New York, at the opening of the May term of court, stated to the jury that the conspiracy trial was a violation of the Constitution. Judge Bond of Baltimore charged a grand jury that persons sitting on military trials for citizens of Maryland not in the armed forces were subject to indictment. General Kautz, a commission member, recalled that "some of my Democratic friends were fond of telling me that when the party got into power again, I would hang for my part in the proceedings."[12]

Rumors also arose during the trial that Johnson was going to set aside the findings, and he was reported by one correspondent to have expressed his regrets that the trial had been military rather than civil. General Thomas Ewing, one of the defense counsel, made this plea to Johnson shortly before the execution but to no avail: "Set aside all their

10. James H. Young (ed.), *Address of Beverley Tucker, Esq., to the People of the United States* (Atlanta: Emory University Library, 1948), 20.
11. Beale (ed.), *Diary of Edward Bates*, 483; New York *World*, May 6, 1865, p. 4; Henry W. Davis to Andrew Johnson, May 13, 1865, in Johnson Papers, Microcopy, Roll 15.
12. Richmond *Whig*, May 22, 1865, p. 1; August V. Kautz, "Reminiscences of the Civil War" (Typescript in August V. Kautz Papers, LC), 112.

unexempted sentences and transfer the causes to the regular judicial tribunal, and by a general order direct all military officers having citizens in custody to obey the writ of Habeas Corpus."[13]

The fact that the trial was to be secret also bothered many people. Here a word of caution is needed, however. One would ordinarily assume that virtually all newspapers would have wished for an open trial in order that they might have afforded it full coverage. Therefore, opposition to the military aspects of the trial is probably a more crucial indicator of the newspapers' views than is their opposition to secrecy.

Antiadministration journals were again in the forefront of those criticizing secret trials. The Albany *Atlas and Argus* said on May 12, "A trial in secret, with Holt for Judge Advocate, a military tribunal as judge and jury, the prisoners deprived of counsel, and hundreds of thousands of dollars offered to witnesses, and other parties interested in convictions! Think of it!" Yet, on the secrecy issue, they were joined just as vehemently by loyal journals. The Chicago *Tribune* told its readers, "The idea that the evidence is only to reach millions of readers through the Senate reporters of the *Congressional Globe*, who pride themselves on remodelling and dignifying paragraphs in decorous style, is simply an absurdity." Other newspapers again raised charges that the proceedings were little better than a star chamber.[14]

Nonetheless, there was some attempt to justify the secret proceedings. Some papers claimed that secrecy was needed to protect the safety of witnesses. Others cautioned patience and an opportunity for the government to vindicate its actions. The comment was sometimes made that the testimony being given in secret involved those not yet captured, and the exposure of this testimony might enable those at large to escape the punishment due their offense.[15]

The secrecy also caused much genuine confusion at the beginning of the trial. The *Intelligencer* said on May 2 that an evening paper had

---

13. New York *Tribune*, June 17, 1865, p. 1; Thomas Ewing to Andrew Johnson, July 4, 1865, in Johnson Papers, Microcopy, Roll 15.

14. Albany *Atlas and Argus*, May 12, 1865, p. 2; Chicago *Tribune*, May 13, p. 2, May 15, 1865, p. 1; New York *Herald*, May 8, 1865, p. 5.

15. Washington *Chronicle*, quoted in New York *Times*, May 14, 1865, p. 5; New York *Times*, May 15, 1865, p. 1; Washington *Daily National Intelligencer*, May 13, 1865, p. 2; Philadelphia *Evening Bulletin*, May 12, 1865, p. 4; T. L. Smith to Edwin Stanton, May 13, 1865, in Edwin M. Stanton Papers, LC.

intimated that the trials were in progress and the hanging would soon begin. It added, "At an earlier period of the world's history we have heard of 'hanging first and trial afterwards'; but such a code does not govern the judiciary of the present." There were other rumors about Herold being on trial, and many incorrect dates given for the commencement of the trial.[16]

Everyone seemed to breathe a sigh of relief when, after beginning the trials in secret, the government decided to open them to the public. The New York papers were especially happy, although the *Times* noted that there were occasions when secrecy was justified, and the government should not bow to popular clamor if that was not in its interest. However the *World* felt that the battle had been only half won, since the military trials continued.[17]

Some newspapers had begun to argue that the real reason for trial secrecy was that the government could not make the charge stick, especially against Confederate leaders mentioned in Johnson's proclamation. However, once the trials actually got underway, such charges began to dissipate in the light of the evidence.[18]

As to responsibility for the proposed secrecy, the onus must apparently rest with Judge Advocate Holt. On May 10, Assistant Judge Advocate Burnett wrote to Stanton reminding him that he had instructed him to publish the charges and specifications to the Associated Press, but that Holt was against it except for a brief synopsis. Stanton advised Burnett to consider himself under Holt and be governed by his opinions. General Comstock also mentioned Holt's arguing vigorously before the commission for secrecy. While some historians surmise collusion between Holt and Stanton, it seems likely, taken in conjunction with other evidence, that Holt was not a mere puppet of Stanton's. To be sure, Stanton as War Department head must bear ultimate responsibility, but it appears that in many matters Stanton relied upon Holt's discretion, and then the judge advocate, largely without Stanton's di-

16. Washington *Daily National Intelligencer*, May 2, 1865, p. 2; New York *Times*, May 1, p. 1, May 3, p. 4, May 4, 1865, p. 4.

17. New York *Herald*, May 9, 1865, p. 4; New York *Times*, May 15, 1865, p. 4; New York *World*, May 15, 1865, p. 4.

18. Albany *Atlas and Argus*, May 13, 1865, p. 2; New York *World*, May 12, 1865, p. 1; Hartford *Daily Courant*, May 17, 1865, p. 2.

rect knowledge, proceeded to make blunders such as relying on perjured testimony.[19]

Many who favored a military trial pointed to a problem that sounds extremely modern—securing a jury in a case that had received so much publicity. This problem existed in the cases of Jefferson Davis and the assassination conspirators. The San Francisco *Alta Californian* told its readers in regard to Davis: "The courts must retrace their steps in the matter of the empanelling of juries, or the system will have to be abandoned altogether. Trial by jury is beginning to be regarded everywhere as the merest farce." The *Herald* added that the normal question asked was whether a man had read, conversed, or expressed opinions as to the accused's guilt or innocence, with those answering in the affirmative being disqualified. "The consequence is that the more stupid a man is the more fitted he is regarded to pass on the question of the life or liberty of his fellow man." Even the *Tribune*, which criticized the *Herald* for fostering party spirit, admitted that sympathy for the murderer might exist in Washington. On Friday, May 26, a letter signed "Punio" appeared in the *Times*, stating that the conspirators could not be convicted by a Washington jury.[20]

What support there was for the military tribunal was generally based on the same point that was brought out at the trials, that Lincoln was killed as commander in chief within the military lines of Washington. Surprisingly, some people who later were regarded as entirely moderate took this view. Journalist Jane Swisshelm, who was involved in the controversy over whether Mrs. Surratt was shackled or not, wrote during the trial to General Hunter, "I shall steadily defend the military trial of the conspirators as necessary to the life of the government." She did add the warning that too much vindictiveness would awaken sympathy in time.[21]

19. Henry L. Burnett to Edwin Stanton, May 10, 1865, in Letters Received, File B 490, JAO, RG 153, NA; Cyrus B. Comstock Diary (MS in Cyrus Comstock Papers, LC), May 8, 1865.

20. San Francisco *Alta Californian*, July 7, 1865, p. 2; New York *Herald*, April 24, 1865, p. 4; New York *Tribune*, April 25, 1865, p. 4; New York *Times*, May 26, 1865, p. 3.

21. New York *Times*, May 13, p. 4, May 15, p. 2, May 16, 1865, p. 4; Osborn H. Oldroyd, *The Assassination of Abraham Lincoln, Flight, Pursuit, Capture, and Punishment of the Conspirators* (Washington: O. H. Oldroyd, 1901), 115; Jane Swisshelm to General Hunter, May 26, 1865, in Holt Papers.

Under the circumstances, many contemporaries concluded in retro-spect that the military court was perhaps the fairest that could have been obtained. General Harris, one of the commission members, made the interesting comment that, given the aroused public sentiment, a civil trial would have resulted in a miscarriage of justice. This was also echoed by Burnett and Speed, while even defense counsel Frederick Stone admitted that "considering it was a Military Court, it was a fair court and one of ability."[22] While these men were intimately involved and thus not entirely impartial observers, one wonders what additional violence might have occurred in 1865 had the jury voted along the same sectional lines as the John Surratt jury did in 1867, thereby thwarting what northerners considered to be the course of justice.[23]

The role of Stanton in the preparation of trial evidence and behind the scenes has also been a matter of long-standing dispute. The New York *World* expressed what has generally become the historical view: "Stanton has all the evidence furnished by his detectives, and doles out, day by day, such as may be necessary to establish his views, and dictates to Holt what each witness is expected to swear to, which is all arranged beforehand with the witnesses." There is no doubt that Stanton had a full share in the pretrial preparation; for as Burnett said, "The investi-gation of the facts was prosecuted under the personal direction of the

22. Thomas M. Harris, *Assassination of Lincoln; A History of the Great Conspiracy Trial of the Conspirators by a Military Commission and a Review of the Trial of John H. Surratt* (Boston: American Citizen, 1892), 82; Henry L. Burnett, "Assassination of President Lin-coln and the Trial of the Assassins," in James H. Kennedy (ed.), *History of the Ohio Society of New York, 1885–1905* (New York: Grafton Press, 1906), 614; James Speed, "The Assassins of Lincoln," *North American Review*, CXLVII (1888), 316, 319; New York *Tribune*, June 17, 1883, p. 4; Clara E. Laughlin, *The Death of Lincoln, The Story of Booth's Plot, His Deed and the Penalty* (New York: Doubleday, Page, 1909), 79. Lawyer-historian Paul J. Sedgwick, "Some Legal Aspects of the Trial of the Lincoln Conspirators," *Lincoln Herald*, LXVIII (1966), 3–10, argues that the Milligan decision notwithstanding, the military commission might well have been legal under Lincoln's nonrevoked proclamation of martial law in 1862. For views opposed to the trial, see John W. Clampitt, "The Trial of Mrs. Surratt," *North American Review*, CXXXI (1880), 229–30; John W. Curran, "The Lincoln Con-spiracy Trial and Military Jurisdiction over Civilians," rpr. from the *Notre Dame Lawyer* (November, 1933), 10–11.

23. Historians have also tended to distort the effect of the military trial, especially regarding the right of the accused to testify. Helen J. Campbell, *The Case For Mrs. Surratt* (New York: G. P. Putnam's Sons, 1943), 183. Francis X. Busch, *Enemies of the State* (Indi-anapolis: Bobbs-Merrill, 1954), 76, claimed erroneously that John Surratt not only could but did testify at his trial in 1867. In reality, as Sedgwick, "Some Legal Aspects of the Trial of the Lincoln Conspirators," 8, points out, in 1865, Maine was the only state that permit-ted a prisoner to testify in his own behalf.

Secretary of War with earnest diligence, until the day the court was ordered to convene." Newspapers also commented on the secretary's diligence, and there exists a draft of the charges and specifications drawn up in the secretary's own hand.[24]

However, with the opening of the trial, the Chicago *Tribune* reported that Stanton's authority in the matter ceased and Holt took over. Many others believed that it was the judge advocate who was responsible for the conduct of the trial. Stanton's secretary, Charles Benjamin, confirmed that the war secretary had no direct connection with the trial of Mrs. Surratt, except for a stiff cross-examination of Weichmann.[25]

Oddly enough, there was even some contemporary doubt as to whether Stanton favored military trials, although why this existed is not exactly clear. Reports did appear in the press that Stanton had opposed the military commission until Holt and the others had won him over. It was apparently such reports that caused James W. White to write Stanton inquiring whether his reported views were correct. Stanton's reply was direct and unequivocal. "I did and do approve of the trial sentence and execution of the assassins and all the action of the government in the cases referred to." Gideon Welles also confirmed that Speed and Stanton had argued vigorously in the cabinet for a military trial.[26]

Although Stanton is usually charged with leading a witch-hunt and rounding up innocent persons indiscriminately, there is evidence that he was more moderate. This harsh picture is usually reinforced by claims of his ill treatment of Mrs. Lincoln and such incidents as his dispute with General Townsend over the photographing of Lincoln's

24. New York *World*, June 2, p. 8, June 9, 1865, p. 4; Burnett, "Assassination of President Lincoln and the Trials of the Assassins," 596; Baltimore *Sun*, May 10, 1865, p. 1; Edwin Stanton, in Draft of Charges and Specifications, N.d., in Holt Papers. Burnett's comment, "until the court was ordered to convene," seems to give some indication that Stanton's role ended there.

25. Chicago *Tribune*, May 16, 1865, p. 2; New York *Herald*, May 14, 1865, p. 4; New York *Times*, May 13, 1865, p. 4; San Francisco *Alta Californian*, June 18, 1865, p. 1; Benjamin Thomas and Harold Hyman, *Stanton: The Life and Times of Lincoln's Secretary of War* (New York: Alfred A. Knopf, 1962), 426; Samuel B. Arnold, *Defence and Prison Experiences of a Lincoln Conspirator: Statements and Autobiographical Notes* (Hattiesburg, Miss.: Book Farm, 1943), 129.

26. Boston Evening *Transcript*, June 20, 1865, p. 2; New York *Times*, June 18, 1865, p. 4; James W. White to Edwin Stanton, July 12, 1865, in Stanton Papers; Beale (ed.), *Diary of Gideon Welles*, II, 303.

remains. However, in many instances, it was Stanton who took a hand in releasing prisoners or allowing them to reclaim their property from Ford's Theatre and other locations. As Laura Keene wrote, "We were released by order of the Secretary of War the moment he heard of our unauthorized detention." Although historians have combed the National Archives files, none has ever mentioned the endorsement appearing on several cases: "It is understood that the Secretary of War does not deem it expedient for the government to incur the trouble and expense of bringing to trial the parties whose offences consist solely in the utterance of words expressing satisfaction at the assassination of the President, their language being unaccompanied by any acts of treasonable character, and no connection with the conspiracy being alleged."[27]

Stanton's treatment of prisoners has also been severely criticized, and historians have speculated upon the reasons for it. Charges of torture have been raised because the prisoners were hooded and ironed and held in solitary confinement. It has been darkly hinted that this was done to prevent those involved in the assassination from revealing what they knew.[28]

On April 29, 1865, General Hancock was given charge of the prisoners and provided with a detailed list of instructions, among which was that all access to and communication with them was forbidden without Stanton's signature, with the exception of visits from the prison governor and medical officer. On the 19th, Stanton had requested Gideon Welles that no one be allowed to communicate with the prisoners on the *Saugus* without written permission signed by both men. This came about following a reprimand to Marshal McPhail for allowing statements made by Arnold to be published.[29]

Despite Stanton's obsession with silence, however, it appears that the prisoners were not hooded during the entire trial, and thus charges that it was done to prevent them from talking fall to the ground. Arnold

27. *The War of the Rebellion: A Compilation of the Official Records of the Union and Confederate Armies* (130 vols., Washington: Government Printing Office, 1880–1901), Ser. I, Vol. XLVI, Pt. 3, p. 952; Laura Keene to Philadelphia *Enquirer*, April 19, 1865, in Benjamin Butler Papers, LC; Ellis Jones, April 25, 1865, Affidavit, in File P 162, JAO, RG 153, NA.

28. Arnold, *Defence and Prison Experiences of a Lincoln Conspirator*, 12, 129; Otto Eisenschiml, *In the Shadow of Lincoln's Death* (New York: Wilfred Funk, 1940), 127–47.

29. Edwin Stanton to Winfield S. Hancock, April 29, Stanton to Gideon Welles, April 19, Stanton to J. L. McPhail, April 18, 1865, all in Stanton Papers.

himself hinted at this when he wrote, "This manner of treatment continued uninterrupted, the hoods never being removed except when I was brought before the court and always replaced on exit, if but a moment intervened, from on or about April 25 to June 10."[30] If the hoods were designed to enforce silence, they would hardly have been removed in the middle of the trial.

A statement by attending physician John P. May reveals that after June 10 the prisoners were not so badly treated. After visiting their cells he noted that they all had hair pillows, and he recommended small boxes or stools for the men and chairs for Mrs. Surratt. He also recommended that they be furnished with reading matter other than newspapers, that the men be given a small portion of tobacco after each meal, and that O'Laughlin be removed to a cell where he could have more light. He felt that the one hour of exercise a day was sufficient and that the diet appeared abundant in quantity and good in quality. Stanton ordered General Hancock to take what measures he could for Mrs. Surratt's comfort. Hangman Christian Rath stated that Spangler and Paine pitched a game of quoits a few feet from where the scaffold stood and that some of his fellow officers used Paine in a joke to scare Rath. It is also apparent that the primary conspirators were not singled out for harsh treatment; Clement Clay at Fortress Monroe was told by his wardens that they had orders from Washington to subject him to the same discipline that Lincoln's assassins underwent.[31]

The military commission has been portrayed as a vindictive group of officers who willingly seized the license they were given to execute the prisoners legally. This view has been reinforced by actions that occurred during the trial, like the two-pronged attack of commission members Hunter and Harris on the integrity of Mrs. Surratt's lawyer, Reverdy Johnson, as insufficient for him to serve as counsel before the commission. General Harris also wrote an account of the proceedings,

30. Samuel Arnold, "The Lincoln Plot," Baltimore *American*, December, 1902, p. 13. Edward Spangler, Statement, N.d., in Ford's Theatre Collection, Maryland Historical Society.

31. John P. May, June 20, Report, and Edwin Stanton to Winfield S. Hancock, June 19, 1865, in Stanton Papers; Chicago *Tribune*, July 10, 1865, p. 1; John A. Gray, "The Fate of the Lincoln Conspirators: The Account of the Hanging, Given by Lieutenant-Colonel Christian Rath, the Executioner," *McClure's Magazine*, XXXVII (1911), 633, 635. Clement C. Clay, January, 1866, Memorandum, in Clement Clay Papers, Duke University Library.

staunchly maintaining the correctness of everything the commission had done and giving verbatim defense of the testimony of such obvious perjurers as Sanford Conover. This has made it extremely easy to picture the entire commission as a group of unthinking, unfeeling military men, who could not have been moved from their purpose by the most relevant evidence in existence.

However, there were other members of the commission who took a much more liberal view. The tone of General Kautz's views can be seen in a comment he made after hearing a lecture by Anna Dickinson. "She is quite elegant but extremely radical and violent in her views." Kautz was greatly moved by the manner in which the prisoners were brought into the courtroom, in chains and hooded, which he said raised visions of the Inquisition in his mind. This made such a bad impression on the court that they were never brought in in this manner again. People opposed to the trial, some of them military men, also approached Kautz and attempted to influence his views. In one instance, he wrote, "General Dawes paid me a visit this evening and talked a great deal about the Commission and its irregularity and error." The attempt to prevent Reverdy Johnson from appearing as counsel also displeased Kautz. He said that Johnson's remarks must have made General Harris regret that he ever objected. Kautz added, "He [Johnson] did the other members great injustice if he supposed they united with General Harris in his ill advised objection."[32]

Kautz's comments also revealed that despite the fact that the commission often upheld the prosecution and overruled the defense, the members were not always uncritically content with what the prosecution was doing. On May 26, he remarked in his journal, "There is much delay by the Judge Advocate Bingham who is constantly objecting to the questions asked by the counsel." He was also upset with Burnett and court recorder Benn Pitman when the suppressed testimony was released and the court had to stop to investigate it.[33]

General Comstock, another officer who was originally on the commission, held similar views. On May 8, 1865, he wrote in his diary, "On

---

32. August V. Kautz Daily Journal (MS in Kautz Papers), May 8, May 9, May 21, May 27, June 9, 1865; Kautz, "Reminiscences of the Civil War," 108–109.
33. August V. Kautz Daily Journal, May 5 and 26, 1865.

Military Commission for trial of conspirators. Hunter president. Wish I could get off. They ought to be tried by Civil Courts—this commission is what is yet worse a secret one I believe." He was also disturbed about the ironing of the prisoners and argued with Holt about the jurisdiction of the court and the limiting of counsel to five arguments. On May 10, Comstock received orders that he was removed from his position on the court, as was Colonel Porter; however, this apparently had no bearing on his liberal position. Rather, both officers were on Grant's staff, and it was not thought right for them to sit on the court when their commander was allegedly one of the intended victims.[34]

Historians have also been extremely critical about the selection of defense counsel for the prisoners. More time should have been allowed the lawyers to prepare their cases and meet with their clients. Although some of the more radical commission members would have denied the prisoners counsel, there is evidence that the government did make efforts to procure counsel for the accused and that as much censure belongs to the legal profession as to the government.[35]

On May 9, Burnett telegraphed Dr. Gerrard E. Morgan that Samuel Arnold desired him as counsel, and he asked Morgan to reply. Similar telegrams and letters were sent on behalf of O'Laughlin, Herold, Dr. Mudd, and Mrs. Surratt. Prospective counsel were also usually informed that a pass would be provided so that they might visit their clients. Actions out of the ordinary were also taken, such as the government sending messages to inform lawyers that particular prisoners wished them to serve as defense counsel. When Reverdy Johnson could not be reached by letter, a telegram was specifically dispatched to him.[36] Despite these efforts, however, in a good many cases the counsel approached declined to act. Even Joseph Bradley, who two years later successfully defended John Surratt, pleaded pressing professional en-

34. Cyrus B. Comstock Diary (MS in Comstock Papers), May 8, May 9, May 10, 1865; Thomas and Hyman, *Stanton,* 424.

35. Edward Spangler, Statement, N.d., in Ford's Theatre Collection.

36. In RG 153, NA: Henry L. Burnett to Gerrard E. Morgan, May 9, to P. H. Maulsby, May 9, to Frederick Stone, May 10, 1865, in Telegrams Sent; Burnett to Reverdy Johnson, to William W. Kirby, to George Mudd, and to Joseph Bradley, May 9, 1865; H. H. Wells to Johnson, May 11, Joseph Holt to William Wood, May 31, D. F. Murphy to Johnson, May 10, 1865, in Letters Sent; Colonel Ingraham to Burnett, May 27, 1865, in Endorsement Book No. 47.

gagements, which turned out to be nothing more than a sensational but ordinary murder trial.[37]

Newspapers also commented on the government's efforts to procure counsel and the difficulties encountered. The pressures brought to bear on lawyers so approached is also evident. The New York *Times* speculated on Mrs. Surratt's boldness in asking for Reverdy Johnson, and believed he would not come. It also wondered why Paine had asked for ex-Confederate Mason Campbell, who had taken the loyalty oath.[38]

Several historians have attempted to make a martyr out of Reverdy Johnson because of the attack upon him by Generals Harris and Hunter. Johnson's withdrawal from the case did create an unfavorable impression on some contemporaries, but this would seem to be all the more reason why he should have remained.[39] There are many indications that Johnson only took the case of Mrs. Surratt so that he might have a showcase for his argument against military tribunals, and that he was really more interested in this than in defending his client. On June 3, the New Orleans *Times-Picayune* correspondent reported that Johnson was absent from the courtroom for this very reason. Similar statements were made at various times by Bingham, Holt, and Harris. While such sources could hardly stand as uncontested proof of the allegation, it was confirmed by fellow defense counsel Frederick Stone in 1883. "He came forward and made an argument against the jurisdiction of the military court, to be read and applauded by the people, and then abandoned the woman." Samuel Arnold also believed that Johnson had bowed to the pressures and excitement of the time.[40]

General Thomas Ewing is depicted as an idealist who nobly defended his clients with all his strength despite overwhelming odds. W. M.

37. In JAO, 1865, RG 153, NA: Joseph H. Bradley to Henry L. Burnett, May 9, in Letters Received, File B 280. See also File B 278, E 281, C 283, Z 288.

38. New York *Times*, May 14, 1865, p. 5; Easton (Pa.) *Free Press*, May 11, 1865, p. 2; New York *Tribune*, May 10, 1865, p. 1; New York *Times*, May 12, 1865, p. 1.

39. David M. DeWitt, *The Assassination of Abraham Lincoln and Its Expiation* (New York: Macmillan, 1909), 106–107; Eisenschiml, *In the Shadow of Lincoln's Death*, 141, agrees that it was wrong for Johnson to withdraw. For newspaper comment on the withdrawal, see New York *Tribune*, May 19, 1865, p. 1; Albany *Argus*, May 19, 1865, p. 2.

40. New Orleans *Times-Picayune*, June 3, 1865, p. 2; John A. Bingham, *Trial of the Conspirators for the Assassination of President Lincoln* (Washington: Government Printing Office, 1865), 10; Joseph Holt, in New York *Tribune*, September 11, 1873, p. 4; Harris, *Assassination of Lincoln*, 111; Frederick Stone, in New York *Tribune*, June 17, 1883, p. 4. Arnold, *Defence and Prison Experiences of a Lincoln Conspirator*, 10.

McPherson wrote to him, "I see your gallantry got you into business as counsel in the *State Trials*; will not Stanton trace that to Sherman and hold him responsible for the murder or at least connected with it through you as his brother-in-law." Nathan Price wrote from Kansas that the press was giving him "hell" for engaging in the conspiracy trials. Nonetheless, a letter to his father near the end of the trials shows he was equally interested in the money he would make. He also thanked Ewing for his help and added, "Your help not only benefitted our clients, but added to the reputation of the firm." Friends wrote praising Ewing for the fame he had gained in establishing himself as a first-class lawyer.[41]

It is also somewhat disconcerting to see the zeal with which Ewing attempted to collect his fees after the conclusion of the trial. John Ford showed his sense of humor when he beseeched him to have patience, for he would pay all: "I can quote Shakespeare better than the Bible but I trust that the sentence above is significant enough." On another occasion he asked Ewing to wait a few more days, explaining, "I mean days as Lawyers mean words when they say, 'one more word.'" Even Mrs. Mudd was forced to reply to a Ewing letter, "It grieves me to know you have been annoyed and nonplussed by our delay in paying the printing bill of Pokenhom. I did not know you were responsible for the amount."[42] No one would deny that Ewing put up one of the ablest defenses of all defense counsel, but he acted for the reasons lawyers have always taken cases. To make him a knight in armor somewhat misses the mark.

There is also some justifiable criticism of the other defense counsel for their handling of the cases. Certainly they were up against a hard task, and they would have been foolish not to recognize the difficulties. But many contemporaries seemed to feel that most of the defense counsel were doing little more than going through the motions. William Doster commented that there were no chances at all for acquittal of his clients Atzerodt and Paine. Herold's defense was not even read by his attorney, Stone, who was out of the city, but by court reporter James

41. William M. McPherson to Thomas Ewing, Jr., June 1, Nathan Price to Thomas Ewing, Jr., August 5, Thomas Ewing, Jr., to Thomas Ewing, Sr., July 7, H. G. Fanh to Thomas Ewing, Jr., July 1, 1865, all in Ewing Family Papers, LC.
42. John T. Ford to Thomas Ewing, August 8, N.d., November 20, and Mrs. Samuel Mudd to Ewing, November 17, 1865, all in Ewing Family Papers.

Murphy. H. L. Burnett felt that "some of the counsel for the accused seemed to be as much convinced as the court of the guilty participation of the rebel authorities at Richmond and their confederates in Canada." Or, as newspaper correspondent Townsend described them, "They either have no chance or no pluck to assert the dignity of their profession."[43]

In retrospect, trial by a military commission appears to have been a mistake. Nonetheless, it was not an entirely unusual procedure under the circumstances. And while the government may have acted in certain irregular ways, the legal profession does not come off unscathed.

43. William E. Doster, *Lincoln and Episodes of the Civil War* (New York: G. P. Putnam's Sons, 1915), 257; Court Martial Record, June 19, 1865, in RG 153, NA; Burnett, "Assassination of President Lincoln and the Trials of the Assassins," 599; George A. Townsend, *The Life, Crime, and Capture of John Wilkes Booth with a Full Sketch of the Conspiracy of Which He Was the Leader, and the Pursuit, Trial, and Execution of His Accomplices* (New York: Dick and Fitzgerald, 1865), 68. For a view that defense counsel were not all that bad, see Washington *Evening Star*, May 12, 1865, p. 2. See also A. Wesley Johns, *The Man Who Shot McKinley* (Cranbury, N.J.: A. S. Barnes, 1970).

12.

Mrs. Mary Surratt

Of all the conspirators brought before the military commission, which convened on May 9, 1865, the most controversial case both at the time and since, was that of Mrs. Mary E. Surratt. The testimony against her may be broken down into three categories. The first was that given by John M. Lloyd, a tenant at her Surrattsville tavern. Lloyd testified that five or six weeks before the assassination, John Surratt, David Herold, and George Atzerodt went to the tavern, whereupon Lloyd secreted two carbines, ammunition, a rope, and a monkey wrench in an upstairs hiding place that John Surratt had shown him. On the Tuesday before the assassination Lloyd was traveling to Washington and met Mrs. Surratt on the road at Uniontown. She allegedly told him to get the "shooting irons" ready, as they would be wanted soon. On April 14, when he returned from court at Marlboro, he met Mrs. Surratt at the tavern and this time she again told him to have the "shooting irons" ready, for there would be some parties to call for them. She also delivered to Lloyd a package that turned out to be field glasses. About midnight on the 14th, Herold and Booth stopped at the tavern and Herold said, "Lloyd, for God's sake, make haste and get those things." After drinking briefly, they took one carbine and the field glasses and proceeded on their way.

The second and generally considered to be the most damaging testimony was that of her son's friend, Louis Weichmann, a boarder at her Washington residence on H Street. His testimony seemed to indicate an intimacy between Booth and both Mary and John Surratt. He testified that on Tuesday, April 11, Mrs. Surratt attempted to borrow Booth's buggy to go to the country, but Booth had sold it and instead provided ten dollars to hire one. Before leaving for Surrattsville on April 14, Mrs. Surratt had been alone in conversation with Booth. Weichmann also told of the Confederate agents and blockade-runners, Mrs. Sarah Antoinette Slater and Spencer Howell, who visited the Surratt home, and the mysterious Baptist preacher called both Wood and Payne, who later turned out to be the assailant of Secretary Seward. He also revealed that he had seen Atzerodt and Herold at the Surratt home.

Weichmann also spoke of a mysterious affair sometime in March when Mrs. Surratt, weeping bitterly, told him John had gone away. John, Booth, and Paine then returned very agitated, and John told Weichmann that his hopes were gone and asked if he could get him a clerkship. Finally Weichmann's suspicions were so aroused that he informed his coworker Captain Daniel H. L. Gleason, who, Weichmann felt, did not take the idea too seriously.

In an affidavit dated August 11, 1865, Weichmann also added some additional damaging recollections about Mrs. Surratt. She had supposedly wept and closed her house on the fall of Richmond. On the way to Surrattsville on April 14, when seeing some pickets, she asked an old farmer if they usually remained all night, and when told they were withdrawn at eight o'clock, she replied that she was glad to know it. She also supposedly made statements about all the rejoicing being turned into mourning and hurried home for a nine o'clock meeting with a caller who, from Anna Surratt's statement at breakfast, Weichmann determined to be Booth.

The third factor against Mrs. Surratt was the strange arrival at her home of Lewis Paine, disguised as a laborer, on the night of her arrest. The arrival at her doorstep of the man who had methodically left the Seward home a bloody shambles hardly made a favorable impression in court.[1]

There is some puzzle among historians as to how detectives arrived at the Surratt house. It has usually been argued by historians that Daniel H. L. Gleason, who worked with Louis Weichmann, supplied information to the War Department that may have caused the Surratt house and some members of the Booth gang to be placed under surveillance, although it was officers of the Metropolitan Police Force led by detective John A. Clarvoe who appeared at the Surratt house on the night of the murder.[2] A recent author has claimed that Gleason's 1911 statement

1. Benn Pitman, *The Assassination of President Lincoln and the Trial of the Conspirators* (New York: Funk and Wagnalls, 1954), 85–86, 113–24, 420–21; Louis Weichmann, August 11, 1865, Statement, in Letters Received, File W 706, JAO, RG 153, NA.

2. Otto Eisenschiml, *Why Was Lincoln Murdered?* (Boston: Little Brown, 1937), 272–73, speculates that the story told by stableman John Fletcher about Herold trying to steal

was inaccurate and that he had informed the authorities about his suspicions of the Surratts only after Lincoln's murder. No arrests were made by the police officers. On April 17, after a Surratt neighbor, J. H. Kimball, had told the military authorities of a statement by the Surratts' black servant, Susan Jackson, that three men had come to Mrs. Surratt's house on Saturday night and that one of them had said John was in the theater, General Augur ordered Colonel Olcott to arrest the members of the Surratt household. Colonel John Foster, who was gathering evidence to be used in the trial in summarizing the testimony, said, "The information derived from this girl led to the arrest of Mrs. Surratt, which was made late in the evening of the 17th." Susan Jackson later contradicted her statements during John Surratt's trial in 1867.[3]

When the conspiracy trial commenced, it created a great deal of public interest. Despite the heat as the oppressive Washington summer dragged on, there were constant references to the distinguished courtroom visitors and the large audience, which included many ladies. Foreign visitors also took an interest in the proceedings, for on June 5, 1865, the consul general of Switzerland requested permission for a Swiss gentleman, Frederick C. Richards, to have a pass to visit the penitentiary while he was in the city.[4]

Reporters demonstrated their feelings about the particular defendants by the descriptions given in the newspapers. On May 14, the New York *Times* described Mrs. Surratt as "fair, fat and forty" but added,

his horse might have alerted authorities to the Surratt house, though this is not certain. Detective James A. McDevitt's claim, in the Washington *Star*, April 14, 1894, p. 17, that an actor whom he believed was John McCullough had told him after the assassination that if he wished to find out everything about the conspiracy, he should watch Mrs. Surratt's house, does not appear to have much merit.

3. William Hanchett, "The War Department and Booth's Abduction Plot," *Lincoln Herald*, LXXXII (1980), 499–508. Colonel John Foster, Summary of Testimony Referring to Various Suspects, N.d., in Evidence Book, File ERB, p. 24. J. H. Kimball, N.d., in Record Book, File K, p. 82, apparently provided the government the first information about Susan Jackson's story. See Mary Surratt, April 17, 1865, Statement, in Record Book, File S, p. 78. All in JAO, 1865, RG 153, NA, where questioners bore down hard on Susan Jackson's allegations and Mrs. Surratt denied them. For her trouble Susan received a five-hundred-dollar reward. See United States Government, *Trial of John H. Surratt in the Criminal Court for the District of Columbia, Hon. George P. Fisher Presiding* (2 vols.; Washington: Government Printing Office, 1867), I, 163, in which Susan said John had been at his mother's on the night of the assassination.

4. New York *Times*, May 18, 1865, p. 1; Washington *Evening Star*, May 20, 1865, p. 2; John F. Citz to Joseph Holt, June 5, 1865, in Joseph Holt Papers, LC.

"we failed to notice that 'cold, cruel gleam in her gray eyes,' which some of the gentlemen of the press have attributed to them." The correspondent also attempted to portray the harshness of Mrs. Surratt by noting her lack of concern over the testimony, while the Washington *Evening Star* said she had lost all hope and was crouched in her corner with her face entirely concealed. At the trial's conclusion the Chicago *Tribune* called her "the perfect type of venomous Southern woman."[5]

One of the major controversies regarding Mrs. Surratt is whether she wore irons during the trial. The New York *Times* of May 15 mentioned that she wore irons on her legs, which was also affirmed by Ben:Perley Poore in his *Reminiscences*.[6] On September 2, 1873, a letter signed "Truth" and written by John T. Ford appeared in the New York *Tribune* accusing Judge Holt of having inflicted unnecessary pain and indignity upon a helpless woman. On September 11, 1873, Holt replied to the letter stating "that no 'manacles' of any kind were upon Mrs. Surratt when in the presence of the court." He included a letter from General Joseph Hartranft, who was now governor of Pennsylvania, verifying his assertion. The controversy was further joined by reporter Jane Swisshelm, who had referred to Mrs. Surratt as a prisoner in chains in 1865 and who now added—admitting that she had not been able to see Mrs. Surratt's feet—"Every time she moved them I heard chains clank." The Washington *Chronicle* denied the charge and also printed a letter from Frederick Aiken, one of Mrs. Surratt's counsel. "I have to say in reply that at no time during her unlawful trial was Mrs. Surratt manacled . . . while in the presence of the court." In an interview published in November, 1873, the court president, David Hunter, claimed to have investigated published reports in 1865 that Mrs. Surratt was ironed and found them to be untrue. Father Jacob Ambrose Walter, the priest who heard her confession, also said of Mrs. Surratt when he first saw her at

---

5. New York *Times*, May 14, p. 4, and May 15, 1865, p. 1; Washington *Evening Star*, May 26, 1865, p. 2; Chicago *Tribune*, July 7, 1865, p. 1.

6. New York *Times*, May 15, 1865, p. 1; Ben: Perley Poore, *Perley's Reminiscences of Sixty Years in the National Metropolis* (2 vols.; Philadelphia: Hubbard Brothers, 1886), II, 184. George A. Townsend, *The Life, Crime, and Capture of John Wilkes Booth with a Full Sketch of the Conspiracy of Which He Was the Leader, and the Pursuit, Trial, and Execution of His Accomplices* (New York: Dick and Fitzgerald, 1865), 63, said that her skirts hid her feet so that he could not determine if they were chained.

the end of the trial, "She was not manacled nor heavily ironed, as has been said."[7]

It is difficult to reach a definite conclusion. Nonetheless, there is some evidence that the prisoners may have all been initially ironed and perhaps even hooded. Both Kautz and Comstock mentioned all the prisoners being chained and hooded, not making any exception for Mrs. Surratt.[8] However, as the trial proceeded and less stringent measures were used, even against the male prisoners, Mrs. Surratt's chains, if she wore them, were removed. In any case, to call this torture or to hint that it was done to maintain prisoner silence is untrue.

It has generally been assumed that Weichmann was almost solely responsible for Mrs. Surratt going to the gallows, and a great deal of contempt has been heaped upon him. There would appear to be an interesting psychological phenomenon involved, for if Lincoln's murder seemed to be parricide, Mrs. Surratt's betrayal by Weichmann has struck historians as matricide. The youth who was treated like a son viciously sent his adopted mother to the gallows.[9]

However, to contemporaries, while Weichmann's testimony was not unimportant, it seemed to be the testimony of Lloyd coupled with Paine's arrival at her house that actually convicted her. The *Chicago Tribune* said on July 18, 1865, "In point of fact the testimony of Weichmann was not at all essential to the conviction of Mrs. Surratt. It was of very small importance as compared with that of Lloyd, and still less consequence as compared with Mrs. Surratt's own conduct when confronted with Paine, after the arrest of that culprit." Even Dr. Mudd,

---

7. New York *Tribune*, September 2, p. 5, and September 11, 1873, p. 4; Joseph Hartranft to Joseph Holt, September 4, 1873, in Holt Papers; Otto Eisenschiml, *In the Shadow of Lincoln's Death* (New York: Wilfred Funk, 1940), 117–19; Washington *Daily Morning Chronicle*, September 19, p. 4, and November 9, 1873, p. 4; Cincinnati *Enquirer*, June 7, 1891, in Ford's Theatre Collection. Another member of the defense counsel, Frederick Stone, in New York *Tribune*, June 17, 1883, p. 4, said, "She was ironed but not heavily like the others."

8. August V. Kautz, "Reminiscences of the Civil War" (Typescript in August V. Kautz Papers, LC), 108; Cyrus B. Comstock Diary (MS in Cyrus Comstock Papers, LC), May 9, 1865.

9. Lloyd Lewis, *Myths After Lincoln* (New York: Harcourt Brace, 1929), 256; Clara E. Laughlin, *The Death of Lincoln, The Story of Booth's Plot, His Deed and the Penalty* (New York: Doubleday, Page, 1909), 203; John T. Ford, Statement, N.d., in Ford's Theatre Collection.

who was extremely bitter at the treatment he had received, wrote of Weichmann that he "seemed, whilst on the stand, to be disposed to give what he believed a truthful statement." On Lloyd's death in 1892, the New York *World* spoke of him as the man whose testimony had been most damaging and had probably condemned Mrs. Surratt. General Harris also recalled that Lloyd's testimony had much more influence upon him than Weichmann's. Weichmann himself wrote to Judge Holt in 1883 that he had not originally believed Mrs. Surratt guilty, adding, "My faith was shaken only when I heard Lloyd's terrible damning evidence." [10]

Although Weichmann has sometimes been portrayed as being nervous, trembling, and unsure of himself on the witness stand, he was evidently the type of individual who made a favorable impression on those who heard him. General Wallace wrote of his testimony, "I have never seen anything like his steadfastness. There he stood, a young man only twenty-three years of age, strikingly handsome, intelligent, self-possessed, under the most searching cross-examination I have ever heard." [11]

Wallace also disavowed Weichmann's involvement in the plot, but in spite of this, there is evidence that he was very likely involved in some manner and that fear probably caused him to color his testimony to bring it more into line with the government's conception of the plot. In Weichmann's letter of May 5, 1865, to H. L. Burnett, he admitted as much when he said, "You confused and terrified me so much yesterday, that I was almost unable to say anything." John Surratt accused Weichmann of having acted out of moral cowardice and pique because he was not more fully included in the kidnapping scheme due to his deficiencies in riding and shooting. Just such a set of circumstances could

10. Chicago *Tribune*, July 18, 1865, p. 1; Nettie Mudd, *The Life of Dr. Samuel A. Mudd, Containing His Letters From Fort Jefferson, Dry Tortugas, Where He Was Imprisoned Four Years for Alleged Complicity in the Assassination of Abraham Lincoln* (Marietta, Ga.: Continental Book, 1955), 45; Eisenschiml, *Why Was Lincoln Murdered?*, 279–80, agreed with Mudd's assessment of Weichmann's testimony. New York *World*, December 22, 1892, p. 2; Thomas M. Harris, *Rome's Responsibility for the Assassination of Abraham Lincoln* (Los Angeles: Heritage Manor, 1960), 25. Louis Weichmann to Joseph Holt, December 18, 1883, Extract of a letter in Holt's handwriting, in Holt Papers.

11. Helen J. Campbell, *The Case for Mrs. Surratt* (New York: G. P. Putnam's Sons, 1943), 158 ff; Lew Wallace, *Lew Wallace: An Autobiography* (2 vols.; New York: Harper Bros., 1906), II, 848.

explain why Weichmann informed Gleason. Not being fully allowed into the conspiracy but aware of its details, he may have grasped the precarious position he was in should anything go wrong and therefore informed Gleason in order to cover himself. William P. Wood, superintendent of Old Capitol Prison, also charged that Weichmann had turned state's evidence, while John T. Ford gave a vivid impression of Weichmann as a moral coward and filled with fear that Stanton had inflicted on him.[12]

These charges were reinforced at the conclusion of the trial by John Brophy, a friend of the Surratt family who repeated the statements Weichmann was supposed to have made to him. Among these were that Stanton and Burnett had threatened him with death if he did not tell all he knew, that if Gleason had not informed on him, the authorities would not have gotten a word out of him, that he had deliberately lied on the witness stand, that Mrs. Surratt neither liked her son John going to Richmond nor particularly cared for the company he kept, and that Weichmann had offered to write a letter avowing Mrs. Surratt's innocence if Brophy would hand it directly to the president. Word of Brophy's allegations reached the newspapers, and on July 17, 1865, Weichmann answered them, saying that the charges had twice been taken to Holt, once to the members of the court, and even to President Johnson. He denied all maltreatment and concluded, "The Government knows best and must make a dread and just example to terrify all enemies to free government."[13]

On top of this, there are indications that Weichmann was a southern sympathizer and that, in addition to his knowledge of the abduction

---

12. David M. DeWitt, *The Assassination of Abraham Lincoln and Its Expiation* (New York: MacMillan, 1909), 97; Louis Weichmann to Henry L. Burnett, May 5, 1865, in Record Book, File W, p. 102, JAO, RG 153, NA; Eisenschiml, *Why Was Lincoln Murdered?*, 280; John Surratt, Washington *Post*, April 3, 1898, p. 11; Laughlin, *Death of Lincoln*, 236; Eisenschiml, *In the Shadow of Lincoln's Death*, 186; John T. Ford, Statement, N.d., in Ford's Theatre Collection; John T. Ford, "Behind the Curtain of a Conspiracy," *North American Review*, XLVIII (1898), 484–93; Edward V. Murphy, "Lincoln Court Trial Reporter Tells His Story," New York *Times Magazine*, April 9, 1916, p. 9.

13. Charles Mason to Andrew Johnson, July 7, 1865, Containing Affidavit of John Brophy, in Andrew Johnson Papers, LC, Microcopy, Roll 15; John Brophy, July 7, 1865, Statement, in File Folder 80, RG 153, NA; Gettysburg *Compiler*, July 24, 1865, p. 2; Washington *Evening Star*, July 17, 1865, p. 1; Philadelphia *Evening Bulletin*, July 17, 1865, p. 2. See United States Government, *Trial of John H. Surratt*, II, 814–20, for testimony of Lewis Carland and James Gifford, who corroborated the Brophy story.

plot, he was passing on information about southern prisoners, acquired through his government job, to John Surratt. Surratt raised such charges in his 1870 Rockville speech, as did his schoolmate Henri B. Ste. Marie. Blockade-runner Augustus (alias Spencer) Howell also said that Weichmann had given him information and that Weichmann had taken the job in the commissary general of prisoners' office with the expressed agreement with Surratt to furnish him information.[14]

The government at first suspected Weichmann of being involved. On April 18, Stanton received a letter from Joseph Clark, a clerk in the adjutant general's office, stating his belief that Weichmann was Booth's accomplice. Colonel Foster, who was involved in the investigation, was also convinced that Weichmann should be placed in custody. However, when he inquired whether Weichmann should be left at large, he was informed by Burnett that Stanton had only ordered his statement to be taken and that "I [Burnett] do not feel warranted in ordering his arrest." Major O'Beirne also wrote, "Weichmann was an accomplice of the conspirators but [his] status was subsequently changed." As late as May 2, the authorities were asking Lyman Bunnel, who saw three persons with Booth on the night of the assassination, to see if Weichmann might not be one of them.[15]

The same suspicion of involvement also centered on Lloyd, especially since he had first denied to the officers who questioned him that anyone had been at the tavern on the night of the assassination. Special Officer George Cottingham summed up the grounds for Lloyd's implication.[16]

Nonetheless, Weichmann and Lloyd both had their status changed from conspirators to star witnesses for the government. On May 14, 1865, we find Holt writing to Stanton, "Lewis J. Weichmann and J. M. Lloyd prisoners at the Old Capitol having faithfully given their testi-

---

14. Laughlin, *Death of Lincoln*, 237; Eisenschiml, *In the Shadow of Lincoln's Death*, 180; Augustus Howell, Affidavit, N.d., in Ford's Theatre Collection; Pitman, *The Assassination of President Lincoln*, 133–35.

15. Joseph Clark to Edwin Stanton, April 16, 1865, in Letters Received, File C 270, JAO, Colonel Foster, Report Concerning Weichmann, N.d., in Record Book, File W, p. 100, JAO, 1865, Foster to Henry L. Burnett, April 30, 1865, Endorsement Book No. 17, all in RG 153, NA; Eisenschiml, *Why Was Lincoln Murdered?*, 292; Lyman Bunnel, May 2, 1865, in Record Book, File B, p. 10, JAO, RG 153, NA.

16. John M. Lloyd, April 22, 1865, Statement, in Letters Received, File L80, JAO, George Cottingham, May 14, 1865, in Letters Received, File A967-AGO-1866, both in RG 153, NA.

mony in the cases now on trial before this court I recommend that they at once be released from custody." In June, Weichmann was asking Colonel Burnett to assist him in getting April's salary and to see that his parole might be extended to Philadelphia so that he might visit his parents. Holt again wrote Stanton recommending that Weichmann's request be granted and all money due him be paid. Weichmann was thus rewarded for services rendered.[17]

There is no necessarily sinister connotation to Weichmann's and Lloyd's immunity, for it merely shows that encouraging a witness to implicate his fellow conspirators is a long and honored tradition in the United States. As the San Francisco *Alta Californian* said so perceptively, "Some objection was made that several of the witnesses were themselves participants in the crime, and therefore unworthy of credence; but if such testimony were not accepted, the punishment of great crimes would be rarer than it is."[18]

Weichmann's subsequent career, as it can be pieced together through his long correspondence with Judge Holt, is extremely interesting. On August 14, 1865, he wrote to Stanton saying he could no longer continue his theological studies and planned to ask for a job in a custom-house or post office. In October, he questioned Holt as to whether he had heard anything about his application, and when Weichmann still had not heard by November, he detailed in a letter the misfortunes he had undergone because he had stood by the government.[19]

Weichmann also wrote to commission member General James A. Ekin on November 24, 1865, and the letter contains an interesting statement. After asking Ekin if he had seen the secretary of war about his application, Weichmann stated, "I am sorry to trouble you so much, but you see I am holding you at your own words." On November 28, he informed Holt that he would accept a position in the Philadelphia

17. Joseph Holt to Edwin Stanton, May 14, 1865, in File Folder 60, Louis Weichmann to Henry L. Burnett, June 11, 1865, in Letters Received, File W 525, JAO, Weichmann to Burnett, June 16, 1865, in Letters Received, File W 692, JAO, Holt to Stanton, June 16, 1865, in Letters Sent, all in RG 153, NA.

18. San Francisco *Alta Californian*, July 20, 1865, p. 2. Such tactics are currently quite common in the United States, and several states have witness immunity laws even in murder cases. Nevertheless, Americans still seem to feel a degree of scorn for the informer.

19. Louis Weichmann to Edwin Stanton, August 4, 1865, in File Folder 70, RG 153, NA; Weichmann to Joseph Holt, October 10, November 12, 1865, Weichmann to Henry L. Burnett, November 20, 1865, all in Holt Papers.

Custom House, and on December 18 notified the judge advocate that he was on the job.[20]

In June, 1866, Weichmann inquired as to the whereabouts of John Surratt, who he feared was lurking in Philadelphia for some dark purpose. When a new collector was appointed at Philadelphia, he again appealed to Holt for the protection of his job. He made more interesting statements, speaking about the "peculiar circumstances under which I was appointed," and also writing to collector W. P. Johnston, "I hold my appointment from the Secretary of the Treasury for services rendered to the War Department and to the Military Commission convened at Washington, May 9, 1865, in the detection and conviction of the assassins of Abraham Lincoln." In December, 1866, Weichmann praised Holt's "Vindication," which he had seen in the Washington *Chronicle* and which was published in pamphlet form, and said that if Holt would send him more pamphlets, they would be given to the proper persons. The "Vindication" attempted to refute charges that he withheld the clemency plea for Mrs. Surratt from President Johnson.[21]

Weichmann finally did lose his job in 1886, when he was notified that he was granted a few days' leave of absence until September 30, at which time his resignation would be accepted. He turned once more to his protector, Holt, even asking him for a loan of $150, though he later regretted this request. There is no indication of whether he ever received the money, but this time Holt could not save his job.[22]

In these later years, Weichmann was also working on a manuscript of his experiences in the events surrounding the assassination. He sent portions of it to Holt for his comments and even asked Holt if he might borrow his copy of George Alfred Townsend's *Caty O' Catoctin*, which he was using as a reference work.[23]

20. Louis Weichmann to James A. Ekin, November 24, 1865, Weichmann to Joseph Holt, November 28, December 18, 1865, all in Holt Papers.
21. Louis Weichmann to Joseph Holt, June 21, August 9, September 1, October 10, October 19, October 20, October 23, December 5, 1866, Weichmann to W. P. Johnston, October 15, 1866, *ibid.*
22. John Cadwalader to Louis Wiechmann, Septmeber 24, 1886, Valentine Brothers to Weichmann, December 18, 1886, Weichmann to Valentine Brothers, December 29, 1886, Weichmann to Joseph Holt, January 5, 1887, *ibid.*
23. Louis Weichmann to Joseph Holt, December 30, 1887, February 1, February 10, 1888, May 24, 1893, February 3, 1887, *ibid.* In 1975 Floyd Risvold published the Weichmann manuscript, which he had obtained from one of Weichmann's heirs, under the title *A True History of the Assassination of Abraham Lincoln and of the Conspiracy of 1865* (New York:

Through the efforts of General Wallace, Weichmann was appointed stenographer and typist for the Indiana Republican State Committee. After the Republican triumph in the elections, he wrote Holt that he had been assured by General Ekin, Colonel Foster, General Wallace, and Judge Bingham, that they would aid him in getting back into government service, and he enclosed copies of recommendations from several individuals. Ekin wrote to Holt saying he had written to Secretary of the Treasury William Windom reminding him of the assurance that Weichmann would be in the public service. "This is in accordance with our understanding which I believe will be carried out. It is my purpose to follow this matter up, if 'it takes all summer!' "[24]

Weichmann felt that his life after the assassination had been a story of cruel suffering. He wrote to Assistant Judge Advocate Bingham in 1889, "My life has been one of trial and persecution;—persecution by the Democratic party and, I regret to say, by leading church dignitaries in the Church in which I was reared. This had made it all the more bitter." He also feared public opinion and what authors might write about his role in the trials, even such friendly authors as General Harris. For example, he wrote to Bingham promising to make a strong defense should defense lawyer John W. Clampitt carry out his threatened personal attacks upon him. He also greatly dreaded the influence that the utterances of Mrs. Surratt's confessor Father Walter might have, although he informed Holt that in Indiana, aside from the Catholic papers, Walter was having little influence. He added, "Public opinion is pretty well made up on that subject, and in the way you and I would have it."[25]

Alfred Knopf, 1975). While the book has been greeted by a great deal of enthusiasm on the part of historians, claims that it brings to light new evidence about the assassination do not stand up to examination. Besides a few interesting anecdotes, it contains little that is new; it is a self-serving defense of Weichmann's position; the editing is very uncritical; and it does little to dispel the notion that Weichmann might have turned states' evidence to save himself. It also should not be regarded as a primary source, since Weichmann kept no notes at the time and the writing was accomplished many years later. His request for *Caty O'Catoctin* shows the dubious type of source he was using to refresh his memory.

24. Louis Weichmann to Joseph Holt, March 5, November 20, 1888, February 18, March 16, April 29, 1889, James A. Ekin to Holt, July 9, 1890, all in Holt Papers; Weichmann to John A. Bingham, February 18, 1889, in John A. Bingham Papers, Ohio Historical Society, Microcopy, Roll 3.

25. Louis Weichmann to John A. Bingham, January 31, 1889, April 5, 1895, in Bingham Papers, Microcopy, Roll 3; Weichmann to Joseph Holt, June 15, 1889, April 5, 1890, June 8, September 10, October 22, 1891, all in Holt Papers.

A letter to Bingham in 1896 further reveals some interesting insight into Weichmann's personality and the assurances he craved that his course had been right: "You, more than any man alive today, are aware of the need of praise to which I am entitled for the sacrifices I made. . . . I have always felt I would like to have some brief expression from you in writing as to what you think of the manner in which I performed my duty to the country and of the reward to which I am entitled in the estimation of all good people."

While he did undergo much persecution—at least of a mental nature—because of his testimony, statements by his sisters that he was fired upon are not verified in his correspondence with Holt. His alleged deathbed statement affirming the truthfulness of all he had done does sound similar to statements he made in letters to many people.[26]

The many attempts to vindicate Mrs. Surratt have been almost entirely by later writers. To contemporaries, the evidence brought out seemed strongly to indicate her guilt. Even the opposition press, on the whole, agreed with this appraisal. The New York *World*, which was so vehemently opposed to military trials, said, "The proceedings before General Hunter and his associates show the gratifying fact that sufficient legal evidence exists to convict all those connected with the plot before any jury in the land." The Albany *Argus* added, "The government had a clear case against the accused; and before any decent court and jury, any fair lawyer could have got a verdict of guilty, which would not only have satisfied justice, but what is quite important in revolutionary times, would have convinced the public mind."[27]

Just as the members of the commission were not all so radical as they have been portrayed, the court proceedings were apparently not so stringent either. There were several reports of kindness extended to prisoners, all the way from their being allowed to remain after court to write letters to being allowed conversations with relatives. The New York *Tribune* also reported that police officers in civilian clothes, not

26. Louis Weichmann to John A. Bingham, September 17, 1896, in Bingham Papers, Microcopy, Roll 4; Lewis, *Myths After Lincoln*, 260–61, 267.

27. Gettysburg *Adams Sentinel*, May 16, 1865, p. 3; *Trial of the Assassins and Conspirators for the Murder of Abraham Lincoln: The Evidence in Full with Arguments of Counsel on Both Sides, and the Verdict of the Military Commission* (Philadelphia: Barclay, 1865), 38, 93–94; New York *World*, May 16, p. 4, May 26, p. 1, May 27, p. 4, June 2, 1865, p. 8; Albany *Argus*, June 15, 1865, p. 2.

uniformed soldiers, sat between the prisoners, in order to make identification more difficult. Other newspapers felt that the court was giving every courtesy to the defense and were favorably impressed when Judge Holt insisted that the daily reading of the record should not be dispensed with. Reporter Noah Brooks described the court as presenting a picture of disorder, with the officers sitting in various negligent attitudes. General Kautz, however, frequently commented that the court had worked long hours.[28]

Despite the initial excitement over the trial, the case began to drag for many people. The accidental discharge of a guard's musket in an upper room on May 25, however, caused considerable disturbance and what the *Tribune* called "Guy Fawkes apprehensions." But comments on the uninteresting nature of the evidence became frequent, although it did not dampen the interest of the Washington spectators. Even while the fate of the conspirators was being decided, there was apparently a lot more interest in the Fourth of July or the situation of the French in Mexico. Some debated whether the onus for delays in the trial rested with the prosecution or the defense.[29]

Nevertheless, some interest was revived by the arguments delivered at the close of the trial, especially those by Reverdy Johnson and John A. Bingham. The interest is indicated in a letter from T. A. Marshall to Holt, asking for a copy of both arguments. "I am anxious particularly to see how you make that a case 'arising in the land or naval forces or in the militia' and by what process of reasoning you sustain the jurisdiction of the Court." Reverdy Johnson's argument, which was read by Clampitt, consisted mainly of an attack upon the commission's jurisdiction and pointed out that the civil courts were open and that even if the president could suspend the writ of habeas corpus, all other rights remained and the defendants should have been tried in the civil courts. The war power that the prosecution had argued justified military commissions was not a prerogative of the executive but of Congress. John-

28. Washington *Daily National Intelligencer*, June 23, 1865, p. 2; Washington *Evening Star*, May 23, p. 2, June 5, p. 2, May 15, p. 2, May 18, 1865, p. 2; New York *Tribune*, May 15, 1865, p. 6; Washington *Daily National Intelligencer*, May 17, 1865, p. 3; Noah Brooks, "The Close of Lincoln's Career," *Century Magazine*, L (1895), 26; August V. Kautz Daily Journal (MS in Kautz Papers), May 15, 1865.

29. New York *Tribune*, May 26, p. 1, June 1, 1865, p. 1; New York *Times*, June 9, p. 1, June 10, p. 8, June 12, p. 4, June 24, p. 1, July 1–5, 1865; Albany *Argus*, July 3, 1865, p. 2.

son's argument did not deal directly with Mrs. Surratt's case but seized upon perhaps the only chance she had, that of destroying the jurisdiction on which the military commission rested. Another defense lawyer, William Doster, later recalled that the attacks on the court's jurisdiction were an unsuccessful attempt to arouse newspapers and public opinion.[30]

Assistant Judge Advocate Bingham's argument, like Johnson's, also addressed constitutional issues more than it did the specific guilt or innocence of those involved. He attempted to show that Lincoln had suspended habeas corpus by Order 141 and that Congress had then legalized this by statute, making the military commission a legal body even under Reverdy Johnson's dictum that only Congress could approve such bodies. Much of the evidence that Bingham reviewed was of alleged southern atrocities and relied heavily on the testimony of Sanford Conover, Montgomery, and Merritt, which later proved to be perjured.[31]

The government also attempted to bolster its case by having Attorney General Speed reduce his argument to writing, and then printing and distributing it separately as well as appending it to the trial record. His predecessor, Edward Bates, was very much opposed to Speed's view and was himself writing an argument against martial law and military commissions, which he had promised Reverdy Johnson.[32]

Public reaction clearly demonstrates that these arguments once again divided people along the lines of progovernment and antigovernment and that jurisdictional questions became almost more important than the actual fate of the individuals involved. Most loyal people would probably have agreed with the New York *Herald* that "to make the plea

30. T. A. Marshall to Joseph Holt, May 31, 1865, in Holt Papers; *An Argument to Establish the Illegality of Military Commissions in the United States . . . Prepared by Reverdy Johnson, One of the Counsel of Mrs. Surratt* (Baltimore: John Murphy, 1865); William E. Doster, *Lincoln and Episodes of the Civil War* (New York: G. P. Putnam's Sons, 1915), 262–63. For General Ewing's argument to the court's jurisdiction, see Pitman, *The Assassination of President Lincoln*, 264–67. See 288–99 for Aiken's specific defense of Mrs. Surratt.

31. John A. Bingham, *Trial of the Conspirators for the Assassination of President Lincoln . . . Delivered June 27 and 28, 1865, Before the Military Commission, Washington, D.C.* (Washington: Government Printing Office, 1865). A. Oakey Hall, "The Surratt Cause Célèbre," *Green Bag*, VIII (1896), 198.

32. James Speed, *Opinion on the Constitutional Power of the Military to Try and Execute the Assassins of the President* (Washington: Government Printing Office, 1865); Pitman, *The Assassination of President Lincoln*, 403–409; Howard K. Beale (ed.), *The Diary of Edward Bates, 1859–1866*, Vol. IV of the Annual Report of the American Historical Association, 1930 (Washington: Government Printing Office, 1933), 499, 520–21.

hold water Mr. Johnson was compelled to ignore the rebellion, and to require the members of the court to recognize it as a legal fact that during the last four years the country has been in a state of profound peace and that all this time no such thing as military law has superseded the civil courts this side of Mexico." The *Herald* also noted the incongruity of Johnson's going through the entire trial before the commission and then coming forward to attempt to deny its jurisdiction. The *Times* said that the question was really one of the past, for the matter of the right to invoke every sovereign war power had been decided during the conflict. *Harper's* admitted that Johnson's argument was able but wondered if the assassin was not to be considered a rebel spy, merely because he was not enrolled in any regimental lists. On the other side the New York *World* said, "This learned and exhaustive argument will convince all except those who wilfully shut their eyes against evidence."[33]

General Kautz wrote of Bingham's speech that it had "for its principle defect the volume of words in which it is enveloped although otherwise well prepared and very conclusive." Union papers were effusive in their praise, and letters poured in to Holt and Bingham favoring the argument. Again the *World* referred to Bingham's argument as "shameful in its perversion of evidence" and said that while it had intended to publish the speech in its entirety, it now felt that publication was not worthwhile. From Wisconsin, Charles A. Eldridge wrote to Holt that he had placed the arguments of Bingham and Speed into the hands of his constituents but asked if his motive was really a nonpartisan informing of the public: "Why did not you and the Secretary of War, include in the distribution, the able argument of Senator Johnson and the other distinguished counsel for the defense?"[34]

If the arguments at the end of the trial seemed to deal more with philosophical issues, however, affairs returned to a very personal basis with the announcement that Mary Surratt, Atzerodt, Paine, and Herold were to be hanged on July 7, one week after the tribunal reached its

33. New York *Herald*, June 29, p. 4, June 20, 1865, p. 4; Philadelphia *Evening Bulletin*, June 6, 1865, p. 4; New York *Times*, June 30, 1865, p. 4; *Harper's Weekly*, July 1, 1865, p. 401; New York *World*, June 20, 1865, p. 4.

34. Kautz Daily Journal, June 27, 1865, in Kautz Papers; Philadelphia *Evening Bulletin*, June 28, p. 3, June 29, 1865, p. 4; Washington *Evening Star*, June 29, 1865, p. 2; M. Simpson to John A. Bingham, August 1, 1865, in Bingham Papers, Microcopy, Roll 1; John Hamilton to Joseph Holt, August 23, 1865, in Holt Papers; New York *World*, July 4, 1865, p. 4; Charles A. Eldridge to Joseph Holt, October 16, 1865, in Holt Papers.

verdict. While the execution aroused much controversy in 1865, a great deal of it occurred, not, as historians have mistakenly claimed, because substantial numbers of people believed that Mrs. Surratt was not guilty, but rather because there existed a great deal of sentiment against hanging a woman.

Some people believed that Mrs. Surratt might be spared; and there were also some lingering doubts over all the hangings, because the sentence had been pronounced by a military court. The New York *Times* said, "Surprise is expressed, almost unanimously, that the excution should be fixed for a day so immediate after the promulgation of the sentence. . . . It is believed that Mrs. Surratt's sentence will be commuted to imprisonment for life." John W. Clampitt also recalled the surprise he had felt when he heard the newsboys on the street crying the news of the execution. Several opposition newspapers expressed the hope that the president would set aside the verdict and order a new trial. On the whole, however, the verdict merely reinforced the beliefs people had about the rightness or wrongness of military trials, instead of causing any drastic changes in opinion.[35]

Most loyal newspapers, believing Mrs. Surratt guilty, however, reported no reason to expect clemency. The New York *Times* even said that there might be some feeling that the punishment of the four conspirators who had merely received life imprisonment had not been harsh enough, but reflection would show the verdict to be just, even though it was tempered with mercy. Others believed that the very rapid execution would provide a stern warning to anyone else contemplating assassination.[36]

The majority of those wishing clemency for Mrs. Surratt still probably considered her guilty. As the New York *Herald* said, "The sympathy in favor of Mrs. Surratt gained ground by discussion, and hundreds who admitted her guilt inveighed bitterly against the mode of her punishment." Guard Henry B. Whitney wrote in his diary at Fort Jefferson,

35. New York *Times*, July 7, 1865, pp. 1, 4. See also Washington *Evening Star*, July 7, 1865, p. 2; John W. Clampitt, "The Trial of Mrs. Surratt," *North American Review*, CXXXI (1880), 234–35; Albany *Argus*, July 3, pp. 1, 2, July 7, 1865, p. 2; New York *News*, quoted in Baltimore *Sun*, July 10, 1865, p. 1.

36. New York *Times*, July 7, p. 4, July 8, 1865, p. 1; San Francisco *Alta Californian*, July 20, 1865, p. 1; New York *Tribune*, July 7, 1865, p. 1; Washington *Daily National Intelligencer*, July 7, 1865, p. 1.

where several of the conspirators were later imprisoned, that while he had no objection to the conspirators hanging, "I think Mrs. S——— ought to have been imprisoned for life. The country is no better for her death in such a manner."[37]

Hangman Christian Rath even had difficulty in getting men to dig the graves. He finally had to rely on soldiers, among whom there were more than an ample number of volunteers. Authorities like Generals Hancock and Hartranft also had hopes that a last-minute reprieve might arrive. George Townsend described spectators at the foot of the scaffold discussing Mrs. Surratt's reprieve. "But few hoped for it, though some were induced by Mrs. Surratt's counsel to believe she would not be hanged today." The delicacy in hanging a woman can be sensed in the comment by the New York *World* reporter: "It was with a shudder, almost a blush, that I saw an officer gather the ropes tightly three times about the robes of Mrs. Surratt, and bind her ankles with cords."[38]

The concurrently occurring murder trial of Mary Harris, who was acquitted on the grounds of temporary insanity, caused many to believe that the trial of the conspirators by military trial had been correct. *Leslie's Illustrated* said, "It is now clear that one certainly, perhaps most of these conspirators, would have escaped the penalty of their crimes, had they been handed over to the judicial Dogberrys and morally-perverted juries of the national capital."[39]

There was a self-congratulatory air about the trials being concluded with so little additional violence, and relief all around that they had ended. On July 8, the *Times* said, "The public desire to hear no more of the revolting subject," and on July 26, after discussion had continued

---

37. New York *Herald*, July 8, p. 1, July 7, 1865, p. 1. Among those mentioning reluctance to hang a woman, see Brooks, "Close of Lincoln's Career," 612, and Hugh McCulloch, *Men and Measures of Half a Century* (New York: Charles Scribner's Sons, 1900), 225. Henry B. Whitney Diary (MS in Whitney Papers, Duke University Library), July 20, 1865.

38. John A. Gray, "The Fate of the Lincoln Conspirators: the Account of the Hanging Given by Lieutenant-Colonel Christian Rath, the Executioner," *McClure's Magazine*, XXXVII (1911), 635; Lafayette C. Baker, *History of the United States Secret Service* (Philadelphia: King and Baird, 1867), 514; Osborn H. Oldroyd, *The Assassination of Abraham Lincoln, Flight, Pursuit, Capture, and Punishment of the Conspirators* (Washington: O. H. Oldroyd, 1901), 204.

39. *Frank Leslie's Illustrated*, August 12, 1865, p. 322; Chicago *Tribune*, July 24, 1865, p. 2; New Orleans *Times-Picayune*, July 28, 1865, p. 4.

because of various controversies, the *Herald* called for a moratorium. Johnson and Holt received praise from newspapers and the public alike for standing firm and carrying out the will of the nation. Many journals saw that a rapid execution had relieved the president of the many pleas for clemency that would have followed any sort of delay.[40]

At the conclusion of the trial, attempts had been made by the counsel and friends of Mrs. Surratt to intervene with the president both on a personal basis and through the courts by means of securing a writ of habeas corpus. Early on the morning of the execution, Aiken and Clampitt applied to Judge Andrew B. Wylie for the writ and he issued it, though with some apprehension, for Clampitt quoted him as saying, "I am about to perform an act which before to-morrow's sun goes down may consign me to the Old Capitol Prison." At 11:30 General Hancock appeared accompanied by Attorney General Speed and returned the writ with President Johnson's endorsement suspending its execution. Orville H. Browning, who was present at the writ's return, said Wylie "should have proceeded against him [Hancock] for contempt, and have seen whether the President would have taken him forcibly from the hands of the Court." William Boyce wrote to Seward on July 29 that he felt Seward had blundered in not allowing the writ in Mrs. Surratt's case. There was additional criticism of both Wylie and Johnson, but the *Intelligencer* said on July 11 that each had merely done his duty according to law and with no animosity.[41]

A controversy was also soon to develop over charges by Mrs. Sur-

40. New York *Times*, July 8, 1865, p. 4; New York *Herald*, July 26, 1865, p. 4; Chicago *Tribune*, July 12, 1865, p. 2; Easton (Pa.) *Free Press*, July 13, 1865, p. 2; Edwin Correr to Johnson, July 8, Thomas Laurie to Johnson, July 8, 1865, both in Johnson Papers, Microcopy, Roll 15; New York *Herald*, July 7, 1865, p. 1; Philadelphia *Evening Bulletin*, July 8, 1865, p. 4.

41. For the habeas corpus maneuverings, see *The Trial of the Alleged Assassins and Conspirators at Washington City, D.C., May and June, 1865, for the Murder of President Abraham Lincoln* (Philadelphia: T. B. Peterson and Brothers, 1865), 209–10. Clampitt, "The Trial of Mrs. Surratt," 236; Petition for Habeas Corpus for Mary E. Surratt, July 7, 1865, Copy, in Holt Papers; James G. Randall and Theodore C. Pease (eds.), *Diary of Orville Hickman Browning* (2 vols.; Springfield, Ill.: Jefferson's Printing and Stationery, 1933), II, 37; *The War of the Rebellion: A Compilation of the Official Records of the Union and Confederate Armies* (130 vols., Washington: Government Printing Office, 1880–1901), Ser. II, Vol. VIII, p. 714; Washington *Daily National Intelligencer*, July 11, 1865, p. 2; Washington *Evening Star*, July 7, 1865, p. 2. Doster also applied for a writ of habeas corpus for Paine and Atzerodt, but because of its suspension in Mrs. Surratt's case, the court refused to act.

ratt's confessor, Father Walter, that he was not allowed to see her until he should agree to make no statements nor allow her to express her innocence. On July 12, the New York *Tribune* charged, "One of the prominent counsel engaged on the late conspiracy trial, asserts positively that spiritual attendants were denied to Mrs. Surratt on the day of the execution, until Secretary Stanton had received from them a promise that they would not on the scaffold proclaim their belief in her innocence." This was followed by a dispatch dated July 16, 1865, charging that Father Walter was denied a pass by General Hardie without first consulting Stanton. He finally received a pass but at the same time mentioned to Hardie his belief in Mrs. Surratt's innocence. He was then informed that since the pass was unsigned by Stanton, it would not admit him to the military prison; if he agreed to say nothing about Mrs. Surratt's innocence, however, he would get the required pass. Father Walter at first refused, but seeing that Hardie remained adamant and that Mrs. Surratt might be executed without spiritual comfort, he finally acquiesced.[42]

Hardie, who was himself Catholic, answered Walter, stating that he had not objected to Walter's protests of Mrs. Surratt's innocence but rather to the extreme bitterness of his language. He denied that he had threatened to revoke the pass but did say that Walter's intemperate language had so aroused him that he was thinking of recommending another priest. He also denied that Stanton had known he had gone to see Walter. Again opinion divided on partisan lines, with friends of Hardie and Stanton rushing to their defense, and opponents like the New York *World* tending to back Father Walter.[43]

42. Otto Eisenschiml, "Addenda to Lincoln's Assassination," *Journal of the Illinois State Historical Society*, XLIII (1950), 208; Eisenschiml, *In the Shadow of Lincoln's Death*, 128, 136, 147. Eisenschiml believed that Stanton used William Wood, superintendent of Old Capitol Prison, to promise Mrs. Surratt through her brother Zad Jenkins that she would not be executed, then broke his word and immediately sent her to the gallows before she could tell what she knew, which would incriminate him. New York *Tribune*, July 12, p. 1, July 17, 1865, p. 1; Jacob A. Walter, "The Surratt Case: A True Statement of Facts," *Catholic Review* (August 29, 1891), 140; John Clampitt, in Chicago *Times-Herald*, March 23, 1895, p. 1; Jacob A. Walter, *The Surratt Case: A True Statement of Facts Concerning This Notable Case*, Read before United States Catholic Historical Society, (N.p., May 25, 1891), 1.

43. Philadelphia *Evening Bulletin*, July 21, 1865, p. 2; New York *Tribune*, July 24, 1865, p. 7; C. S. Noyes to Edwin Stanton, July 14, 1865, in Edwin M. Stanton Papers, LC; S. Wickerson to James Hardie, July 18, 1865, in James A. Hardie Papers, LC; New York *World*, July 18, 1865, p. 4.

General Hancock also became involved and went to see Archbishop Martin John Spalding. The Archbishop then wrote to Hardie: "I am convinced that you acted with the best motives and in what you believed to be the best interests of the Church, of which you have been a staunch friend. While I say this, I may be permitted to express regret at your having thought it necessary to employ certain expressions in regard to Rev. Mr. Walter, which were scarcely called for by the argument."[44]

These relatively minor controversies are insignificant compared to the clemency plea that five members of the court signed in Mrs. Surratt's case. Historians have long debated whether the president saw the plea or whether it was willfully kept from him, allowing an innocent woman to go to her death. The matter did not become important until 1867, during the trial of John Surratt, when public knowledge of the petition first became widespread. Then, prosecutor Edwards Pierrepont promised to show that the matter of clemency to Mrs. Surratt, rather than having been prevented from being presented to the president, was taken up at a cabinet meeting and that the execution received the approval of all present. However, when he did not make good his promise, defense lawyer Richard T. Merrick chided him, "Why didn't you bring it in? Did you find at the end of the record a recommendation to mercy in the case of Mrs. Surratt that the President never saw?" Pierrepont later explained that Judge Holt had told him that the clemency plea was before the president when he signed the execution order, although Merrick then asked why the clemency plea had not been published with the official trial record. President Johnson, after learning of the existence of such a document, supposedly sent for it and read its contents for the first time. While there was some controversy in the press at the time, the matter then lay dormant for a period of six years.[45]

On August 26, 1873, however, Holt published an article in the Washington *Daily Morning Chronicle*, which was almost immediately incor-

44. Winfield S. Hancock to Edwin Stanton, July 21, 1865, in Stanton Papers; Archbishop Spalding to James Hardie, July 23, 1865, in Hardie Papers.

45. United States Government, *Trial of John H. Surratt*, II, 1207, 1249, 1320–21, 1368; DeWitt, *Assassination of Abraham Lincoln*, 223–24; George L. Sioussat (ed.), "William G. Moore, Notes," *American Historical Review*, XIX (1913), 108; W. Winthrop to Joseph Holt, August 12, 1867, in Holt Papers; New York *Times*, August 7, p. 5, August 8, p. 4, August 9, p. 4, August 10, 1867, p. 4.

porated into a pamphlet entitled *Vindication of Hon. Joseph Holt Judge Advocate General of the United States Army.* Holt attempted to gather evidence in the form of various letters that he felt bolstered his case. James Wright and Frank Howe, clerks in the Bureau of Military Justice, confirmed that the pages of the court record were bound together in such a way that it would have been all but impossible for Johnson not to have seen the clemency petition. General Reuben D. Mussey, Johnson's private secretary, also affirmed that the president had spoken to him about such a petition. James Harlan, former secretary of the interior, said that while the plea had not been formally before the cabinet, it had been informally discussed by cabinet members. The Reverend George Butler recalled that when he had spoken to Johnson after the execution, the president had mentioned pressure for clemency but said he had remained firm because Mrs. Surratt had "maintained the nest that hatched the egg." Attorney General Speed wrote that he had seen the trial proceedings, with the petition attached, in the president's office. And Bingham stated that Stanton and Seward had informed him that both Johnson and the cabinet had seen the plea but were unanimous in denying it. However, because Stanton and Seward were now both dead, his story remained uncorroborated.[46]

On November 12, 1873, Johnson broke his long silence to reply to Holt's allegations. He very vigorously denied that he had ever seen the plea, though he did admit that in the course of a conversation, Holt strongly urged upon him that the fact that one of the conspirators was a woman should have no bearing on her case. Johnson also said that since Holt came to see him alone and he signed the death sentence in Holt's presence, there could have been no cabinet meeting before the execution, and none was held until July 7. Johnson further wondered why Holt had not secured direct evidence from Seward and Stanton while they were alive rather than only indirectly from Bingham after

---

46. Joseph Holt, *Vindication of Hon. Joseph Holt Judge Advocate General of the United States Army* (Washington: *Daily Morning Chronicle*, 1873); R. D. Mussey to Joseph Holt, August 19, 1873, in Holt Papers; Holt to John A. Bingham, February 18, 1873, in Bingham Papers, Microcopy, Roll 1; Bingham to Holt, August 1, 1888, in Holt Papers; Thomas M. Harris, *Assassination of Lincoln: A History of the Great Conspiracy Trial of the Conspirators by a Military Commission and a Review of the Trial of John H. Surratt* (Boston: American Citizen, 1892), 408; "New Facts About Mrs. Surratt: Correspondence of Judge Holt and Hon. James Speed," *North American Review*, CXLVII (1888), 83–94.

their death. He also questioned why court stenographer Pitman, who had included other extraneous material in his trial edition, had not included the clemency petition.[47]

Parenthetically it should be mentioned that some historians question the exact manner in which Pitman compiled his work, although the charge that he edited the testimony to coincide with a government version of events is easily disproved by examining his correspondence. On July 11, 1865, Pitman wrote to defense lawyer Ewing inquiring if he wished any change made in his argument for Spangler and also thanking him for his argument in the Mudd case. Also, on August 24, he acknowledged receipt of the corrected argument and said that although everything was in type, it could probably still be included. He added, "The book is 7/8 done. I think you will be pleased with it. I am conscious of having done the work carefully and fairly." Pitman also corresponded with President Johnson in 1873, claiming, as he had in a letter to Holt, that the clemency plea was not part of the record and admitting that he was not even aware of its existence until Assistant Judge Advocate Burnett informed him of it after the execution. On November 22, 1873, Pitman told Holt he had compiled his book either from the *Daily Intelligencer* copy or the copy of his own notes. And Burnett claimed that once he gave the record to the judge advocate, he never saw it again until 1873 or 1874. While Pitman's trial version was compiled haphazardly and was somewhat condensed, with all the defects this entails, it seems readily apparent that there was no purposeful censorship involved and that the defense had as much opportunity to edit the final version as the prosecution.[48]

Holt replied to Johnson's defense in the *Chronicle*, on December 1, 1873. He again attacked Johnson's conduct in the matter and included a letter from General Ekin saying that Holt had told him the entire case, including the clemency plea, had been laid before the president.

47. Washington *Daily Morning Chronicle*, November 12, 1873, p. 5; Washington *Weekly Chronicle*, November 12, 1873, p. 1.
48. Vaughan Shelton, *Mask for Treason* (Harrisburg: Stackpole Books, 1965), 67–73; Benn Pitman to Thomas Ewing, August 24, 1865, in Ewing Family Papers, LC; Andrew Johnson to Pitman, April 16, Pitman to Johnson, April 20, 1874, all in Johnson Papers, Microcopy, Roll 38; Joseph Holt to Pitman, November 20, Pitman to Holt, November 22, 1873, all in Holt Papers; Horatio King, "Open Letter: Judge Holt and the Lincoln Conspirators," *Century Magazine*, XXXIX (1890), 956; John T. Ford, Statement, N.d., in Ford's Theatre Collection.

He also included Pitman's letter stating that the plea was not part of the record and a letter by General David Hunter expressing his confidence that Johnson had seen the petition. Friends and supporters came forth to tell Holt that they felt his vindication was now complete, and some offered to distribute the *Vindication* where it might do the most good.[49]

The entire affair boils down to whether Johnson or Holt was telling the truth. Several individuals provided evidence that seemed to favor Johnson's version of events. William Wood, superintendent of Old Capitol Prison, said that he had spoken to Johnson about the innocence of Mrs. Surratt and that Johnson had said he regretted not giving her the benefit of executive clemency and expressed "his detestation of what he termed the 'infamous conduct of Stanton' in keeping these facts from him." Orville H. Browning had asked the president and cabinet on August 9, 1867, about the plea, and all declared that they had never heard of it until it was brought out during the trial of John Surratt. It is also apparent why Holt never asked Gideon Welles about the plea, for the former navy secretary had written Johnson on November 5, 1873, "I am confident that I never saw the record of the trial, the decision of the court, or the petition for clemency, nor was I ever present at any consultation in regard to either, or any matter touching her trial and execution."[50]

However, while the evidence is strong that Holt did suppress the petition, there are indications that Johnson must have known about it before the John Surratt trial. Contemporary rumors about a clemency plea abounded in 1865. The Easton (Pa.) *Argus* of July 20, 1865, said, "It seems that five of the military judges who sentenced Mrs. Surratt,

49. Washington *Daily Morning Chronicle*, December 1, 1873, pp. 2–3; to Joseph Holt: T. S. Bell, August 27, and Horatio King and John J. Speed, August 28, 1873, all in Holt Papers. For friends congratulating Johnson, see Andrew J. Kellar to Andrew Johnson, December 6, A. H. Garland to Johnson, December 6, 1873, both in Johnson Papers, Microcopy, Roll 37.

50. DeWitt, *Assassination of Abraham Lincoln*, 136–37, argued very convincingly that the irregular manner in which the death sentences were added at the end of the proceedings could well have meant that Johnson didn't notice the petition among the papers he signed. Washington *Gazette*, Clipping, N.d., in Eisenschiml, *Why Was Lincoln Murdered?*, 289. Among others mentioning Johnson's regret at hanging Mrs. Surratt is Thomas N. Conrad, *A Confederate Spy: A Story of the Civil War* (Lynchburg, Va.: Artcraft Printing, 1961), 137. Randall and Pease (eds.), *Diary of Orville Hickman Browning*, II, 155; Gideon Welles to Andrew Johnson, November 5, 1873, in Johnson Papers, Microcopy, Roll 37.

signed a paper asking for a commutation of her sentence to life imprisonment." General Kautz also wrote to Colonel H. B. Burnham in 1873, "The idea at once occurred to me how he could have failed to see it when it was published in the newspapers at the time." Even more startling was the fact that Weichmann knew of the plea in 1866, for, as he wrote to Holt on October 23, "Mr. Johnson . . . resisted the desire of the Commission that her punishment might be commuted into imprisonment for life on account of her age and sex." Further corroboration of this point came from James May, a friend of Orville H. Browning, who wrote to Johnson in 1873 saying he had been told by Ekin that Bingham had written out the plea. May had always felt that Bingham had suppressed it. He asked Johnson to explain the matter and reminded the president that he had once said to him: "I do assure you, that I did not see or hear of that document, until some days *after*, the execution of Mrs. Surratt. . . . Some short time after the execution of Mrs. Surratt, I noticed, quite an excitement expressed in the newspapers, which induced me, to send for the papers, referring to the case. *Then*, it was, for *the first time*, I saw the paper, you refer to, and even then, that paper was *not attached* to the *verdict*, but it was a *loose* paper, *by itself*." The effect of this evidence is to make it appear inconceivable that Johnson did not know of the clemency plea shortly after the execution, but he, too, was capable of suppression if it was to his political advantage.[51]

In some respects, despite all the attention devoted to it, the clemency plea is also a false issue. While severe censure is due to Holt for withholding it, its effect on Johnson is far from certain. In view of the hanging mood that both the president and the country were in, it seems probable that the plea would have had little effect. Although some of his actions were perhaps due to his illness, the president refused to see

51. Easton (Pa.) *Argus*, July 20, 1865, p. 1; Hartford *Weekly Times*, July 15, 1865, p. 2; August V. Kautz to H. B. Burnham, December 17, 1873, in Holt Papers. Kautz's claim that the petition was published in 1865 has never been substantiated. Louis Weichmann to Joseph Holt, October 23, 1866, February 10, 1874, both in Holt Papers; James May to Andrew Johnson, September 6, 1873, in Johnson Papers, Microcopy, Roll 37. Easton (Pa.) *Sentinel*, July 25, 1867, p. 2, reported during the John Surratt trial that the plea was nothing new to the well-posted friends of Mrs. Surratt. See also *The Great Conspiracy, A Book of Absorbing Interest! Startling Developments . . . and the Life and Extraordinary Adventures of John H. Surratt, the Conspirator* (Philadelphia: Barclay, 1866), 180.

Anna Surratt or Herold's sisters when they came pleading for mercy, and referred them to Holt. And as Father Walter wrote of Holt, "He had no more feeling for the poor daughter than a piece of stone, he referred her to the President." Mrs. Winfield Scott Hancock said that her husband never understood why he was held responsible by the public for Mrs. Surratt's death, because he had several times presented Johnson with the reasons why she should be pardoned, but Johnson had ignored them. John Ford also came to Washington with a letter urging commutation, which former Postmaster General Montgomery Blair later assured him had reached the president on that day. As the Albany *Argus* saw so perceptively, the president was in some ways a victim of circumstance. "It would not do for him, profiting as he does in one sense, by the crime of these conspirators, to appear to be lenient to their offense, or indifferent to their punishment." Since Johnson did consider one of the arguments in the petition, sex, and rejected it, it does not appear that he would have changed his mind, although a plea signed by five members of the court would have presented him an easy out had he wished to take it.[52]

Although there was duplicity on the part of both men, Johnson still comes out better than Holt. Johnson never did try to shift the blame away from his own responsibility even in later political campaigns. Noran Maynard wrote Holt in 1873 that when Johnson was assailed during a Congressional campaign for his treatment of Mrs. Surratt, he replied manfully and not apologetically that she had been tried and sentenced by a constitutional tribunal and he had seen no reason not to carry out the sentence. Yet Holt, whom defense lawyer John Clampitt charged was one of those most responsible for influencing the commission to vote for the death penalty for Mrs. Surratt, attempted to avoid his responsibility. Holt's protestation has a rather hollow ring to it: "I

---

52. *Trial of the Assassins and Conspirators for the Murder of Abraham Lincoln*, 90; New York *Times*, July 7, 1865, p. 2; Townsend, *Life, Crime and Capture*, 79; Walter, "The Surratt Case: A True Statement of Facts," 140. It is interesting that Johnson referred the petitioners to Holt, not Stanton. When lawyers Aiken and Clampitt asked for Mrs. Surratt's body, Stanton also referred them to Holt. New York *Tribune*, July 17, 1865, p. 1; Joseph Holt to R. D. Mussey, July 9, 1873, in Holt Papers; Albany *Argus*, July 13, 1865, p. 2; Almira R. Hancock, *Reminiscences of Winfield Scott Hancock* (New York: Charles L. Webster, 1887), 109, John T. Ford, Manuscript, N.d., in Ford's Theatre Collection; Albany *Argus*, July 7, 1865, p. 2.

should have shuddered to propose the brief period of two days within which the sentences should be executed, for with all the mountain of guilt weighing on the heads of those wretched culprits, I still recognized them as human beings with souls to be saved or lost."[53]

Once again, there is no evidence that Stanton was very heavily involved in Holt's deceit, though he was in favor of Mrs. Surratt's hanging. Secretary Welles was no doubt correct when he wrote Johnson that Stanton and Holt did not desire peace and conciliation, and though he felt they were leagued together, he was forced to admit, "I have no positive proof of the fact, and I should not . . . feel justified in placing him [Holt] before the public." On August 29, 1873, S. B. Sanders wrote to Johnson, "I and others have always charged the murder of Mrs. Surratt to Holt and Stanton, particularly the former." Stanton, like Johnson, was also ill at the period of the execution and therefore physically incapable of becoming too involved.[54]

Historians have attempted to make a connection between Stanton's dismissal from the cabinet and the discovery by Johnson that there was a clemency plea. But as far as can be determined, contemporaries never suggested such a connection; and Johnson, in a confidential executive document dated December 12, 1867, made it clear that his dismissal of Stanton was the culmination of a long series of events, and he made no mention of the clemency plea.[55]

In many respects, the execution of Mrs. Surratt was symbolic. Defense lawyer William Doster wrote, "More than all, it was the period proper for punishment of the rebellion, and somebody must be hanged for example's sake." Judge Levi Turner, speaking to Samuel Mudd of his innocence, said that somebody had to suffer and it was just as well Mudd should as anybody else. General Kautz saw the same factor at work but added very perceptively, "It was apparent to me . . . that there

---

53. Noran Maynard to Joseph Holt, November 14, 1873, in Holt Papers; John W. Clampitt, in Chicago *Times-Herald*, March 23, 1895, p. 1; Kautz, "Reminiscences of the Civil War," 111; DeWitt, *Assassination of Abraham Lincoln*, 247.

54. Benjamin Thomas and Harold Hyman, *Stanton: The Life and Times of Lincoln's Secretary of War* (New York: Alfred A. Knopf, 1962), 430; Eisenschiml, *In the Shadow of Lincoln's Death*, 131; Gideon Welles to Andrew Johnson, July 27, 1869, in Johnson Papers, Microcopy, Roll 37; Baltimore *Sun*, July 4, 1865, p. 1

55. Thomas and Hyman, *Stanton*, 549; Presidential Executive Documents, Confidential, E, 40th Cong., 2nd Sess., in Stanton Papers.

would be a reaction and those who were instrumental in her execution, would regret that they had permitted Mrs. Surratt to be hung."[56]

There remains some question of Mrs. Surratt's role in the abduction plot. Many have suspected before and since that she, like Weichmann, could hardly have been ignorant of all knowledge about it, but this is not clearly proven. Viewed today, there seems to be much in her favor as regards the murder, including the statements of people like Paine that she was not involved, the legitimate business she had at Surrattsville, her poor eyesight, and the conflicting testimony of the arresting officers about her alleged confrontation with Paine.[57]

In any case, the evidence clearly shows that historians' arguments that a military versus a civil trial was a key to the outcome is untrue, except in the broad sense that the Supreme Court decision *ex parte Milligan* might be construed to invalidate the entire proceedings on constitutional grounds. However, Mrs. Surratt before a civil jury in 1865 could hardly have expected to receive less than life imprisonment, which is exactly what she would have gotten from the commission had the wishes of the court been carried out. In reality, the excited and violent nature of the times were much more of a factor, for as Benjamin Williams wrote in 1964, "In an attempt to find the reasons for Mrs. Surratt's execution it is necessary to examine much more than the legal aspects of the case. Three elements . . . conspired . . . the temper of the times, the political ramifications of the trial, and the state of law when the events happened."[58] Had historians examined all of these elements, they would not have presented a distorted picture of the case of Mrs. Surratt.

---

56. Doster, *Lincoln and Episodes of the Civil War*, 258–59; N. Mudd, *Life of Dr. Samuel A. Mudd*, 239; Hal Higdon, *The Union vs. Dr. Mudd* (Chicago: Follett, 1964), 71; Kautz, "Reminiscences of the Civil War," 111.

57. Albany *Argus*, July 18, 1865, p. 2; Robert J. Donovan, *The Assassins* (New York: Harper Bros., 1952), 273; Oldroyd, *Assassination of Abraham Lincoln*, 130–31; Richard M. Smoot, *The Unwritten History of the Assassination of Abraham Lincoln* (Clinton, Mass.: W. J. Coulter, 1908), 70. For those defending her innocence completely, see Campbell, *Case For Mrs. Surratt*; DeWitt, *Assassination of Abraham Lincoln*, 230, 257; Eisenschiml, *In the Shadow of Lincoln's Death*, 101; Samuel B. Arnold, *Defence and Prison Experiences of a Lincoln Conspirator: Statements and Autobiographical Notes* (Hattiesburg, Miss.: Book Farm, 1943), 63; Gray, "The Fate of the Lincoln Conspirators," 635.

58. For comments on the Milligan decision, see DeWitt, *Assassination of Abraham Lincoln*, 145, 162; A. Oakey Hall, "The Surratt Cause Célèbre," *Green Bag*, VIII (1896), 201; Benjamin Williams, "The Trial of Mrs. Surratt and the Lincoln Assassination Plot," *Alabama Lawyer*, XXV (1964), 23.

13.

Dr. Samuel A. Mudd

In the same way that Mrs. Surratt's case has elicited much sympathy from historians, so has that of Dr. Samuel A. Mudd. For, again, there is much uncertainty as to the exact nature of his involvement. Most historians have believed, and with apparent justification, that if Booth had not broken his leg as he jumped from Lincoln's box, the name of Dr. Mudd would never have been mentioned in relation to the assassination.

Louis Weichmann was again one of the primary witnesses testifying for the prosecution. He related that on January 15, 1865, he and John Surratt had been passing down Seventh Street when someone had called out, "Surratt, Surratt." It turned out to be Dr. Mudd, who was walking with John Wilkes Booth, whom he introduced. The group went around to the National Hotel to Booth's room, from which Surratt and Mudd went into the corridor for a private conversation with the actor. Then, as they sat around a table, Booth took out an envelope and made marks on it that appeared to be roads or lines, though Weichmann claimed he could not see or hear exactly what they were doing. Mudd also admitted in statements to authorities that in November, 1864, Booth had been in Bryantown, supposedly buying horses, and had spent a night at his house.[1]

The testimony of the officers involved in Mudd's arrest, the validity of some of which is doubtful, also made a bad impression in his case. William Williams, who went to Mudd's home on Tuesday, April 18, said that Mudd was uneasy and unwilling to given information. He ne-

1. Benn Pitman, *The Assassination of President Lincoln and the Trial of the Conspirators* (New York: Funk and Wagnalls, 1954), 16, 114; Samuel A. Mudd, April 21, 1865, Statement, in Letters Received, File M 315, JAO, RG 153, NA. See Nettie Mudd, *The Life of Dr. Samuel A. Mudd, Containing His Letters from Fort Jefferson, Dry Tortugas, Where He Was Imprisoned Four Years for Alleged Complicity in the Assassination of Abraham Lincoln* (Marietta, Ga.: Continental Book, 1955), 42.

glected to mention that the officers had proceeded to his home because they were informed by Mudd himself, through his cousin, Dr. George Mudd, that some suspicious men had been at his house. Detective Simon Gavacan testified that Mudd had flatly denied that two men had come to his house on the Saturday morning following the assassination. Colonel H. H. Wells also gave his impression of the unwilling and embarrassed attitude of Mudd.

Dr. Mudd's slaves also painted an unflattering picture of their master, with tales of rebels hiding down in the woods the previous summer, one of them being Surratt. Mudd also allegedly talked of the Baltimore Plot to kill Lincoln. He was also portrayed as a cruel man who had shot one of his slaves while threatening to send some others to Richmond.

Other damaging testimony was given by Daniel Thomas, who testified that Mudd had told him that Lincoln and the entire cabinet were abolitionists and that they and Union men in Maryland would be killed in six or seven weeks. William Evans testified that the previous winter he had seen Mudd go into Mrs. Surratt's house, and Marcus Norton said that on March 31, Mudd had entered his room in the National Hotel looking for Booth.[2]

It is again obvious that, given the circumstances of 1865, Mudd's setting of Booth's leg and his previous connection with him made the evidence seem formidable. Nonetheless, defense testimony seemed to show that many of the witnesses against Mudd were of a dubious character. The incident described by the slaves, of rebels hiding in the woods, was shown to have taken place in 1861, and John Surratt was not involved. Other witnesses severely impugned the veracity of Daniel Thomas, among them his brother, who was a physician and who testified that Thomas had suffered a paralytic attack about six years before and was not now always right mentally. Jeremiah Mudd, his cousin, also testified that on December 23, 1865, the doctor and he had gone to Washington, and Mudd later verified that it was at this time, not in January, that the meeting which Weichmann described had taken place. Family and slaves also testified that Mudd had not been away overnight from March 1 through 5 and therefore could not have been in Washing-

---

2. Pitman, *The Assassination of President Lincoln*, 88–90, 168–77.

ton on March 3, when Norton testified that he had seen him. A great deal of testimony was also taken in an attempt to prove that it was not clearly known even on Saturday, April 15, 1865, who the assassin was.

However, the witness most favorable for Mudd was his cousin Dr. George Mudd, who brought out, after some objection by the judge advocate, that it was Mudd himself who had asked him to go and inform the authorities of the suspicious men. Mudd's case was a prime example of the pernicious effect the large rewards could have, with the detectives coloring their story in order to play up their own role in the capture and thus to share a larger portion of the reward.[3]

Initially, the prospects of Dr. Mudd, like those of the other conspirators, were not good. The New York *Tribune* announced to its readers on April 28, 1865, "That Doctor is in jail in Washington, to be tried forthwith by Military Commission for a crime the pre-announced and sure penalty of which is death." The testimony of witnesses like Weichmann also bore heavily on Mudd, and on May 15 the New York *Times* correspondent described Mudd, "against whom it was at first supposed but little if anything of guilt could be shown, but against whom now the testimony thus far seems fearfully pointing."[4]

The press recorded the prisoner's reaction to the testimony in an attempt to indicate his guilt or innocence. When Colonel Wells testified, the New York *Times* said that his evidence was clear and comprehensive and fixed the guilt of Dr. Mudd as Booth's accomplice beyond a doubt. "It disturbed the defendant. . . . Mudd winced manifestly as Col. Wells detailed the defendant's prevarications and evasion, and his final acknowledgement of damaging facts." The following day, when it was brought out that Booth had purchased a horse on Mudd's recommendation, "the prisoner Mudd was visibly affected, his face becoming very red, his eyes discovering great uneasiness, and his general expression denoting consternation."[5]

However, it became apparent that as evidence was introduced to contradict some of the more damaging prosecution testimony, doubts

3. *Ibid.*, 179, 181–90, 193–97, 201–11.
4. New York *Tribune*, April 28, 1865, p. 4; New York *Times*, May 15, 1865, p. 1.
5. New York *Times*, May 17, p. 8, May 18, 1865, p. 1.

began to occur. The Washington *Evening Star* of May 29 said, "Mudd seems to be in good spirits, apparently gathering encouragement from the evidence in his behalf on Saturday to the effect that the clandestine gatherings in the pines near his residence were of parties avoiding arrest by General Sickles as long ago as 1861." The testimony of Thomas and Norton also greatly contributed to the weakening of the prosecution's case. The New York *Times* and New York *Tribune* correspondents both commented on the apparent unreliability of Thomas and showed a disinclination to see anyone convicted on the strength of such testimony. The *Times* attempted to weaken the importance of Thomas' testimony by pointing out that it was cumulative and did not elicit many new facts. The Chicago *Tribune* said Norton was evidently mistaken in his identity of Mudd and called Evans "an erratic individual" whose testimony was "worthless, and discredited by all who heard him testify." The New York *Tribune* correspondent summarized the defense testimony on May 31, saying it was weak, except in Mudd's case.[6]

There was obviously much more contemporary uncertainty about Mudd's guilt than about Mrs. Surratt's, and this undoubtedly had much to do with his escaping the gallows. The members of the commission were also divided. General Kautz commented that Mudd's guilt had not been proven, although General Harris, relying on phrenology, noted that Mudd possessed the bump of secrecy, which firmly convinced him of Mudd's guilt.[7]

In this case, as with some of the evidence against Jefferson Davis and other rebels, the government must have been aware that the testimony of certain witnesses was not very reliable. Daniel Thomas claimed that prior to the assassination he had informed the government of Mudd's utterances; but on May 25, J. N. Holland forwarded to Burnett Thomas' letter, which contained no mention of Lincoln's assassination and merely stated that Dr. George Mudd was not a good Union man.

6. Washington *Evening Star*, May 29, 1865, p. 2; New York *Times*, June 4, p. 1, June 7, 1865, p. 1; New York *Tribune*, May 19, 1865, p. 1; Chicago *Tribune*, June 7, 1865, p. 1; New York *Tribune*, May 31, 1865, p. 1.

7. August V. Kautz, "Reminiscences of the Civil War" (Typescript in August V. Kautz Papers, LC), 110; Thomas M. Harris, *Assassination of Lincoln: A History of the Great Conspiracy Trial of the Conspirators by a Military Commission and a Review of the Trial of John H. Surratt* (Boston: American Citizen, 1892), 80.

Nevertheless, the prosecution attempted to rely strongly on this testimony.[8]

Even now, however, despite evidence that Mudd was at least not involved in the manner the government believed he was, there remain certain questions regarding his conduct. One of these is how he could have failed to recognize Booth, whom he had previously known and who had spent a night under his roof. Mudd claimed that Booth had worn false whiskers when he came to his house, although no one else reported Booth being disguised, and he boldly rode out of Washington giving his correct name. On the other hand, one factor that seems to argue in favor of this story and that would verify Mudd's own assertion that he only became suspicious when Herold asked for a razor so Booth might shave his moustache, was that Mrs. Mudd had mentioned this to Lieutenant Alex Lovett the first time he talked with her and before Dr. Mudd had returned home. This would seem to lend credence to the tale, unless she and her husband had agreed upon the story they would tell.[9]

It has been suggested that Mudd's failure to identify Booth might have been due to the fact that government detectives were using a photograph of his brother Edwin, not only while pursuing the assassin but also during the conspiracy trials. It seems inconceivable that such a deception could have been maintained throughout the entire conspiracy trial, unless it was run in a very stringent manner, which it was not. Also, when they were clean shaven, the Booth brothers bore such a striking resemblance to each other that Colonel Conger at Garrett's barn momentarily mistook John for Edwin. According to the Washington *Evening Star*, "His [Edwin's] likeness to his brother, J. Wilkes Booth, is quite noticeable, he having the same classical features and finely cut chin." Such a transformation of the assassin's appearance as removal of his moustache might have caused could have been one fac-

8. Daniel J. Thomas, Statement, N.d., in Letters Received, File T 315, J. N. Holland to Henry L. Burnett, May 25, in Letters Received, File H 362, both in JAO, 1865, RG 153, NA.

9. Hal Higdon, *The Union vs. Dr. Mudd* (Chicago: Follett, 1964), 13, is probably the most balanced treatment of the subject. Dr. Samuel Mudd, April 21, 1865, Statement, in Record Book, File M, p. 66, Alex Lovett to Henry L. Burnett, May 2, 1865, in Record Book, File L, p. 59, both in JAO, RG 153, NA; Sarah Mudd to Joseph Holt, September 14, 1865, in Joseph Holt Papers, LC; N. Mudd, *Life of Dr. Samuel A. Mudd*, 32.

tor in persuading the government to use a picture of Edwin, whom he now more closely resembled than he did his own pictures with a heavy black moustache.[10]

If anything, however, sent Dr. Mudd to the Dry Tortugas, the impression of reluctance and hesitation he gave to those with whom he came in contact, the fact that a good case was made for his being a southern sympathizer, and the fact that he, like Mrs. Surratt, answered the need for someone to suffer for the crime are very likely responsible. In a letter to Mrs. Mudd on April 12, 1867, her brother, Jeremiah Dyer, mentioned a letter from General Hunter allegedly stating that neither he nor any of the court felt Dr. Mudd had anything to do with the crime but that he "was the victim of his own timidity." Mrs. Mudd also mentioned a conversation related to her by Mrs. Browning in which General Wallace had said, "If Booth had not broken his leg, we would never have heard the name of Dr. Mudd." However, he added, "The deed is done; somebody must suffer for it, and he may as well suffer as anybody else." R. A. Watts, in an article published in 1922, captured this contemporary perception very well. "All or nearly all the witnesses for the defense were either active sympathizers with the rebellion or at best of most doubtful loyalty to the government. . . . Every one of the defendants were most bitter in their hatred of Mr. Lincoln . . . what a boon to Arnold, Spangler, and Mudd, would a fair reputation for loyalty have been."[11]

Also, as with Mrs. Surratt, the suspicion arises that Mudd might have been involved in one of the abduction plots directed against Lincoln. Even those who were not entirely convinced that Mudd was involved in the president's murder seemed to find it hard to believe that Booth's previous association with Mudd concerned merely the pur-

---

10. Otto Eisenschiml, *In the Shadow of Lincoln's Death* (New York: Wilfred Funk, 1940), 68, and *Why Was Lincoln Murdered?* (Boston: Little Brown, 1937), 265, ignores this similarity between the Booth brothers and states that if Colonel Conger mistook John for Edwin, then the individual killed at Garrett's could not have been the assassin. Photograph marked BOOTH'S PHOTOGRAPH, in Exhibits, RG 153, NA; Washington *Evening Star*, May 31, 1865, p. 1. See George S. Bryan, *The Great American Myth* (New York: Carrick and Evans, 1940), 186–87, for argument that Edwin's photo may merely have been misfiled among materials on John as well as the fact that some initial rumors identified Edwin as the assassin.

11. N. Mudd, *Life of Dr. Samuel A. Mudd*, 37–38, 353–54; R. A. Watts, "The Trial and Execution of the Lincoln Conspirators," *Michigan History Magazine*, VI (1922), 109.

chase of horses or land. However, Samuel Arnold said of that relationship, "He [Booth] said he had been down in their neighborhood to purchase horses, and had a nice time there. This was the only time I ever heard Booth mention Dr. Mudd's name."[12]

Mudd himself, although he and his family naturally remained quite bitter about what had happened to him, saw quite clearly the effect that aroused opinion in 1865 had had on his case. "Owing to the excitement and influence prevailing at the time of my trial, I could excuse much; but since time has elapsed for a sober, dispassionate consideration of the matter, I am becoming vexed at my protracted exile. I suppose it is all human."[13]

Appended to the Pitman edition of the trial is the statement of Captain George W. Dutton, in whose custody Mudd was placed on the way to Fort Jefferson. Dutton claimed that Mudd confessed having known Booth when he came to his house and that Weichmann had told the truth about the meeting with Booth. Mudd wrote bitterly of this in August, 1866: "The conduct of Judge Holt . . . his attempt through a parcel of false and perjured statements, to bring public opinion to bear upon my case, after the trial was over, and when I had no power to rebut, shows his animus and is unpardonable for one occupying his position. I am ignorant of the laws, but certainly this act does not appear to me like justice."[14]

Historians have also questioned the reason why the conspirators were finally sent to Fort Jefferson, Dry Tortugas, instead of Albany Penitentiary, which was their original destination. However, the rather simple explanation for this seems to be that in the Dry Tortugas the prisoners would not be subject to a court order for release on a writ of habeas corpus. This is exactly the strategy that defense attorney Thomas Ewing had in mind, for he wrote to his father on July 7 that he hoped

12. Osborn H. Oldroyd, *The Assassination of Abraham Lincoln, Flight, Pursuit, Capture, and Punishment of the Conspirators* (Washington: O. H. Oldroyd, 1901), 58, 260, claimed that he was told by an unquestionable authority that a short time before his death Mudd admitted that he was connected with the original plot to kidnap the president. Unfortunately, he did not identify his source. Samuel B. Arnold, *Defence and Prison Experiences of a Lincoln Conspirator: Statements and Autobiographical Notes* (Hattiesburg, Miss.: Book Farm, 1943), 29.

13. N. Mudd, *Life of Dr. Samuel A. Mudd*, 172.

14. Pitman, *The Assassination of President Lincoln*, 421; N. Mudd, *Life of Dr. Samuel A. Mudd*, 202–203.

to apply to the district judge in Maryland under provisions of the act of 1863, and "if this application fails I expect to go to New York as soon as the prisoners are taken to that state for imprisonment, and there apply to Judge Nelson for a writ of habeas corpus." Orville H. Browning wrote to Ewing on July 19, 1865, after the place of imprisonment had been changed: "The Authorities have probably determined that the question shall not be brought before the judicial tribunals, and have made this disposition of the prisoners to preclude a hearing upon habeas corpus. If their destination is as supposed, they are beyond the reach of the law, and will have to await the course of events to bring them relief." There seems no reason to doubt that the government anticipated the defense tactics and took action accordingly.[15]

The New York *Herald* correspondent caught sight of the prisoners at the arsenal taking their afternoon recreation on July 15, 1865, and they were mingling freely with other prisoners, including Confederate General Harris. If this report is correct, it is again apparent that the government had nothing to hide, or else the prisoners would hardly have been allowed to communicate with a captive rebel general.[16]

That sentiment regarding Mudd was divided ought not to obscure the fact that a majority of northerners probably still considered him guilty and felt that the harsher climate of the Dry Tortugas was a more fitting punishment. A friend of General Ewing wrote to him: "I wonder at your success in mitigating Mudd's sentence. He was proven more guilty than Mrs. Surratt. Your argument on the facts was ingenious and very able, but did not convince me that the d——d rascal ought not to have been hung provided the trial had been by an authorized tribunal."[17]

Indeed the Dry Tortugas was hardly a pleasant place for any prisoner, but charges that the Lincoln conspirators were more harshly treated than other prisoners are untrue. Such a view has been fostered because of Samuel Arnold's bitter statements about cruel treatment being di-

---

15. Easton (Pa.) *Sentinel*, July 27, 1865, p. 2; New York *Herald*, July 19, 1865, p. 1. Eisenschiml, in *Why Was Lincoln Murdered?*, 469, of course believed that this was one more part of the plot to silence the conspirators. Baltimore *Sun*, July 21, 1865, p. 2; Thomas Ewing, Jr. to Thomas Ewing, Sr., July 7, 1865, Orville H. Browning to Thomas Ewing, Jr., July 19, 1865, in Ewing Family Papers, LC.

16. New York *Herald*, July 15, 1865, p. 1.

17. J. M. Connell to Thomas Ewing, July 17, 1865, in Ewing Family Papers.

rectly ordered by Stanton and his belief that a prisoner with yellow fever was deliberately placed near the conspirators so that they might contract the disease and die. However, fellow prisoner Ed Spangler said that the commanding officer of Fort Jefferson had told him there were no more stringent orders in his case than in that of any other prisoners. Some of the more stringent treatment they received was due to Dr. Mudd's attempt to escape. But while harsh by our standards, the treatment of the conspirators was comparatively mild when compared to that of other prisoners who were forced to carry cannonballs, were strung up by their thumbs, and were half-drowned in the ocean. On August 31, 1867, the Washington *Star* described the prisoners as being lodged like all others in the second tier of casements in cool, dry, and airy quarters. "They manage to live pretty well on the government rations although they were a little thinner than usual, but considering everything they were better off than many other prisoners had been." [18]

While confined in the Dry Tortugas, Mudd took quite an interest in the John Surratt trial and public reaction to it. On January 15, 1867, he wrote: "The arrival of Surratt will be the advent of new excitement, and the reiteration of every species of lie and slander which were given currency at our trial and subsequently, and serve as a pretext to continue my unlawful and unjust imprisonment." On March 25, he commented on the bearing of the John Surratt trial on his own case. "Should Surratt have a speedy and impartial trial, I have more hopes from its results than from everything else, for I know it is bound to lead to my entire exculpation, and it will be impossible for those in power to hold me against the will of an enlightened public." He also realized very clearly the changed conditions between 1865 and 1867 when he wrote, "Had Surratt been on the same trial that I was, he would certainly have been hung though innocent—no amount of evidence in his favor could have saved him." At the end of the trial Mudd concluded that they had tried Surratt for murder and proved without doubt the innocence of Mrs. Surratt. He wondered why the newspapers did not take up his own case. [19]

18. Arnold, *Defence and Prison Experiences of a Lincoln Conspirator*, 86, 109; Edward Spangler, Statement, N.d., in Ford's Theatre Collection, Maryland Historical Society; Washington *Evening Star*, quoted in Baltimore *Sun*, August 31, 1867, p. 4.
19. N. Mudd, *Life of Dr. Samuel A. Mudd*, 220, 230–45, 250, 314.

In 1867, the Assassination Committee, during its attempts to gather evidence on which to impeach Andrew Johnson by connecting him with the assassination plot, determined to interrogate the prisoners to ascertain what, if anything, they could reveal. Congressman Ben Butler wrote General John Pope on September 10, 1867, that the committee could call the prisoners to Washington, but he felt that unless any of the evidence proved to be material enough to be examined in full committee, it would be better to examine them at Fort Jefferson in order to avoid expense, trouble, and the danger of escaping. He therefore dispatched William H. Gleason, notary public of Florida, to examine them. Mudd, Spangler, and Arnold were all interviewed, but Mudd revealed little that was new. He merely stated that he had never heard expressed a desire favorable to the assassination, never had a personal knowledge of the proposed assassination, was not acquainted with Mrs. Surratt, knew Booth and John Surratt but not intimately, and did not know O'Laughlin, Spangler, Paine, Herold, or Atzerodt prior to the assassination.[20]

Almost immediately after their imprisonment, efforts had been made to procure a pardon for Mudd and his fellow prisoners. Mrs. Mudd appealed to Holt, but apparently she found the judge advocate a hard man to deal with. She did, however, write to him on September 14, 1865, "Your dignified and reserved manner somewhat awed me, I thought I could see through the reserve a kind heart, and you felt for me on my distress." Efforts were also made to bring a writ of habeas corpus to bear even in the Dry Tortugas, and A. S. Ridgely, attorney for Mudd's brother-in-law, Jeremiah Dyer, made application to Chief Justice Chase. In case Chase had any doubt as to his jurisdiction, Ridgely asked that a date might be set when he and Reverdy Johnson might argue before him as to why he should get involved. However, on December 28, 1866, Chase replied, "The within application has been considered and is denied."[21]

The president had proven equally powerless to act. Dyer wrote to his sister that when John Ford had seen Johnson in February, 1866, the

20. Benjamin Butler to John Pope and to William H. Gleason, September 10, 1867, Gleason, December 19, 1867, Statement, Samuel A. Mudd, December 3, 1867, Statement, all in Benjamin Butler Papers, LC.

21. Sarah Mudd to Joseph Holt, September 4, 1865, in Holt Papers; A. S. Ridgely to Salmon P. Chase, December 28, 1866, in Salmon P. Chase Papers, LC.

president had told him that Mudd was merely a victim of circumstances and ought not to have been imprisoned. However, while he would try to release him when he could, at the present such action would merely provide the Radicals more fuel to use against him. On April 9, 1866, Dyer expressed hope that the Milligan decision might aid Mudd. Mrs. Mudd attributed similar sentiments to Johnson, although he did promise her that he would issue a pardon before his term of office ended. However, when she finally received the message to come for the pardon in 1869, and asked Johnson how she might send it to the Dry Tortugas, he washed his hands of the matter.[22]

However, by 1869, there had been some shift of opinion regarding Mudd, much of it coming about because of the work he had done at Fort Jefferson during a yellow fever epidemic. A few days before his release some soldiers aboard a transport belonging to the 3rd Artillery saw him walking on the parapet and cheered him. Spangler and Arnold were also freed with Mudd, but for Michael O'Laughlin the pardon came too late, as he had perished a victim of yellow fever. Mudd returned to Bryantown to take up his farming and somewhat diminished medical practice and was soon joined by Spangler. In January, 1883, he took sick with a cold and died.[23]

Historians have long viewed Mudd as a victim of military justice, in the same way they have Mrs. Surratt, although because he escaped the gallows, his case has not aroused the same intense sympathy. There is certainly more evidence that Mudd was not involved, and some of this registered with contemporaries. Nonetheless, the circumstantial evidence and southern sympathies attributed to Mudd make it apparent that under the circumstances he was fortunate to have escaped more severe punishment.

22. N. Mudd, *Life of Dr. Samuel A. Mudd*, 165, 174; Oldroyd, *Assassination of Abraham Lincoln*, 251; Watts, "The Trial and Execution of the Lincoln Conspirators," 106.
23. Higdon, *Union vs. Dr. Mudd*, 203. The Mudd family has keenly felt what they consider a great wrong done to their ancestor, and Mudd's grandsons have been waging a campaign at the state and federal level to win exoneration for their grandfather.

14.

Paine, Herold, Atzerodt, O'Laughlin, Arnold, and Spangler

The other alleged conspirators have received less historical notice than either Mrs. Surratt or Dr. Mudd, but among these, one of the most fascinating has always been Lewis Paine. However, there appeared to be little need to devote much attention to his case, or at least to the question of his guilt or innocence. It seemed quite apparent that Paine, who also used the alias of Wood and whose real name was Louis Thornton Powell, had boldly entered the Seward home, attacked the secretary of state, and wounded several members of his household. He was fully identified by several of the individuals involved and freely confessed his guilt to various people including Major Eckert and his lawyer, William E. Doster. The defense lawyers could do little more than admit their client's guilt and fall back on a plea of insanity in order to mitigate his actions, although such a plea met with very little success. While historians could muster some degree of sympathy for Paine because he had undergone a military trial and his youth was so needlessly wasted, the facts in his case seemed fairly conclusive.[1]

As some historians have noted, the authorities initially exhibited confusion as to who had committed the assault on Seward. Booth, John Surratt, and George Atzerodt were all mentioned as candidates, but all three differed radically in appearance from Paine. On some of the reward posters the description of Booth was very brief, whereas that of

---

1. William Bell, Statement, N.d., in Evidence Book, File B, p. 4, George F. Robinson, April 21, 1865, Statement, in Evidence Book, File R, p. 74, both in JAO, 1865, RG 153, NA; Benn Pitman, *The Assassination of President Lincoln and the Trial of the Conspirators* (New York: Funk and Wagnalls, 1954), 154–60, 161–68, 308–17; William E. Doster, *Lincoln and Episodes of the Civil War* (New York: G. P. Putnam's Sons, 1915), 266–72; United States Congress, House, Committee on the Judiciary, *Impeachment Investigation, Testimony Taken Before the Judiciary Committee of the House of Representatives in the Investigation of the Charges Against Andrew Johnson*, 39th Cong., 2nd Sess., 40th Cong., 1st Sess. (Washington: Government Printing Office, 1867), 381, 674. See Vaughan Shelton, *Mask for Treason* (Harrisburg: Stackpole Books, 1965), 401–403 for a view that Paine was innocent.

Paine was so full as to include details such as soft and small hands and a voice that was thin and inclined to tenor.[2]

Such details have led some to charge that the reward posters might have been prepared after the suspects were in custody; but the posters appeared on April 17, before Paine could possibly have been apprehended, as both the Washington *Evening Star* and Boston *Evening Transcript* carried copies on that date. There is also no puzzle as to where Paine's description came from, for Britten A. Hill provided this information in a note to Stanton, after talking with Seward's soldier nurse, George Robinson, and servant, Bell. The description coincides almost exactly with the reward poster even down to Bell's statement that the assassin had a thin, fine voice.[3]

It is not surprising that with a murderous assault occurring, there was some confusion as people struggled for their lives. Nonetheless, the events can be pieced together pretty well from the recollections of participants. The secretary's daughter, Fanny, who was in the room with her father, said that she saw her brother Fred, who was dazed and bleeding, enter the room with the assassin and that they, along with nurse Robinson, struggled around the bed. She did not see her other brother, Augustus, enter the room, but when she did see him his forehead was covered with blood. Augustus' presence was also confirmed by attending physician Dr. Tullio Verdi. "His injuries, however, were comparatively light—one was from a blow with the butt-end of a pistol, on the upper and middle part of the forehead; the other a cut over the metacarpal bone of the thumb on his right hand."[4]

Fanny Seward and her mother both verified that State Department messenger Emrick Hansell had been stabbed by Paine as he rushed down the stairs—a fact that Hansell himself reportedly related to Rob-

2. *The War of the Rebellion: A Compilation of the Official Records of the Union and Confederate Armies* (130 vols., Washington: Government Printing Office, 1880–1901), Ser. I, Vol. XLVI, Pt. 3, pp. 782–83; New York *World*, April 17, 1865, p. 8; New Orleans *Times-Picayune*, April 20, 1865, p. 4—all described either Atzerodt or Surratt as the assailant and mentioned his beard. Shelton, *Mask for Treason*, 40–42, 47.

3. Britten A. Hill to Edwin Stanton, April 16, 1865, in Edwin M. Stanton Papers, LC. For charges of tampering with reward posters, see David Balsiger and Charles E. Sellier, Jr., *The Lincoln Conspiracy* (Los Angeles: Schick Sunn Classic Books, 1977), 200.

4. Patricia C. Johnson (ed.), "I Have Supped Full on Horrors: Diary of Fanny Seward," *American Heritage*, X (1959), 98; Western Saint Louis *Homeopathic Observer*, quoted in New York *Times*, May 18, 1865, p. 1.

inson. Fanny's assertion that she had first opened the door from her father's room to see what was going on in the hall readily explained how the assassin knew which room the secretary was occupying. This was confirmed by her mother and Robinson. The two Seward women also indicated the severity of the secretary's previous injuries from his carriage fall, including a broken arm and jaw. Two dental experts who treated the secretary also mentioned his jaw fracture, although it is still not clear whether, at the time of the attack, he was wearing a steel collar, which might possibly have saved him from greater harm.[5]

Another interesting figure in the Seward case was George Robinson, a man about whom little has been known and many misstatements have been made, including the claim by one historian that he was black. The Robinson case is a good example of how historians have made errors by making exaggerated claims based on little or no research. There was really no reason for this, because an easy search in the National Archives would have revealed his long career in government service—a career that was enhanced because of his efforts to protect Seward. Robinson, like Louis Weichmann, was apparently not a man to let the government forget what he had done for his country.

Robinson had been drafted August 15, 1863, at Bangor, Maine, and assigned to Company B, 8th Maine Volunteers. On May 20, 1864, he was wounded at Bermuda Hundred near Bottom Church, Virginia, and after spending some time at Fortress Monroe and Hammond Hospital, he was assigned to Douglas General Hospital to await transfer to Maine. While stationed there, he was detailed, on April 12, 1865, to serve as nurse for William Seward, an assignment that was to propel him into the national limelight.[6]

On May 19, 1865, he was discharged with the rank of private, and on June 6 he was appointed a clerk in the Treasury Department, where he

5. Johnson (ed.), "I Have Supped Full on Horrors," 64–65, 97–98; Frederick W. Seward, *Seward at Washington as Senator and Secretary of State* (New York: Derby and Miller, 1891), 279; Washington *Evening Star*, April 18, 1865, p. 1. See also Richmond *Whig*, April 22, 1865, p. 4. John K. Lattimer, "The Stabbing of Lincoln's Secretary of State on the Night the President Was Shot," *Journal of the American Medical Association*, XVIIXCII (1965), 102.

6. George Robinson, Enlisted Service Record, in RG 94, "Records of the Adjutant General's Office," NA. For his biography see *In Memoriam: George Foster Robinson* (San Francisco: Military Order of the Loyal Legion of the United States, 1907), in Letters Received, File 5979, ACP, 1872, RG 94, NA. Hartford *Weekly Times*, April 22, 1865, p. 2.

remained until his resignation in November, 1866. He returned to his farm in Island Falls, and he also applied for and received a pension for the injuries he received during the war and also for his wounds in defending Secretary Seward. Grateful citizens in New York offered him a farm in the West and collected $1,600 for him.[7]

On January 8, 1869, he reentered government service, being appointed a clerk in the Quartermaster General's Office of the War Department. In response to a request by the Maine legislature, Congress awarded him a gold medal and $5,000 on March 1, 1871.[8]

The backing he received because of the Seward incident is quite evident. His request to be appointed a paymaster on January 21, 1875, was endorsed by Colonel N. P. Chipman, Vice President Hannibal Hamlin, Senator Lot Morrill, and Joseph Holt. Frederick Seward added, "I do not doubt that if appointed, he would discharge the duties of that responsible position with assiduity and fidelity, creditable to himself and to the Government." On June 23, 1879, he was finally appointed a paymaster with the rank of major in the United States Army.[9]

Robinson and his wife were also not reticent about playing on the event for future advancement. In 1895, Robinson wrote to the adjutant general, George D. Ruggles, asking why his name did not appear in the *Army Register* among those receiving medals. The adjutant general finally ordered that his name would appear in the 1896 register. Also in 1895, Mrs. Robinson wrote to President Grover Cleveland in an attempt to gain for her husband the rank of paymaster general, and in the letter she urged the protection of Seward's life as one of the prime reasons he should be promoted; however, she was not successful. Robinson retired from the army in 1896 and made his home in Pomona, California. On April 23, 1906, he was promoted to lieutenant colonel on the retired

7. *In Memoriam: George Foster Robinson*, George F. Robinson, in Pension File, Application Nos. 69800, 897284, Certificate Nos. 67463, 692089, RG 94, NA; Haverhill (Mass.) *Gazette*, July 7, 1865, p. 2; Boston *Evening Transcript*, May 16, 1865, p. 3.

8. *In Memoriam: George Foster Robinson*, George F. Robinson, "Major George F. Robinson, Paymaster, U.S. Army as to His Name Being Omitted From the 'Medal of Honor' List as Published in the Army Register" (Typescript), both in RG 94, NA; Washington *Evening Star*, September 20, 1892, in Ford's Theatre Collection, Maryland Historical Society.

9. George F. Robinson to Ulysses S. Grant, January 21, 1875, Frederick W. Seward to Secretary of War, February 18, 1875, and *In Memoriam: George Foster Robinson*, all in RG 94, NA.

list, and on August 16, 1907, he died.[10] Several historians would have avoided some basic errors if they had checked Robinson's record more closely.

If Lewis Paine was initially something of an enigma for people in 1865, the aura of mystery about him continued even after he admitted to being Louis Thornton Powell and was executed. At first there was an attempt to link him with the notorious Payne family of Kentucky and Canada; one of the members of this family was at the time in custody in New York for alleged complicity in the Saint Albans raid. This attempt failed, though the spelling *Payne* was often used to refer to him, despite the fact that he had signed his name Paine on an oath of allegiance to the government.[11]

There were many rumors about Paine's antecedents, including his supposed relationship to Robert E. Lee or Jefferson Davis. In an interesting letter to Stanton dated February 26, 1866, General Ethan Allen Hitchcock wrote, "Gen. Baker stated to me just prior to my writing that note, that Mr. Doster had attempted to perpetrate a fraud upon the public for the purpose of confirming the then general belief that the criminal's name was Payne and not Dan Murray Lee." The following day Hitchcock wrote Stanton about his own belief that Paine was Dan Murray Lee and added that he had been identified by members of the Williams family with whom Hitchcock had been residing and also by a nurse. "The nurse was sent for by your order, though you have never seen her, and after an interval of a day or two, she was confronted with Payne, and beyond all possibility of doubt she thought him a son of Smith Lee."[12]

Not satisfied with Paine's identity, Hitchcock had, on August 1, 1865, written Q. A. Gillmore to ascertain if there was a White Oak Station in Florida and if a clergyman named Powell lived near there. The matter was referred to General Israel Vodges, who sent Captain Adam C. Nutt

10. George F. Robinson to G. D. Ruggles, August 22, 1895, Mrs. Robinson to Grover Cleveland, March 26, 1895, both in RG 94, NA.

11. For correspondence regarding the Payne connection, see A. B. Newcombe, April 28, 1865, in Letters Received, File N 209, W. Hunter, May 1865, in Letters Received, File H 350, John A. Foster, N.d., in Record Book, File P, p. 69, 1865, all in JAO, RG 153, NA.

12. Ethan A. Hitchcock to Edwin Stanton, February 26, February 27, 1866, in Ethan Allen Hitchcock Papers, LC.

to investigate. Nutt obtained a copy of a daguerrotype of Paine that was supposed to be forwarded to Washington. Unfortunately, the picture had still not reached Hitchcock by October 30, and if it ever did there is no evidence of its survival or current location. Even though Hitchcock retained his doubts, those who investigated were evidently convinced that Paine was Powell, although admittedly they had never seen him.[13]

Although this doubt about Paine has been perpetuated by some historians, recently discovered materials in the National Archives can be used conclusively to show that Lewis Paine and Louis Thornton Powell were the same individual. Attempts were made to locate other signatures of Paine, besides the one on the oath of allegiance, but apparently not one was discovered. However, on a clothing record for Mosby's Regiment for 1864 appears a name that seems to be S. T. Powell. But on the receipt for the clothing, the name is clearly L. T. Powell, and a comparison of the formation of the *L* with that on the oath signed by Lewis Paine would seem to leave little doubt that Powell and Paine were the same individual.[14]

One other occurrence that may have caused some confusion was the affair of the mysterious Portuguese blockade runner, Joao Celestino. He had apparently made statements about wishing to assassinate Seward, and on April 18, 1865, he was arrested in Philadelphia. The unusual circumstance is that he was initially held on the monitors with the other conspirators and was included in Stanton's draft of the charges and specifications. Stanton informed the Portuguese ambassador, who

13. Ethan A. Hitchcock to Q. A. Gillmore, August 1, Adam C. Nutt to S. L. McHenry, August 26, J. K. Stickney to I. Vodges, August 28, I. Vodges to Ethan A. Hitchcock, August 29, Ethan A. Hitchcock to Edwin Stanton, October 30, 1865, all in Hitchcock Papers, LC.

14. Clothing and Extra Duty Rolls, Virginia Cavalry, Mosby's Regiment, 4th Quarter, 1864, in RG 109, "War Department Collection of Confederate Records," NA. Shelton tried to cast doubt in *Mask for Treason* about Paine's identity, but most of those involved identified Wood and Paine as being the same man. See Honora Fitzpatrick, John T. Holahan, Margaret Branson, Mrs. Martha Murray, Testimony, in Court Martial Record, 1371, 1718, 3075–76, 3919, 3659, Anna Surratt, April 28, 1865, Statement, in Record Book, File S, p. 79, JAO, all in RG 153, NA. Anna was a little more vague than the others as to Paine's identity.

checked into the matter, that there was definite proof of Celestino's implication in the assassination.[15]

There was no great mystery in 1865 about Celestino's arrest, for he had evidently been so vehement in his denunciation of Seward that people logically connected him with the deed. However, there exists great mystery as to the grounds on which he was held and his subsequent release without trial.[16]

While contemporaries were fascinated by Paine and had some doubts about his identity, to them his case seemed to be extremely simple. The New York *Herald* said at the trial's conclusion on July 7, "In the cases of Payne, Herold and Atzerodt there is a great concurrence of opinion." It also noted the great interest in Paine. "The first question asked by the newcomers 'Which is Payne?' he being by common consent the king villain of them all." The New York *Tribune* said of him on May 16, "Payne is obviously one of those brutes at large who would just as readily have undertaken to kill Davis as Seward if he had been hired for that job."[17]

Paine himself seemed ready to die, and his lawyer, Doster, repeated the remark one of the court members had made at lunch: "Well Payne seems to want to be hung, so I guess we might as well hang him." The plea of insanity met with very little success, although Doster argued in his memoirs that before a civil court Paine would have been acquitted by reason of insanity or else would have received a long prison term.[18]

The evidence, however, hardly bears out this contention, especially

15. Edwin Stanton, in Draft of Charges and Specifications, N.d. in Joseph Holt Papers, LC; DeFiganiere to Joao Celestino, May 3, 1865, in File Folder 12, RG 153, NA.

16. New York *Tribune*, April 17, 1865, p. 1; Chicago *Tribune*, April 19, 1865, p. 1; New York *Times*, April 19, 1865, p. 1. As Philip Van Doren Stern notes, there is some possibility that Celestino was a secret service agent or informer, in "The Unknown Conspirator," *American Heritage*, VIII (February, 1957), 54–59.

17. New York *Herald*, July 7, 1865, p. 1; New York *Tribune*, May 16, 1865, p. 1.

18. Doster, *Lincoln and Episodes of the Civil War*, 259–60, 281–82. As the president's Commission on the Causes and Prevention of Violence (1969) suggests, the treatment of assassins in regard to insanity pleas seems to depend to a very great degree on whether the assassins succeed or fail. Thus, when Richard Lawrence failed in his attempt to kill Andrew Jackson, a very liberal definition of insanity was applied and he was declared insane. Paine, who was perceived as intimately connected with Booth's murder of Lincoln, and was himself responsible for a vicious attack on Seward, stood little chance of escaping the consequences of his actions by any insanity plea.

since Doster, failing to show that Paine had the physical characteristics of insanity, argued a sort of environmental insanity in which Paine's southern background made him think there was nothing wrong in killing his enemy. Given the inflamed feeling against the South, such a tactic could hardly have succeeded before either a military or civil court. The Philadelphia *Evening Bulletin* could see no particular insanity in Paine's actions. "Payne was insane just as tens of thousands of other admirers and supporters of slavery were insane, taking woman-beating as the test, and he was insane just as Jeff. Davis, Jacob Thompson, Dr. Blackburn, Booth, Beall, Kennedy and the whole crew of secession butchers were insane." Commission member General Kautz said of Doster's argument: "It was rather a remarkable defense. The deeds charged were not denied."[19]

Paine's own alleged statements, as carried in the newspapers, did not win him much sympathy. On July 8, 1865, the New York *Times* reported that Paine had told Colonel Dodd that he believed himself acting under orders from the rebel authorities. Reverend A. D. Gillette, the minister who visited Paine before the execution, also said that Paine told him he had been in the rebel secret service, journeying between Richmond, Washington, and Baltimore. While there is some doubt about the authenticity of these reported statements, their publication certainly did Paine's case little good with the general public.[20]

Nevertheless, Paine's manly bearing on the scaffold and the fact that many people felt that slavery had killed his good spirit created sympathy for him. A few people, like Orville Browning, went so far as to argue that even Paine's execution was murder, since it was ordered by a military commission.[21]

Paine's alleged utterances that he had been well treated by the authorities and comments that Mrs. Surratt was innocent also gained some attention. However, the *Alta Californian* said, "Assertions are

19. Pitman, *Assassination of President Lincoln*, 308–17; Philadelphia *Evening Bulletin*, June 3, p. 4, June 27, 1865, p. 4; August V. Kautz Daily Journal (MS in August V. Kautz Papers, LC), June 21, 1865.

20. New York *Times*, July 8, 1865, p. 4; Amy Bassett, *Red Cross Reveries on the Home Front and Overseas* (Harrisburg: Stackpole, 1961), 88–89.

21. New York *Herald*, July 8, 1865, p. 1; Chicago *Tribune*, June 13, 1865, p. 2; James G. Randall and Theodore C. Pease (eds.), *Diary of Orville Hickman Browning* (2 vols.; Springfield, Ill.: Jefferson's Printing and Stationery, 1933), II, 37.

frequently made in regard to criminals, and are entitled to little credit unless corroborated, as this is not."[22]

Of the remaining conspirators, little needs to be said. Testimony seemed to indicate that David Herold had ridden out of Washington just shortly after Booth, had accompanied him in his flight, and then was discovered with him at Garrett's barn. His aiding of the assassin meant that he was doomed. The defense's attempt to show that he was a lightheaded, trifling boy could have no more effect than the insanity plea did for Paine.[23]

George Atzerodt's case was also similar. He admitted that he had been involved with the conspirators and had been approached to assassinate Johnson but had declined. The affidavit of Frank Monroe as to Atzerodt's alleged confession aboard the monitor, which the defense tried unsuccessfully to introduce, would appear to have been much more damaging than helpful to his cause. His own contention that he was not involved in the murder carried little weight, as did Paine's statement that Atzerodt was innocent. *Frank Leslie's Illustrated* summed up his case: "If this plea, in its technicalities, shall save the scoundrel, then we may relinquish our native ideas of justice."[24]

Ed Spangler, Ford's Theatre scene shifter, found himself a victim of circumstances; he was in the wrong place at the wrong time and also had previous connections with Booth. Among the many people who felt that Booth must have had help in the theater was General Kautz, who wrote, "An accomplice seemed to have been absolutely necessary to enable Booth to accomplish his purpose." Testimony of several individuals including Joseph Dye, Joseph Stewart, and Jacob Ritterspaugh—a soldier, a member of the audience, and a theater employee, respectively—bore very heavily against him.[25]

---

22. Washington *Evening Star*, July 7, 1865, p. 2; San Francisco *Alta Californian*, July 20, 1865, p. 2.

23. Otto Eisenschiml, *Why Was Lincoln Murdered?* (Boston: Little Brown, 1937), 253; Pitman, *Assassination of President Lincoln*, 85, 96–97.

24. See Pitman, *Assassination of President Lincoln*, 113, 118, 130–32, 139, 144–50, 234, for evidence concerning Atzerodt. See also Frank Monroe, April 23, Affidavit, in Letters Received, File M 26, H. H. Wells, April 25, in Letters Received, File W 550, George Atzerodt, Confession, N.d., in Record Book, File B, Evd. B. p. 2, all in JAO, 1865, RG 153, NA; *Frank Leslie's Illustrated*, July 15, 1865, p. 258.

25. Kautz Daily Journal, May 16, 1865. Pitman, *Assassination of President Lincoln*, 73–75, 79–81, 97–98; Joseph Dye, April 22, 1865, Statement, in Record Book, File D, p. 12;

On May 16, the New York *Times* correspondent said of Spangler, "So far the evidence fastens guilt upon him too strongly to be removed." However, on May 24, the Chicago *Tribune* said that Spangler had become part of the plot only a few hours before the murder and that if he did anything, it was to prepare the way for Booth's escape. While there was, therefore, some doubt over Spangler's role, it is surprising that he received only a six-year sentence, since contemporaries viewed him as one of the guiltiest of the conspirators.[26]

The two conspirators whose cases made the most favorable impression were Michael O'Laughlin and Samuel Arnold. The Washington *Evening Star* said on May 26 that O'Laughlin remained despondent "despite the strong effort made yesterday by the defence to prove an alibi for him." General Kautz concluded that neither Arnold's nor O'Laughlin's part in the murder had been shown. On June 26, the Washington *Daily National Intelligencer* praised lawyer Walter Cox's speech in behalf of his two clients, which it said "won golden opinions from all sorts of people here, who, with pardonable local feeling are proud of his abilities and of the eminent position which he occupies in his profession." It is readily apparent that a good many people believed that Arnold and O'Laughlin were engaged only in Booth's kidnapping scheme and were not convinced by the testimony that they were involved in murder. Therefore, there was satisfaction with their sentences of life imprisonment.[27]

Christian Rath, the hangman, astutely summarized the cases in 1898: "I believe that justice was meted out properly. The four persons surely guilty were executed. The remaining four . . . were not in the affair as

---

Robert Cooper, April 22, 1865, Statement, in Record Book, File C, p. 9, 1865, all in JAO, 1865, RG 153, NA.

26. New York *Times*, May 16, 1865, p. 1; Chicago *Tribune*, May 24, 1865, p. 2. See Pitman, *Assassination of President Lincoln*, 99–112, for defense testimony. *Trial of the Assassins and Conspirators for the Murder of Abraham Lincoln: The Evidence in Full with Arguments of Counsel on Both Sides, and the Verdict of the Military Commission* (Philadelphia: Barclay, 1865), 38, lumped Spangler with Mrs. Surratt, Mudd, and Atzerodt, while General Kautz called him an unwitting tool. See August V. Kautz, "Reminiscences of the Civil War" (Typescript, in August V. Kautz Papers, LC), 110–11.

27. Washington *Evening Star*, May 26, 1865, p. 2; Kautz, "Reminiscences of the Civil War," 110–11; Washington *Daily National Intelligencer*, June 26, 1865, p. 3. See also Albany *Argus*, June 12, 1865, p. 2; Chicago *Tribune*, June 13, 1865, p. 1.

deeply as the others. I do not think that they knew of the plot to kill, only to kidnap the President and his Cabinet." With the exception of Mrs. Surratt and Dr. Mudd this would appear to be a fair estimate.[28]

As in the case of Mrs. Surratt and Dr. Mudd, the trials of the other conspirators ended pretty much as they would have in a civil trial. Interestingly enough there was a great deal more discrimination between the defendants on the part of the public and the military judges than historians have been willing to admit and more than one might reasonably expect, given the aroused circumstances of 1865. Those who were perceived to be less deeply involved in the murder received lighter sentences, while the rest went to the gallows.

28. New York *Press*, September 4, 1898, p. 15.

15

A Trial Within a Trial: Testimony Concerning the Involvement of Southern Leaders

While the specific testimony introduced against the conspirators was not an unimportant factor in their convictions, another trial was occurring simultaneously, that of the Confederate leaders, many of whom were not yet in custody. The evidence introduced along these lines was also an extremely important factor in the trial's outcome.[1]

Historians have been quick to criticize the wide latitude of testimony permitted during the trial, yet in 1865 many people viewed the court, which was attempting to get to the bottom of a vast conspiracy, somewhat as we viewed the Warren Commission. On June 1, the New York *Herald*, saying how dull the regular testimony had become, added, "Now that the government has presented its case, the trial, so far as the prisoners in court are concerned, is scarcely more interesting than an ordinary prosecution for murder." Earlier the New York *Times* had said: "The trial now in progress is not a trial for simple murder. Its object is not merely to punish one or more individuals for a specific act of crime. The government seeks to unravel a conspiracy—to follow every clue that may be offered for the detection and arraignment of every person in any way connected, directly or indirectly, with the extended and formidable conspiracy, in which the assassination of the President was only one of the objects sought."[2]

Many people realized that the evidence elicited would not have been strictly legal before a civil court; but this merely served to reinforce the feeling that a military trial was correct, for as the Boston *Evening Transcript* said on June 23, 1865, "It is now abundantly proved that a court confined within strictly legal bounds, and never travelling out of the

---

1. Guy W. Moore, *The Case of Mrs. Surratt: Her Controversial Trial and Execution for Conspiracy in the Lincoln Assassination* (Norman: University of Oklahoma Press, 1954), 115.

2. David M. DeWitt, *The Assassination of Abraham Lincoln and Its Expiation* (New York: MacMillan, 1909), 113; New York *Herald*, June 1, 1865, p. 4; New York *Times*, May 15, 1865, p. 4.

narrow limits of merely technical investigation, could not have developed the full extent of the hideous plot." Confederate officer Henry Kyd Douglas expressed his belief that the focus of the trial had in fact become the effort to link the Confederates with the assassination conspiracy.[3]

Immediately after the assassination, the government had collected a great deal of evidence seeming to implicate Davis and the Confederates in Canada in the murder. An affidavit of one Godfrey Hyams was forwarded on May 11 by Alfred Russell, United States district attorney for the Eastern District of Michigan. Hyams claimed to have knowledge of Booth's being in Canada at various times in 1864 and also claimed to have taken part himself in a plot to introduce yellow fever into the United States by means of infected clothing. Hyams stated that the leading spirit behind this plot was Dr. Blackburn. This alleged yellow fever plot received a great deal of attention and investigation. Dr. Francis Tumblety, a quack medicine man, was taken into custody on suspicion that he was the infamous Blackburn, but he was eventually released, denying all knowledge of the crime and expressing only abhorrence for Lincoln's murder.[4] Other individuals like Hosea Carter and John Deveny also provided evidence that Booth had been in Canada in company with leading rebels in the fall of 1864. There was an abundance of such evidence and some of it was not even introduced during the trial.[5]

Davis' alleged utterances were also brought to the government's attention. Important among those who testified on this point was Lewis F. Bates, who claimed that Davis had said when informed of the assas-

3. Boston *Evening Transcript*, June 23, 1865, p. 2. Henry K. Douglas, *I Rode with Stonewall, Being Chiefly the War Experiences of the Youngest Member of Jackson's Staff from the John Brown Raid to the Hanging of Mrs. Surratt* (Chapel Hill: University of North Carolina Press, 1940), 342. A. Oakey Hall points out that of a total of 147 prosecution witnesses, 60 testified on the character of the rebellion, "The Surratt Cause Célèbre," *Green Bag*, VIII (1896), 197.

4. Alfred Russell, May 11, in Letters Received, File R 345, Godfrey F. Hyams, May 30, Letters Received, File H 437, all in JAO, 1865, RG 153, NA; On Tumblety, see Colonel J. Baker, May 16, 1865, Letters Received, File B 261, JAO, in RG 153, NA; New York *Times*, June 10, 1865, p. 2.

5. In RG 153, NA: James B. Fry, June 3, 1865, Record Book, File F, p. 53, John Deveney to Edwin Stanton, April 22, 1865, Statement, in Letters Received, File D 55, D 61, all in JAO, John A. Dix to William Seward, April 19, 1865, in File Folder 43, James Peadon to Dix, June 7, in Letters Received, File P 686, Evidence Against Booth, File B Evd. B, p. 2, both in JAO, 1865. Pitman, *Assassination of President Lincoln*, 38–39.

sination, "If it were to be done at all, it were better that, it were well done." Samuel P. Jones, a blind man from Richmond, also testified to having heard rewards offered by private secessionists for Lincoln's head and said Davis was behind the plot.[6]

There was also a great deal of evidence introduced concerning general rebel atrocities such as town and steamboat burning, mysterious cipher letters, and supposedly incriminating documents discovered in the rebel archives. For example, Edward Frazer testified to his own involvement in attempts to burn bridges and steamboats on the Mississippi River. The Reverend W. H. Ryder had picked up some papers in Richmond on April 29 that also related to the burning of towns and shipping. During his testimony Major Eckert expressed his belief that a cipher found by Assistant Secretary of War Charles A. Dana in the offices of Confederate Secretary of State Judah Benjamin was the same as one found in Booth's trunk.[7]

Quite naturally, the cipher letters with their hidden meanings held much fascination for the public. General Dix had forwarded, even before the assassination, the Charles Selby letter picked up in a New York streetcar by Mrs. Mary Hudspeth, and Charles Duell found another letter at Moorehead City, North Carolina, saying that "Pet" had done his work and old Abe was in hell. Equally mystifying was the so-called Lon letter addressed to J. W. B. and discovered by Charles Dawson, clerk at the National Hotel. A government detective by the name of Purdy, who had been mentioned in the letter, testified that it had been written by Lon McAleer, who had been involved with rebel spies.[8]

The Confederate archives also yielded documents such as General Order 111, which outlawed General Butler, and copies of documents organizing the Secret Service Bureau and providing for the capture and

6. Lewis F. Bates, May 29, 1865, Statement, in Joseph Holt Papers, LC; Benn Pitman, *The Assassination of President Lincoln and the Trial of the Conspirators* (New York: Funk and Wagnalls, 1954), 37–38, 46–47; Samuel P. Jones, May 4, 1865, Statement, in Record Book, File J, p. 56, JAO, RG 153, NA.

7. Edward Frazer, April 24, 1865, Statement, in Record Book, File F, p. 55, JAO, L. Polk to Jefferson Davis, February 27, 1864, File Folder 40, W. H. Ryder to General Sweet, May 8, 1865, in Letters Received, File R 365, JAO, all in RG 153, NA; Pitman, *Assassination of President Lincoln*, 47–50; *The Trial of the Alleged Assassins and Conspirators at Washington City, D.C., May and June, 1865, for the Murder of President Abraham Lincoln* (Philadelphia: T. B. Peterson and Brothers, 1865), 78.

8. John A. Dix, November 17, 1864, in Letters Received, Filed with Exhibits Court Martial Record; Charles Duell, N.d., in Letters Received, File D 366, JAO, 1865. For

destruction of enemy property by land or sea. Also discovered was a letter from Lieutenant Alston that offered to rid the Confederacy of some of its deadliest foes by striking at the heart's blood of her enemies.[9]

Suspicion was also cast on the rebel army when Henry Von Steinacker, who claimed to have been on the staff of General Edward Johnson, testified that the assassination conspiracy was well known in the army. He testified to a meeting between Booth and officers of the Stonewall Brigade, the purpose of which was to send men north to release prisoners, burn cities, and assassinate the president and cabinet.[10]

Also extremely important were statements by Union prisoners about alleged utterances of their captors and also their mistreatment. Some of this evidence was solicited by the government, but a good deal of it was given voluntarily. Marshal McPhail was especially active in gathering this type of information and suggested that a committee be appointed to take additional testimony. Special attention was devoted to Libby Prison, where the rules were particularly stringent and where powder was supposed to have been placed under the prison to blow up the inmates should Union armies move on Richmond and attempt to free them.[11]

Most of the foregoing testimony was given in open court, with the exception of that by Von Steinacker, who testified secretly on Friday,

Purdy's involvement, see Robert Purdy, June 4, 1865, in Letters Received, File P 463, File B 479, File C 480, all in JAO, RG 153, NA. James T. Fairburn to Joseph Holt, N.d., Robert Purdy to Holt, N.d., Leonidas McAleer, William French, Charles M. French, James M. Brady, Joseph Shriver, June 7, 1865, Statements, H. A. Myers, Statement, N.d., all in Holt Papers; Pitman, *Assassination of President Lincoln*, 39–40, 42–43.

9. Hugh Tradger, May 29, Record Book, File S, p. 53, Confederate Documents Numbers 1 and 2, Record Book, File C, p. 11, all in JAO, 1865, RG 153, NA; Pitman, *Assassination of President Lincoln*, 52.

10. Henry Von Steinacker, April 25, 1865, Statement, in Letters Received, File V 510, JAO, RG 153, NA.

11. R. E. Higginson, April 25, in Letters Received, File H 63, James M. Deems to Joseph Holt, May 29, in Letters Received, File D 412, Marshal McPhail to Henry L. Burnett, May 24, in Letters Received, File Mc 656, all in JAO, 1865, RG 153, NA. For evidence regarding Libby Prison, see *The War of the Rebellion: A Compilation of the Official Records of the Union and Confederate Armies*, (130 vols., Washington: Government Printing Office, 1880–1901), Ser. II, Vol. VIII, p. 551, hereinafter cited as *OR*; R. Bartley to Joseph Holt, May 14, in Letters Received, File B 360, Henry W. Halleck, May 19, in Letters Received, File H 689, both in JAO, 1865, RG 153, NA; Pitman, *Assassination of President Lincoln*, 57–63.

May 12; the transcript was released on Monday, May 14. However, three major government witnesses, Richard Montgomery, James Merritt, and Sanford Conover, testified behind closed doors. The testimony was released only when Conover's statements were leaked to the Cincinnati *Enquirer* by court reporter Pitman.

Montgomery testified that while he was in Canada he had been in contact with various Confederate leaders and that the chief Confederate commissioner in Canada, Jacob Thompson, had told him he could have Lincoln put out of the way any time he wanted. In January, 1865, Thompson disclosed a plot to kill Lincoln and other leading northerners and said he favored it but was waiting to see how the Richmond government would receive it. Montgomery also claimed that he had seen Paine in Canada, talking to former Alabama Senator Clement Clay, and that after the murder, Confederate agent Beverley Tucker told him Lincoln should have been killed long ago and it was a shame the boys had not been allowed to act.

Merritt testified to similar dealings with the Confederates in Canada and said that Confederate agent George Young had told him old Abe would never be inaugurated. Assassination was freely discussed among the rebels in Montreal, and another Confederate, George Sanders, had said that there was plenty of money for the purpose and that Jeff Davis had given his authorization by letter. Merritt also claimed to have seen Herold in Canada, using the name of Harrison, and heard the names of Booth, Harrison, "Port Tobacco" (Atzerodt's nickname), and Surratt as being among those of others who were ready to assassinate Lincoln. Merritt added that a man named Harper had told him that he and others were leaving for the United States to assassinate Lincoln, and Merritt had then attempted to convey the information to a justice of the peace.

However, the star witness was Sanford Conover, alias James Watson Wallace, whose real name was Charles Dunham. Conover, a self-appointed correspondent for the New York *Tribune*, claimed to have passed for a rebel in Canada and to have been very freely admitted to rebel meetings. He had seen Booth and Surratt in company with Thompson and George Sanders. Surratt had supposedly brought dispatches from Judah Benjamin and a letter from Davis at which Thompson exclaimed, "This makes the thing all right." Conover also claimed that Thompson had told him that Booth would be commissioned to perform the deed and that although he had informed the *Tribune* of the plot, it would not publish his letter. He also testified to having knowledge about Dr. Blackburn's yellow fever plot and about plans to poison and blow up the Croton Reservoir in New York.

However, Conover was not through testifying, for rumors arose that there were many discrepancies in his testimony. Conover had claimed as part of his background and credentials that he had testified at the Saint Albans trial under the name of James Watson Wallace. On June 10, in the Montreal *Evening Telegraph*, the real James Watson Wallace swore that he was the person who had testified before the Saint Albans Commission. The individual who had testified before the military commission under the name of Sanford Conover was an imposter, and he, the real Wallace, had never been associated with the rebels in Canada. Conover then had to be returned to the witness stand on June 27 to explain that his testimony on the Saint Albans trial had been mixed with that of another individual who had testified, James Wallace. After his testimony on May 20 and May 22 at the conspiracy trial, Judge Holt had sent Conover to Canada to procure a certified copy of his testimony at the Saint Albans trial. He saw the leading rebels in Canada who again made incriminating remarks, but they then learned of the testimony he had given at the conspiracy trial. A group of men including Sanders and Tucker made him swear under threat of death that he had never made such statements before the commission. Nathan Auser, a witness who was apparently coached by Conover to back up his story, was put on the stand to verify that he was present at these events.[12]

The effect of the testimony concerning rebel involvement was enormous. General Kautz made several comments in his diary, showing the impact that the testimony had on him. On May 12, 1865, the day that Montgomery, Von Steinacker, Mrs. Hudspeth, and Samuel Jones testified, he wrote, "We worked hard today and took a great deal of evidence. Some of it was very important, and implicates Jeff. Davis, Jake Thompson and Sanders, Clay, and Cleary." Of Conover's testimony of May 20 he said, "An important witness was called and his testimony

---

12. Pitman, *Assassination of President Lincoln*, 24–37; *Trial of the Alleged Assassins*, 132–42, 155, 156, 173; Nathan Auser, June 19, 1865, Statement, in Holt Papers.

was taken with closed doors. He very strongly implicates the rebels in Canada."[13]

If such testimony could so influence a more liberal member of the court, one can imagine its tendency to strengthen the preconceptions of those already inclined to believe in rebel involvement in Lincoln's murder. When, during the course of an objection to a statement by witness George McGee, Thomas Ewing asked if Samuel Arnold had entered the rebel service to assassinate the president, Judge Advocate Bingham responded, "Yes, he entered into it to assassinate the President; and everybody else that entered into the rebellion, entered it to assassinate everybody that represented the Government, that either followed the standard in the field, or represented its standards in the councils." In similar fashion, when Confederate General Edward Johnson attempted to testify in order to refute some of Von Steinacker's statements, he was attacked by Generals Howe and Ekin because of his rebel service and particularly because a party of which he was a member had fired on and killed some of Howe's men.[14]

The testimony concerning the mistreatment of Union prisoners caused particular consternation in the North, for as the Philadelphia *Evening Bulletin* said, "If any further evidence was needed of the rebel savagery exhibited towards our prisoners of war, in their hands, it was furnished by the testimony taken in the trial of the assassins in Washington yesterday." However, there were some doubts, even in 1865, as to whether such testimony was really relevant to this trial.[15]

Revelations concerning the yellow fever plot caused even more horror and interest. The Philadelphia *Evening Bulletin* reminded citizens of the city of brotherly love how they had aided Virginia ten years earlier when the fever raged there and how they had been repaid for their kindness. The *Bulletin* added that this atrocity was even worse than the assassination of the president. The testimony apparently caused the

---

13. August V. Kautz Daily Journal (MS in August V. Kautz Papers, LC), May 12, May 20, 1865.

14. Pitman, *Assassination of President Lincoln*, 64–65; *Trial of the Alleged Assassins and Conspirators at Washington City, D.C.*, 86; DeWitt, *Assassination of Abraham Lincoln*, 112. The correspondent for the New York *Times*, May 31, 1865, p. 1, said that General Howe's actions seemed to astonish everyone.

15. Philadelphia *Evening Bulletin*, May 26, 1865, p. 4. See also New York *Times*, May 8, p. 2, May 26, 1865, p. 1; Chicago *Tribune*, May 26, 1865, p. 1.

same uproar that talk of germ warfare does today, because the intro-duction of pestilence would have directly involved many innocent ci-vilians. As the New York *Tribune* said, "This evidence seemed to send a thrill of horror through all." Godfrey Hyams, rather than receiving credit for his testimony, called down criticism upon himself for his ad-mitted involvement. The Toronto *Globe* called him a criminal of the worst sort who should be deported under the Alien Act, while the New York *Times* correspondent noted that the reaction of the audience seemed to be that while they believed Hyams, if they had their way he too would be hanged for his part in the affair.[16]

The letters found in the rebel archives as well as the cipher dispatches also made a marked impression. When the Alston letter was intro-duced, there were expressions of "Oh, the monster! Oh, horrible! Shame, shame!" The New York *Times* also criticized certain news-papers, which it did not name, for trying to play down the importance of the letter picked up by the Reverend W. H. Ryder, which detailed the burning of towns and shipping. The evidence given about the cipher convinced many people that there was a connection between Booth and the Richmond government.[17]

The release of the suppressed testimony further reinforced this view. The *Times* greeted the first installment with the headlines: REVELA-TIONS CONCERNING THE ORIGIN OF THE MURDER PLOT, IT WAS DE-CIDED UPON JUST AFTER THE REBEL DEFEAT AT GETTYSBURG, CURI-OUS LETTERS DROPPED IN A THIRD AVENUE CAR, BOOTH'S VISIT TO CANADA AND INTERCOURSE WITH SANDERS, and THE ASSASSINATION LONG CONTEMPLATED BY THE REBEL LEADERS IN RICHMOND. The Chicago *Tribune*, believing that the evidence was strong, added that the military commission had been correct in suppressing the evidence, and it called for an apology from the New York *Tribune*, *World*, and *Evening Post*, who had been attacking this course of action.[18]

On May 29, the *Times* correspondent reported that all the closed door testimony would soon be released, and on June 5, largely because Pit-man had leaked it to a Cincinnati newspaper, the testimony was given

16. New York *Tribune*, May 30, 1865, p. 1; Philadelphia *Evening Bulletin*, May 16, p. 4, May 27, 1865, p. 4; Toronto *Globe*, quoted in New York *Times*, May 7, 1865, p. 2.

17. New York *Times*, May 23, 1865, p. 8. See also Albany *Argus*, May 26, 1865, p. 2; San Francisco *Alta Californian*, June 20, 1865, p. 1.

18. New York *Times*, May 17, 1865, p. 1; Chicago *Tribune*, May 20, 1865, p. 2.

to the public. The majority of newspapers that supported the Union now felt that the evidence was conclusive that the rebels had been involved in the assassination. There was also some criticism of Pitman for endangering the lives of witnesses who had testified, and speculation as to what might be done to him.[19]

Even in 1865, however, there were doubts about some of the evidence and especially about Conover's incredible conduct after he had testified. Also defense attorney Cox charged that the "Lon" letter was a forgery, and because of this Purdy, a government detective whose veracity was doubtful, was called to testify. Confederate officer Henry Kyd Douglas wrote of Von Steinacker's testimony, "It was such an absurd tissue of lies and so transparent that the wonder is that even that Court could listen to it with patience."[20]

As noted, those accused in Johnson's proclamation vehemently denied the charges against them, and George N. Sanders wrote on May 22 to "Titus Oates" Holt care of E. M. Stanton, decrying the character of the villains who had testified against him. Clement Clay also expressed his confidence that he could prove the testimony to be false, and a friend expressed his willingness to go before a grand jury in an effort to indict Conover for perjury. A letter to the New York *World* on June 2 summed up the feeling that many people had, especially those opposed to the government. "The evidence against the real plotters and their accomplices is very full and explicit, nor is it necessary to trust the government spies to establish it; but against Davis, and Clay, and Thompson, it is halting and has a suspicious appearance."[21]

While there was even some initial caution expressed about Conover's testimony, doubt became much more widespread after his return to Canada and the printing of the confusing James Watson Wallace state-

19. New York *Times*, May 29, p. 1, June 6, 1865, pp. 1, 8; New York *Tribune*, June 5, p. 1, June 7, 1865, p. 1; Easton (Pa.) *Free Press*, June 8, 1865, p. 2; Chicago *Tribune*, June 9, 1865, p. 2. During the trial there were reports of prosecution witnesses being assaulted because of their testimony, but virtually all of these proved to be unfounded. See, for example, Chicago *Tribune*, May 11, 1865, p. 2.

20. New York *Tribune*, June 3, 1865, p. 1; New York *Times*, June 14, 1865, p. 1; Pitman, *Assassination of President Lincoln*, 42–43; Douglas, *I Rode With Stonewall*, 340–41.

21. James Young (ed.) *Address of Beverley Tucker, Esq., to the People of the United States* (Atlanta: Emory University Library, 1948), 30; William H. Carroll to Clement C. Clay, October 26, 1866 [1865], Clay to his wife, January 1, 1866, both in Clement C. Clay Papers, Duke University Library. See also New York *Herald*, June 10, 1865, p. 1; New York *World*, June 2, 1865, p. 8.

ments. On June 8, the Albany *Argus* questioned the motives in Conover's return to Canada. Several newspapers also printed the letter from accused conspirator William Cleary, secretary of the Confederate Commission in Canada, which pointed out alleged discrepancies in testimony between this trial and the Saint Albans trial.

When Conover finally returned to the stand in an attempt to clarify his conduct, the *Argus* said, "The evidence was listened to with a great deal of curious interest, and it was hard to say, when the witness concluded, whether he was James Watson Wallace or somebody else." The Chicago *Tribune* was particularly bitter in denouncing Conover and printed a letter from Conover to Jacob Thompson dated March 20, which showed that whereas Conover was reporting conversations with Thompson in February, 1865, as of March 20, he had not even met him.[22]

The Reverend Stuart Robinson also produced a pamphlet in which he did much to destroy the effect of Conover's testimony. Robinson denied Conover's allegations that he was involved with Dr. Blackburn in the yellow fever plot, asking what good it would do to spread such pestilence, for it would rage within the lines of both sides. He also pointed out the falsehoods of Conover and Montgomery, adding: "Thus the miserable fictions of this villain's appendix, under the manipulation of Mr. Holt, like the whole work in chief of the three witnesses, is seen to be not only an unmitigated lie, but a stupid lie, so contrived that the whole structure of falsehood drops to pieces by reference to places and dates; thus easily making the perjury manifest to the humblest capacity of the people by the very short and conclusive method of proving an alibi." Former Attorney General Bates wrote that while he did not feel that Robinson had made the most of his case, "yet he has matter enough, if perspicuously and tersely stated, to overwhelm both the witnesses with shame."[23]

Robinson also charged that there was no excuse for the Bureau of Military Justice not knowing that such evidence was perjured, and in-

22. Albany *Argus*, June 8, p. 2, June 29, 1865, p. 2; Chicago *Tribune*, July 1, p. 2, July 11, 1865, p. 1.
23. Stuart Robinson, *Infamous Perjuries of the "Bureau of Military Justice" Exposed* (Toronto: N.p., 1865); Howard K. Beale (ed.), *The Diary of Edward Bates, 1859–1866*, Vol. IV of the Annual Report of the American Historical Association, 1930 (Washington: Government Printing Office, 1933), 493.

deed there is some justification for this view. The government evidently had some doubts about Conover's veracity, for Holt telegraphed S. H. Gay of the *Tribune* on June 7, 1865, "What could you state if examined as a witness, as to the general character of Sanford Conover for integrity and truth." General Dix also wrote Stanton about Conover on June 24: "They [papers found in his trunk] show that he wrote for the Montreal *Telegraph* a most atrocious and vindictive article on the assassination of Mr. Lincoln. His character, in other aspects, is bad; and his testimony where he is known, will have no weight unless it is corroborated by witnesses of unquestionable credibility."[24]

Dr. Merritt also came in for his share of suspicion. On June 14, the Richmond *Whig* stated that Clement Clay had positively not been in Canada on the date that Merritt claimed to have heard him in conversation. A writer from Ayr, Canada, informed the New York *Times* of his belief that Merritt was as guilty as those who had committed the murder if he had concealed knowledge of it. On June 7, Judge Holt received information from the Justice of the Peace before whom Merritt was supposed to have sworn out his affidavit, that he had no knowledge of Merritt. In a similar fashion the government should have had some reason to suspect that Von Steinacker's testimony was tainted.[25]

On the whole, however, the perjured testimony produced relatively few ripples of dissent and did very little to shake people's faith in the government's case, for as *Harper's Weekly* said, "In the absence of any other proof, there is nothing improbable in Conover's statements. Look at another page of this paper, and see how these same rebels treated our prisoners of war." Conover and the others gave testimony which so completely harmonized with what people wanted to believe

---

24. Robinson, *Infamous Perjuries*, 6. See Seymour J. Frank, "The Conspiracy to Implicate the Confederate Leaders in Lincoln's Assassination," *Mississippi Valley Historical Review*, X (1954), 629–56, for argument that Holt and Stanton were acting in concert and were little more than willful suborners of perjury. Joseph Holt to S. H. Gay, June 7, 1865, in Telegrams Sent, JAO, RG 153, NA. See also Sanford Conover, June 28, 1865, Receipt for $240, in Letters Received, File C 727, JAO, RG 153, NA; John A. Dix to Edwin Stanton, June 24, 1865, in Edwin M. Stanton Papers, LC.

25. Richmond *Whig*, June 14, 1865, p. 2; New York *Times*, June 17, 1865, p. 2; "Court Martial Proceedings," 149, H. W. Hunter to Joseph Holt, June 27, 1865, in File Folder 28, D. H. Cockerill, May 8, 1865, Statement, Record Book, File C, p. 10, JAO, all in RG 153, NA; Pitman, *Assassination of President Lincoln*, 64–69.

that they could not bring themselves to see that it was not true; or else, if their confidence was shaken in certain specific testimony, there still seemed to be an ample amount of unshakeable corroborative evidence to support the charges.[26]

Unfortunately for Joseph Holt, however, the attempt to implicate the southern leaders did not end with the conspiracy trial. Holt kept on gathering "evidence" in the Bureau of Military Justice, partially spurred on by Clement Clay's assertions that he could prove he was not in Canada when alleged conversations had taken place. Aided by Conover, Holt discovered several additional witnesses including William Campbell, Joseph Snevil, Farnum B. Wright, Campbell Montgomery, Albert Ross, Sarah Douglass, Mary Knapp, and John H. Patten. In the light of this additional testimony, Holt apparently felt confident in informing Stanton that the charges against Clay, Davis, and Burton Harrison could be made to stick. On March 20, 1866, he wrote to Stanton, "With these depositions the preparation of the case by this bureau is properly terminated, and in as much as both the criminals and the proofs of their crime are now in the hands of the Government, it only remains for me respectfully, but most earnestly, to renew my former recommendation that Davis and Clay be arraigned and tried before a military commission."[27]

The Judiciary Committee of the House, however, was becoming increasingly interested in the charges on which Davis and Clay were being held, and on April 17, 1866, James Wilson asked Stanton for the evidence implicating these individuals. Holt had already appeared before the committee on April 14 and reaffirmed his belief in the guilt of Davis and others as charged. He stated, when asked if the investigation had been pursued on his own initiative or had the approval of the president and secretary of war, that it was voluntary on his part, although he added, "but pursued with the approval of the Secretary of War." This would again make it appear that Stanton had given Holt some general authority to proceed with his investigation, but had left the details to Holt's discretion. If Stanton had been directly involved, it also appears

26. *Harper's Weekly*, June 17, 1865, p. 371.
27. *OR*, Ser. II, Vol. VIII, 812–91 *passim*, 940; Sanford Conover to Joseph Holt, July 26, August 2, 1865, in Benjamin Butler Papers, LC. See also Depositions, in Holt Papers.

that there would have been no need for the extremely detailed reports that Holt made of this activities.[28]

The committee also called Dr. Merritt and Richard Montgomery to testify. They remained relatively unscathed, but on May 8, Holt's evidence began to crumble, for when the committee called William Campbell, he admitted that his deposition made before Holt was false and that he had been coached by Conover as to what he would say, in the hope of receiving money. On May 24, Joseph Snevil also admitted that he had been lying.[29]

Conover, who had himself testified on May 8, was confronted with the evidence, and while denying all that Campbell had said, he refused to make a formal statement. Holt then had to return before the committee on June 18. He claimed that Stanton had concurred in all that he had done, and declared, "My confidence in the testimony was strengthened by my knowledg that it was in accord with and seemed to be, in a large degree, a natural sequence from other facts which had been testified to as having occurred in Canada by witnesses known to the Government and whose reputation has not been and cannot it is believed, be successfully assailed." Nonetheless, he withdrew the testimony from the committee's consideration.[30]

Incredible as it now seems, the majority report of the committee, issued in July, 1866, ignored all this damaging testimony and concluded that the evidence was still sufficient to implicate Davis. However, while the committee tried to make it difficult for its minority member, A. J. Rogers, even to examine the evidence, he revealed the perjured testimony to the country. As Rogers concluded:

> I do not say that 'Judge Holt' did originate the charges or organize the plot or perjurers, because I do not know that he did; I merely say that a

28. *OR*, Ser. II, Vol. VIII, 898. On January 29, 1866, M. Howard had advised Holt not to reveal the evidence on which Davis was being held to the House because counter-evidence could then be manufactured. In Holt Papers. Joseph Holt, April 14, 1866, Testimony, in Butler Papers. The comment "but pursued with the approval of the Secretary of War" appears with an omission notation, so it is difficult to tell whether Holt added this as an afterthought or whether it was added later. There is another similar notation in the course of the same testimony.

29. James B. Merritt, April 20, Richard Montgomery, May 1, William Campbell, May 8, Joseph Snevil, May 24, 1866, Testimony, all in Butler Papers. See also *OR*, Ser. II, Vol. VIII, 921–22; Levi C. Turner to James F. Wilson, June 2, 1866, in Holt Papers.

30. Sanford Conover, May 8, Joseph Holt, June 18, 1866, Testimony, both in Butler Papers.

plot based on the assassination was formed against Davis, Clay and others, and that the plotters did, and even yet, operate through the Bureau of Military Justice, and that the argument forwarded by Mr. Holt to the Committee of the Judiciary looked to be like a shield extended over the plotters—extended, it may be, from no personal animosity to Messrs. Davis, Clay, and the others—extended, it may be with a desire to save certain officers of the government from the charge of having been betrayed into the mistakes of a vague apprehension, the blunders of an excitement, which it was their power to allay or control, not to increase or share.

Edward Bates wrote in his diary of the minority report by Rogers, "He discloses the perjury of the witnesses and the wicked subornation of certain high officials, to the point of nausea."[31]

Beginning on August 12, 1866, the New York *Herald* carried a series of letters between Conover and the perjured witnesses, mentioning sums of money and making statements that placed Judge Holt in an extremely bad light. Holt had already grasped the precarious position in which the committee's report and these letters had placed him. On July 3, 1866, he wrote to Stanton in an effort to convince him of his entire innocence in the matter.[32]

Over the objections of Attorney General Stanbery and Secretary Stanton as well as W. W. Winthrop and other advisors at the Bureau of Military Justice, Holt decided as on other occasions that his only course was to clear his name. Holt therefore published his vindication in the Washington *Daily Morning Chronicle* of September 3, 1866, which statement was later incorporated in pamphlet form. Holt also made a significant attempt to have this article and pamphlet widely distributed. For example, Frank Ballard wrote to Holt on September 10: "I duly recd your letter and the accompanying copies of the vindication. The latter have all been properly placed and I could use more to your advantage and that of the truth. In distributing I have tried to reach some of our papers with what success I cannot yet tell."[33]

---

31. *House Reports*, 39th Cong., 1st Sess., No. 104, p. 36; Beale (ed.), *Diary of Edward Bates*, 494.

32. New York *Herald*, August 12, p. 5, August 24, p. 2, September 21, 1866, p. 8; Joseph Snevil to Sanford Conover, November 14, Report of William Campbell to Joseph Holt, November 15, Campbell to Holt, November 15, Campbell to Conover, November 19, 1865, all in Holt Papers; *OR*, Ser. II, Vol. VIII, 931–45.

33. W. W. Winthrop to Joseph Holt, August 6, August 18, 1866, both in Holt Papers. While government officials had advised him to ignore the criticism, Holt's brother had

Ballard went to the New York *Herald* and saw their correspondent, Putnam, about the letters his paper had been publishing. Ballard reported to Holt that Putnam claimed no desire to injure him but that the paper was merely pandering to public interest in Davis, but Ballard questioned Putnam's protestations. Holt himself wrote to *Herald* editor James Gordon Bennett claiming that he had never seen the letters printed in the *Herald* on September 21; and Ballard informed Holt that the *Herald* would print his letter, adding, "For once, then, the antidote will follow the poison pretty directly." Holt also tried to get possession of the letters, but Putnam said that several, including two signed by Conover, had now disappeared.[34]

Members of Congress also came forward to vindicate Holt, saying that he had insisted on bringing the witnesses before the committee and had immediately withdrawn the testimony when it proved to be false. While the *Herald* remained quite critical of Holt, the Washington *Daily Morning Chronicle* defended the judge advocate, relying mainly on his own assertion that there was a move on foot to defame him and the Bureau of Military Justice, primarily to help bring about Davis's release.[35]

Also incredible, even after Campbell's and Snevil's revelations, was that Conover was allowed to proceed to New York with an officer, whom he eluded, and then disappeared. Holt dispatched Levi Turner to see if Conover could be found and also to track down Campbell and Snevil, who had also made themselves scarce after giving their testimony. Turner located the latter two and took depositions from them that the *Herald* letters were forgeries. Turner also secured a warrant for Conover's arrest and he was apprehended in early November. After his

---

warned him that he must vindicate himself. See R. S. Holt to Joseph Holt, August 22, 1866, *ibid.*; Joseph Holt, *Vindication of Judge Advocate General Holt from the Foul Slanders of Traitors, Their Aiders, Abettors, and Sympathizers, Acting in the Interest of Jefferson Davis* (N.p., September 4, 1866); Frank W. Ballard to Joseph Holt, September 10, 1866, in Holt Papers.

34. Frank W. Ballard to Joseph Holt, September 28, Holt to James G. Bennett, September 22, Ballard to Holt, September 24, J. D. R. Putnam to Marshal Murray, December 5, Murray to Levi C. Turner, December 5, 1866, all in Holt Papers.

35. George Boutwell to Joseph Holt, September 13, Levi C. Turner to Holt, September 10, James F. Wilson to Holt, September 29, 1866, all in Holt Papers; Washington *Daily Morning Chronicle*, September 3, 1866, p. 2; *OR*, Ser. II, Vol. VIII, p. 962.

arrest, Conover also denied the validity of the letters and said that he had acted to revenge himself on Davis, who had had him imprisoned in Castle Thunder for six months. He still affirmed that Davis was connected with the assassination.[36]

In addition to the *Vindication*, Holt also asked for a court of inquiry. His brother had written him on September 29, as to the advisability of his course of action. Stanton pressed the matter before the cabinet, but the majority was opposed. Secretary Welles advised that this type of criticism was something that those in public life must be willing to bear.[37]

Much can be understood through a look at Holt's psychological makeup. As Secretary Welles wrote so perceptively in his diary: "I long since was aware that Holt was severe and unrelenting, and am further compelled to think that, with a good deal of mental vigor and strength as a writer he has a strange weakness. He is credulous and often the dupe of his own imaginings. Believes men guilty on shadowy suspicions, and is ready to condemn them without trial. Stanton has sometimes brought forward singular papers relating to conspiracies, and dark and murderous designs in which he had evident faith, and Holt has assured him in his suspicions." Holt could never stand criticism and had been involved since late 1865 in a dispute with former Postmaster General Montgomery Blair, in which, again despite the advice of friends, he had attempted to sue Blair for some statements Blair had made about him. Holt also employed Merritt from January, 1866, to May, 1867, in an attempt to procure a letter from one Chapman, which was supposed to strongly implicate Davis in the assassination. Holt's credulity often led him to take actions that bordered on the point of criminal negligence. He was much too thin-skinned to be a public of-

36. Levi C. Turner to Joseph Holt, October 1, October 2, October 3, 1866, William Campbell and Joseph Snevil, October 18, 1866, Statements, Levi C. Turner to Joseph Holt, October 24, October 30, November 8, 1866, all in Holt Papers; *OR*, Ser, II, Vol. VIII, p. 973.

37. Joseph Holt to Edwin Stanton, September 11, Stanton to Joseph Holt, November 14, R. S. Holt to Joseph Holt, September 29, 1866, all in Holt Papers; *OR*, Ser. II, Vol. VIII, p. 964; James G. Randall and Theodore C. Pease (eds.), *Diary of Orville Hickman Browning* (2 vols.; Springfield, Ill.: Jefferson's Printing and Stationery, 1933), II, 95; Howard K. Beale (ed.), *Diary of Gideon Welles* (3 vols.; New York: W. W. Norton, 1960), II, 601.

ficial. Holt believed that Davis and the rebels in Canada were guilty, and nothing could ever shake that belief.[38]

However, a subtle shift now began to manifest itself on the part of the Judiciary Committee, for while the emphasis had previously been on implicating Davis, the Radicals now turned to an effort to implicate Johnson in the assassination. In 1865, the Albany *Atlas and Argus* had wondered whether Booth's leaving of his card at the Kirkwood House had not been a move to cast suspicion upon the vice-president. It will also be remembered that Sanders and Tucker had said that there was much more ground for suspecting Johnson of the murder than there was for suspecting them.[39]

Dark hints also began to creep into speeches on the floor of Congress that Johnson might have come to the presidential chair by more than merely fortuitous circumstances. Representative James M. Ashley said: "Sir, a man of Mr. Johnson's antecedents, of his mental and moral caliber, coming into the Presidency as he came into it—and I say nothing now of the dark suspicion which crept over the minds of men as to his complicity in the assassination plot nor of the fact, that I cannot banish from my mind, the mysterious connection between death and treachery which this case presents."[40]

The capture of John Surratt and preparation for his trial also brought rumors that Johnson was afraid of what Surratt might reveal. The Springfield (Mass.) *Daily Republican* said:

> Those who have a taste for the horrible will find satisfaction in a new Washington rumor to the effect that the secret mission of Fred Seward on the steamer 'Gettysburg' is for the purpose of intercepting the 'Swatara,' and offering to John Surratt the promise of a pardon from President Johnson if he will not implicate the president in the assassination of Mr. Lin-

38. Beale (ed.), *Diary of Gideon Welles*, II, 423; to Joseph Holt: James B. Merritt, January 9, May 1, October 10, 1866, February 26, April 22, 1867, and E. W. Dennis, September 24, 1866, April 30, 1867, all in Holt Papers; *OR*, Ser. II, Vol. VIII, p. 978.

39. Albany *Atlas and Argus*, April 20, 1865, p. 2; Young (ed.), *Address of Beverley Tucker*, 9. See also George S. Bryan, *The Great American Myth* (New York: Carrick and Evans, 1940), 386; Otto Eisenschiml, *Why Was Lincoln Murdered?* (Boston: Little Brown, 1937), 389; New York *Herald*, May 6, 1865, p. 1.

40. *Congressional Globe*, 40th Cong., 1st Sess., 18, 19. See also *Congressional Globe*, 39th Cong., 1st Sess., 444; DeWitt, *Assassination of Abraham Lincoln*, 174. This speech was quite a reversal from Ashley's note to Johnson on April 15, 1865: "The telegraph has just announced the gratifying fact that you are inaugurated." See James Ashley to Andrew Johnson, April 15, 1865, in Andrew Johnson Papers, LC, Microcopy, Roll 13.

coln. Young Seward is supposed also to have a filial motive for wishing to induce Surratt to keep silence, as it is part of the horrible theory that Secretary Seward was in the assassination plot, and consented to be almost killed in order to disarm suspicion!

Johnson did have some worries along these lines, for as Secretary Welles revealed, the president feared that the Radicals might offer Surratt a pardon and that in his desperate circumstances Surratt might make almost any statement in order to save himself from hanging as his mother had.[41]

There was good reason for Johnson's fears of the Radicals, for they attempted to use Conover, who was incarcerated in the same prison as Surratt, to implicate Johnson. However, in the end there were so many plots and counterplots involved that the public was extremely confused about just what had happened. On May 8, 1867, William Rabe, who had been in jail with Conover but had received a pardon from Johnson, offered to reveal to the president the details of a conspiracy being raised against him. William Moore, Johnson's secretary, wrote to Rabe that he would be pleased to see him on the subject of his communication. In his statement, Rabe said that Conover had told him that he and Ashley were going to use William Cleaver, who testified during the John Surratt trial, to implicate Johnson before the Judiciary Committee. Overtures had also been made to Surratt, but he declined, since he felt that his counsel could get him acquitted. Ashley had visited with Conover on seven different occasions.[42]

Meanwhile, Conover had applied to Johnson for a pardon, basing his plea on the manner of impaneling the jury, which had been declared illegal in the Surratt trial. On July 29, after falling out with his Radical friends, who he evidently felt were about to betray him, Conover wrote to Johnson and revealed to him the details of the plot. He also apparently supplied Johnson with copies of the documents involved, many of which are still preserved in Johnson's papers. Even after Conover

41. Springfield (Mass.) *Daily Republican*, January 28, p. 2, April 29, 1867, p. 2; Beale (ed.), *Diary of Gideon Welles*, III, 31. See also Alfred Isacsson, "John Surratt and the Lincoln Assassination Plot," *Maryland Historical Magazine*, LII (1957), 334; Washington *Daily Morning Chronicle*, August 29, 1873, p. 5.

42. William Rabe to Andrew Johnson, May 8, William Moore to Rabe, May 8, Rabe, R. Water, Bell Coleman, May 10, 1867, Statements, all in Johnson Papers, Microcopy, Roll 27.

went to the Albany Penitentiary, his wife forwarded his letters to Johnson, and Conover was still extremely bitter at Congressmen Butler and Ashley, who he maintained had led him into schemes of forgery.[43] In July, Congressman Albert Gallatin Riddle had, with Holt's concurrence, also applied for Conover's pardon. This apparently was to make it look as if Johnson granted the pardon to insure Conover's silence, once the existence of the forged documents should be revealed.[44]

The president brought this evidence he was gathering before at least a part of the cabinet, and they agreed that the best course of action was to have the documents published. This material was released to the newspapers on August 10, 1867, and caused quite a furor in the press. While people were contemplating what such revelations meant, another set of documents was released on August 15, charging that Nathan Anser (Auser) had been approached by two Democrats, General Roger A. Pryor and Ben Wood, to swear falsely that Holt and Conover had induced him to give perjured testimony. Auser refused but James E. Matterson took three hundred dollars. It was also revealed that Congressmen Rogers, Radford, and certain other Democrats had applied for a pardon for Conover.[45]

On August 15, the *Times* headlined an editorial THE TABLES TURNED— WHO THE CONOVER CONSPIRATORS REALLY ARE. Other newspapers also supported Ashley and Holt and denounced the Conover maneuverings as a Democratic plot. However, some newspapers severely attacked Holt, among the most vehement of which was the Washington *Daily National Intelligencer*. The *Intelligencer* reprinted an article from the Philadelphia *Age* calling for military discipline for Holt's offenses, but urging no muffling and handcuffing. The *Intelligencer* itself had said on August 13, "Why should not the conspirators against the life of

43. Charles A. Dunham to Andrew Johnson, July 26, July 29, W. B. Matchett to Dunham, April 26, James M. Ashley to Dunham, April 28, July 8, Ashley to Joseph Holt and Albert G. Riddle, July 22, Matchett to Holt, August 3, Dunham to his wife, August 15, December 15, December 22, 1867, February 16, March 1, April 13, June 7, 1868, Dunham to Robert Johnson, November 24, 1867, all *ibid.*, Rolls 27, 28, 29, 30.

44. Albert G. Riddle to Andrew Johnson, July 23, 1867, *ibid.*, Roll 28.

45. Beale (ed.), *Diary of Gideon Welles*, III, 195; Randall and Pease (eds.), *Diary of Orville Hickman Browning*, II, 152–53; New York *Times*, August 10, p. 1, August 15, 1867, p. 1.

President Johnson be arrested, imprisoned, tried by military commission, and be ignominiously executed?"[46]

Those accused of being involved also attempted to defend themselves. Congressman Riddle denied that he had been part of any plot and said he had signed Conover's pardon plea at Mrs. Conover's urging, only because of the information that Conover had so freely supplied to the government. Pryor and Wood also swore to affidavits denying the charges against them.[47]

On the whole, however, this time there was a great deal of caution expressed on both sides, and most people had evidently had their fill of Conover. The New York *Tribune* called for an end to affidavits and counter-affidavits. The Chicago *Tribune* said about the affair, "It is, without exception, the most unclean thing that has ever been thrust before the eyes of the American people." Perhaps the San Francisco *Alta Californian* summed up the state of opinion best. "Public opinion is about equally divided as to whether the plot was really one of Ashley, Butler and others against the President, or of the President, with the aid of Conover, against the former."[48]

Judge Holt denied that he had anything to do with the publication of the documents of August 15, although such protestations hardly convinced the *Intelligencer*. Clearly, Holt was well aware of the existence of such material, since W. B. Matchett had informed him of the existence of such statements on June 28, 1867. Holt's papers also contain copies of the statements of Auser, James Matterson, Francis McFall, and other individuals supposed to be involved, as well as a copy of Riddle's letter to Seward in Holt's own handwriting. While he was aware of their existence, there is evidence that Holt may not have been directly involved in their publication, for Thomas F. Barr, apparently in reply to Holt's request, informed him that the statements were copied from the

46. New York *Times*, August 15, 1867, pp. 1, 4; *Harper's Weekly*, August 31, 1867, p. 546; New York *Herald*, August 12, p. 4, August 18, 1867, p. 4; New York *Tribune*, August 12, 1867, p. 4; Philadelphia *Age*, quoted in Washington *Daily National Intelligencer*, August 15, 1867, p. 2. See also August 13, pp. 1, 2, August 17, p. 2, August 27, 1867, p. 2.

47. New York *Times*, August 17, p. 4, August 18, 1867, p. 6; Randall and Pease (eds.), *Diary of Orville Hickman Browning*, II, 156, 157; Baltimore *Sun*, August 17, 1867, p. 4; New York *Times*, August 16, 1867, p. 4.

48. New York *Tribune*, August 16, 1867, p. 4; Chicago *Tribune*, August 20, 1867, p. 2; San Francisco *Alta Californian*, August 13, 1867, p. 1.

originals by General Henry Boynton, correspondent of the Cincinnati *Gazette*, and made public by him.[49]

General Butler had also managed during the course of the Surratt trial to have a select committee appointed, with himself as chairman, to investigate the assassination. Butler had indicated, when he clashed with Congressman John A. Bingham in a celebrated debate the preceding March, that he was one person who was very much interested in getting to the bottom of the mystery surrounding the assassination. In this debate Butler pressed charges that Booth's diary had been suppressed and also that pages had been removed, while charging that Bingham had sent an innocent woman, Mrs. Surratt, to the gallows. This incident created some public interest as gauged by the number of letters Butler received.[50]

The establishment of the committee also elicited much comment from the press, especially regarding the offer made to solicit testimony that promised immunity to any individuals who might have to incriminate themselves. The *Intelligencer* caustically greeted the news. "General Butler the chairman of this appropriately-named committee, which seems to have been raised for the purpose of assassinating the reputation of men, has advertised for witnesses." The Easton (Pa.) *Sentinel*, noting that previous government witnesses had received positions, money, or trips in and out of the penitentiary, added that the individual's reward seemed to be "owing to the value of the testimony and the ability of the witness when he has told his lie, of sticking to it." Even the Springfield (Mass.) *Republican*, which felt Butler might provide the country with good service if his committee was conducted properly, warned against making it a mere partisan vehicle.[51]

49. New York *Times*, August 16, p. 4, August 20, 1867, p. 1; Washington *Daily National Intelligencer*, August 20, 1867, p. 2; W. B. Matchett to Joseph Holt, April 30, June 28, 1867, Francis McFall, John Martin, James Matterson, Nathan Auser, May 17, 1867, Statements, Albert G. Riddle to Andrew Johnson, July 23, Thomas F. Barr to Joseph Holt, August 23, 1867, all in Holt Papers.

50. *Congressional Globe*, 40th Cong., 1st Sess., 263–64, 363, 522; to Benjamin Butler: John J. Davenport, March 28, Oliver Potter, April 15, R. Ould, April 10, 1867, all in Butler Papers.

51. Washington *Daily National Intelligencer*, July 25, p. 2, July 29, 1867, p. 2; Easton (Pa.) *Sentinel*, August 1, p. 2, July 18, p. 2, August 15, 1867, p. 2; Memphis *Daily Appeal*, July 14, 1867, p. 2; Springfield (Mass.) *Weekly Republican*, July 13, 1867, p. 2. See also Samuel B. Arnold, *Defence and Prison Experiences of a Lincoln Conspirator: Statements and Autobiographical Notes* (Hattiesburg, Miss.: Book Farm, 1943), 116–17, where Arnold

While the committee did take some testimony and received letters from people who indicated that they could furnish evidence to implicate Johnson, no report was ever made. Some further testimony was taken before the Judiciary Committee during the impeachment investigation in an attempt to use such evidence against Johnson, but nothing further came of this either.[52]

It must always be kept in mind that two trials were occurring simultaneously in 1865, one involving those actually in the dock and the other that of the Confederate leaders. To contemporaries the cases of those on trial were generally quite straightforward and simple, and the feeling seemed to be that the government had proven its case. There was, however, some comprehension that the guilt of all eight defendants was not equal and that some might have been involved in a kidnapping plot with Booth and not so deeply in the murder. There thus seemed to be widespread satisfaction when those perceived to be the guiltiest were hanged and those with lesser involvement received prison sentences.

The second trial, consisting of evidence against Confederate leaders, has been dismissed by historians because the testimony of several witnesses turned out to be perjured. However, to contemporaries this evidence was every bit as important as the case against the other conspirators whose guilt seemed proven. It reinforced the view that those who had committed treason against their country and had committed many atrocities were certainly capable of assassination. With the public so persuaded, it is not unusual that the military commission handed down the sentences that it did.

---

charges that Gleason, whom the committee sent to take statements at Fort Jefferson, virtually made an open offer to any of the convicted conspirators if they would agree to implicate Johnson.

52. Hans L. Trefousse, "Belated Revelations of the Assassination Committee," *Lincoln Herald*, LVIII (1956), 13–16; to Benjamin Butler: Justice, October 23, George B. Hutchison, April 16, William M. Kelley, August 27, 1867, all in Butler Papers. U.S. Congress, House, Committee on the Judiciary, *Testimony Taken Before the Judiciary Committee of the House of Representatives in the Investigation of the Charges Against Andrew Johnson*, 39th Cong., 2nd Sess., 40th Cong., 1st Sess. (Washington: Government Printing Office, 1867), 1191, 1194, 1195, 1196–98, 1203.

16.

Pursuit and Trial of John Surratt

Immediately after Lincoln's assassination, suspicion fastened itself upon John Surratt as Seward's assailant. However, much to his good fortune, he was not apprehended. On July 7, 1865, the New York *Times* reported that Paine had called Surratt a coward for not returning to die with his mother. There were also reports that the defense had attempted to bring Surratt to testify if he could be given protection, but Stanton had refused, since Surratt was so deeply involved. General Kautz and Congressman Albert Riddle both stated that Mrs. Surratt would have been spared had John Surratt been tried, but it is not really clear whether there is any truth to these allegations or whether they were mere suppositions.[1]

What is clear is that historians have gone further and charged that once Surratt had fled, the government had no desire to return him for trial and punishment. Surratt himself said in an interview in the Washington *Post* in 1898: "Now, as a matter of fact, our government did not want me in the United States. They were willing and anxious for me to remain abroad and hoped I would continue to do so. While I was in London, Liverpool, and in Birmingham our consuls of those ports knew who I was, and advised our State Department of my whereabouts, but nothing was done." Such charges have occurred partly because on November 24, 1865, Stanton withdrew the reward for Surratt. These charges echo those made at the time of Surratt's trial that certain persons were extremely afraid of what Surratt might be able to reveal.[2]

---

1. New York *Times*, July 7, 1865, p. 1; Albany *Argus*, July 7, p. 1, July 1, 1865, p. 2; August V. Kautz, "Reminiscences of the Civil War" (Typescript in August V. Kautz Papers, LC), III; Albert G. Riddle, *Recollections of War Times* (New York: G. P. Putnam's Sons, 1895), 340. See also David M. De Witt, *The Assassination of Abraham Lincoln and Its Expiation* (New York: MacMillan, 1909), 121.

2. Otto Eisenschiml, *In the Shadow of Lincoln's Death* (New York: Wilfred Funk, 1940), 256, 266–67; Theodore Roscoe, *The Web of Conspiracy* (Englewood, N.J.: Prentice-Hall, 1959), 507; Washington *Post*, April 3, 1898, p. 11; Denver *Evening Post*, April 9, 1898, p. 4; *House Executive Documents*, 39th Cong., 1st Sess., No. 90.

The story of Surratt's escape and capture reads very much like a dime novel, except that it is true. He made his way to Canada, then to England and the Papal States where he became a Papal Zouave. However, he was recognized by a fellow Zouave, Henry Ste. Marie, who reported Surratt's presence to the American minister, Rufus King. While the government was deciding what action it should take and conducting negotiations with the Papacy for Surratt's arrest, the papal government took action on its own account to have him seized on November 7, 1866. When he was being transferred from the barracks at Veroli, he leaped over a precipice and made his way to Naples, where he boarded a ship for Alexandria. While King was foiled in efforts to have Surratt apprehended along the route of his flight, he was able to alert Consul Hale at Alexandria, who possessed full extraterritorial powers, and it was there that Surratt was arrested on November 27, 1866. On December 21, he was sent back to the United States aboard the gunboat *Swatara* to stand trial.[3]

Historians also note that the government did know Surratt's exact whereabouts but took no action at all to capture him. There were many contemporary rumors, some of them erroneous, of his flight to Canada and to Europe. Vice-Consul Henry Wilding at Liverpool, who conveyed news of Surratt's presence directly to the government, was informed on October 13, 1865, by acting Secretary of State William Hunter that "upon a consultation with the Secretary of War and Judge Advocate General, it is thought advisable that no action be taken in regard to the arrest of the supposed John Surratt at present."[4]

Again, however, while some historians have hinted at vast conspiracies, the real reason for the hesitation and delay was the uncertainty in the process of arresting and extraditing the fugitive. In the original dealings with the papal government, one of the points at issue had been the lack of an extradition treaty between the two governments and the reluctance of the American government to have to accept a favor. Con-

3. *House Executive Documents*, 39th Cong., 2nd Sess., Nos. 9, 25; *House Reports*, 39th Cong., 2nd Sess., No. 33; United States Court of Claims, *Henry B. Ste. Marie vs. the United States, Amended Petition No. 6415*, May 6, 1873; Leo F. Stock (ed.), *United States Ministers to the Papal States: Instructions and Despatches, 1848–1868* (2 vols.; Washington: Catholic University Press, 1933), I, 359, 360, 367, 377–78, 381–82, 388, 401.

4. New York *Times*, April 27, p. 4, May 19, 1865, p. 4; Philadelphia *Evening Bulletin*, May 22, 1865, p. 2; James A. McDevitt and R. P. Bigley to A. C. Richards, April 20, 1865, in Letters Received, File B 47, JAO, RG 153, NA.

sul George P. Marsh at Florence had first notified Seward on November 18, 1866, that the Italian government would probably surrender Surratt, but only on the stipulation that he should not receive the death penalty. On November 24 he added, "My present impression, judging from my last interview with the secretary general of foreign affairs, is that the accused would not have been surrendered; and it would therefore be fortunate if he should be found in the Turkish Empire, where the extra-territorial jurisdiction of the consuls would empower them to arrest and detain him without offense to the Turkish government!" Consul W. Winthrop ran into similar difficulties when he attempted to arrange to have Surratt apprehended if the ship on which he was traveling touched at Malta. Consul Thomas Dudley at Liverpool forwarded an extract from the London *Times* of December 6, 1866, which mentioned the problem of political asylum and a political murderer. Both Hunter and Holt expressed their opinion before the Judiciary Committee that it would have been useless to attempt to apprehend Surratt anywhere within the British possessions.[5]

Stanton also testified in a plausible manner before the same committee that the reward had been withdrawn because, after so much time had elapsed, the capture would most likely have to be by government officials who he did not feel should receive a substantial reward for doing their duty, and the withdrawal of the reward might put the fugitives off their guard and induce them to return to the United States. He also said that positive identification of Surratt was a necessity, and given the delicate extradition situation, this would seem to make much sense. The government did, in fact, take some measures to verify Surratt's identity through the use of photographs and also attempted to ascertain whether Henry Ste. Marie, who had identified Surratt, was a reliable witness. It must also be remembered that even though the reward had been withdrawn, Ste. Marie still received ten thousand dollars for the information he had given.[6]

5. *House Executive Documents*, 39th Cong., 2nd Sess., No. 25, pp. 6, 7, 22, 17–18; *House Reports*, 39th Cong., 2nd Sess., No. 33, pp. 3, 4, 9–11, 13.
6. *House Executive Documents*, 39th Cong., 2nd Sess., No. 39, pp. 9–10; Stock (ed.), *United States Ministers to the Papal States*, I, 383; U.S. Congress, *H. B. Sainte-Marie: Letters from the Secretary of War Ad Interim Relative to a Claim of Saint-Marie for Compensation*

Even the charge that the *Swatara* was extremely slow in returning the prisoner to the United States can be explained by the fact that for economy reasons coal could not be used on the open seas, and given no other orders, the ship proceeded under sail. Since the weather was stormy at this time of year, it took forty-five days from Villefranche to the Virginia capes.

Nonetheless, the Judiciary Committee on March 2, 1867, determined that there had been some negligence on the government's part in not identifying Surratt and not pursuing him when it knew where he had gone. Of course, much of this criticism was designed to embarrass Johnson. The newspapers again raised dark hints that even now, when the government had Surratt in custody, it really had no desire to bring him to trial.[7]

However, on June 10, 1867, John Surratt was finally brought to trial before a civil jury for the murder of Abraham Lincoln. To some people, the maneuverings by the prosecution seemed to substantiate the newspaper rumors. Almost immediately the prosecution attempted to quash the panel of jurors for not having been drawn in strict accordance with the procedure set down by law. Edwards Pierrepont, for the prosecution, merely said that the government wished everything to be in proper order so that there could be no charges of unfairness.

The defense was not pleased with these proceedings or, particularly, with the effect they might have on public opinion, for as Surratt's lawyer Richard Merrick argued, "I suggest to your honor, whether it is probable a jury against whose qualifications nothing is alleged, who were summoned without regard to this case, and before it was anticipated it might be tried, are not better fit to do justice than any summoned in anticipation of the case."

On June 12, Judge George P. Fisher set aside the panel and ordered the marshal of the District of Columbia to summon more talesmen. The difficulty in empaneling a jury from among those now called is

Furnished in the Surratt Case, 40th Cong., 2nd Sess., 24; *Congressional Globe*, 40th Cong., 2nd Sess., 602. See also Eisenschiml, *In the Shadow of Lincoln's Death*, 248.

7. George D. Barton, "John Surratt's Capture," in New York *Sun*, May 20, 1916, p. 6; *House Reports*, 39th Cong., 2nd Sess., No. 33, pp. 2, 15–16; Eisenschiml, *In the Shadow of Lincoln's Death*, 248–49, 266–67.

seen in the number who either were challenged or else disqualified themselves on such grounds as having formed an opinion about the trial or holding views opposed to capital punishment.[8]

The trial testimony fills two large volumes. Assistant District Attorney Nathaniel Wilson opened for the prosecution by saying that it would prove "to your entire satisfaction, by competent and credible witnesses, that at that time the prisoner at the bar was then present aiding and abetting the murder; and that at twenty minutes past ten o'clock that night he was in front of the theatre in company with Booth." The prosecution then began by introducing the testimony of individuals like Surgeon General Barnes, Major Rathbone, Joseph Stewart, and James Ferguson, as to the details of the assassination. Barnes's testimony was particularly vivid, for he identified the bullet and bits of bone taken from the head of Abraham Lincoln.

The first significant prosecution witness was Sergeant Joseph Dye. During the conspiracy trial he had testified to seeing two men outside the theater with Booth, engaged in calling the time and in other suspicious activities. At that time he indicated that one of these men very closely resembled Spangler, except that he wore a moustache. Now he testified that it was John Surratt who had been in front of the theater calling the time and whose thin, pale face had so impressed him that he afterwards saw it in his dreams. He also added a detail not previously brought out—that as he was returning to camp, a woman whom he now believed was Mrs. Surratt had raised her window and asked Sergeant Cooper, who was with Dye, what was going on downtown.

To counter this evidence, Merrick attacked Dye during cross-examination by showing that at the conspiracy trial Dye had said that the smallest of the three men had called the time. Dye could only answer lamely that by the smallest he had meant thinnest, that is, Surratt. Positive testimony was also introduced that the group of three in front of the theater was composed of stage carpenter James Gifford, actor C. B. Hess, who was to sing a patriotic song, and costumer Louis Carland. Hess, not wanting to be late for his performance, had called for the time and Carland had told him what it was. Mrs. Frederika Lambert

8. United States Government, *Trial of John H. Surratt in the Criminal Court for the District of Columbia, Hon. George P. Fisher Presiding* (2 vols.; Washington: Government Printing Office, 1867), I, 5ff., 18, 27, 34, 41, 51, 69–70, 75.

also testified, and was supported in this by her servant, that she had an encounter with two soldiers on the evening of April 14, quite similar to the one described by Cooper and Dye.[9]

Numerous witnesses testified that Surratt had been in Washington on April 14. These included detective John Lee; David C. Reed, who identified Surratt by the clothes he wore; Benjamin Vanderpoel, who claimed to have seen Booth, Surratt, and others in a music hall where there was a woman dancing; Charles Wood, a barber, who saw Surratt in his shop with Booth and Michael O'Laughlin on the morning of the assassination; Susan Ann Jackson, who saw Surratt at his mother's house; William Cleaver, and several others.

The major defense against this identification was the testimony of individuals in Elmira, New York, that Surratt had been there on April 13 and 14. Particularly important was Dr. Augustus Bissell, who stated categorically that he had seen Surratt in Elmira on April 14. Confederate General Edwin Lee was also put on the stand to prove that Surratt was engaged in spying for the Confederate government in Elmira and had made a report to him on his return, but the testimony was not allowed. William Failing also testified that Surratt's signature appeared on the register of the Webster House in Canandaigua, New York, for April 15, but since the register had not been properly safeguarded for the past two years, Judge Fisher would not allow this evidence to stand.[10]

Louis Weichmann and John Lloyd were also significant witnesses, as they had been during the conspiracy trial. Weichmann presented basically the same testimony that he had given in the conspiracy trial with some additional embellishments, such as Anna Surratt's alleged statement at breakfast on April 15 that the death of Lincoln was no more than the death of any Negro in the army. Weichmann again got into trouble with some of his dates, for he said that Paine came to Mrs. Surratt's for the second time on March 13, which was an impossibility since Paine was under arrest at the time. He also included the testimony that he had given in his deposition after the conspiracy trial.

9. *Ibid.*, 118, 121–57 *passim*, 551, 557–76, 661–69. For corroboration of Dye's testimony by Sergeant Cooper, see 183–89.
10. *Ibid.*, 158, 162, 176, 195–200, 204–16, 240–42, 489, 494, 498, 500, 501, 520, 723–28; II, 729–45, 761–71, 780–82, 863–92.

The defense made some attempt to impeach Weichmann by showing that he had sworn to things happening on different dates during the two trials. More significant, however, was the use of witnesses like Carland, Gifford, and John Ford to show that Weichmann had been pressured and threatened into making the statements that he did make. Other boarders at the Surratt house also contradicted many of the statements Weichmann had made.

John Lloyd repeated his story, though reluctantly, that Mrs. Surratt had spoken to him about shooting irons and had delivered the package containing the field glasses. He again had to admit that he had been drunk and had lied to the authorities. Interestingly, when defense lawyer Bradley argued that Lloyd was himself probably implicated in the conspiracy, prosecutor Pierrepont said that he agreed and that the witness' reluctance to testify made his testimony all the more valuable.[11]

Another important prosecution witness was Dr. Lewis McMillan, surgeon of the steamship *Peruvian*, the ship on which Surratt had traveled to England. McMillan repeated certain damaging statements that Surratt supposedly made, including one that he and a woman had murdered four or five escaping Union prisoners in cold blood. Surratt also said that he hoped to live to serve Andy Johnson as Lincoln had been served. Henry B. Ste. Marie, who had been so instrumental in Surratt's apprehension, testified that Surratt told him he had escaped from Washington on the night of the assassination. This contradicted one of Ste. Marie's earlier letters, which said that Surratt had been in New York. William Cleaver, who identified Surratt as being in Washington on April 14, also added that Surratt had made comments at his livery stable about bloody work to do and killing Abraham Lincoln, the damned old scoundrel.

To counter McMillan the defense relied mainly on Stephen Cameron, chaplain and sometime Confederate secret service agent, who said McMillan had told him that Surratt was in Elmira on the day of the assassination and then went to a town in upstate New York with an Indian name he could not remember (Canandaigua) and that Surratt was innocent. Cleaver and Ste. Marie were mainly attacked as to their credibility as witnesses.[12]

11. *Ibid.*, I, 276–302, 369–437, 698, 716; II, 745, 814–15, 820, 835, 1282.
12. *Ibid.*, I, 206, 461–84, 492–93; II, 794, 806.

A great deal of testimony was introduced to the effect that on Tuesday, April 18, 1865, two men had slept in the Burlington, Vermont, railroad depot, and Charles Blinn, the night watchman, had discovered after they left a handkerchief marked J. H. SURRATT 2. Others testified to seeing a man who looked very much like Surratt in Saint Albans, Vermont. The defense, however, produced John Holahan, a boarder at Mrs. Surratt's, who had proceeded with detectives to Canada after the assassination in search of Surratt. He testified that he had in his possession one of Surratt's handkerchiefs, which was marked in the manner described, and that he had lost it in the Burlington depot on April 20.[13]

Some testimony was also introduced about Mrs. Surratt, and both sides clashed over that unfortunate woman. District Attorney Carrington took severe exception to the remarks by defense counsel that Mrs. Surratt had been murdered. On the other side Joseph Bradley said the defense hoped to do "something in the way of vindicating the pure fame of [Surratt's] departed mother," and Merrick said that Mrs. Surratt's spirit was present in the court. "We have felt our blood run cold as the rustling of the garments from the grave swept by us." The prosecution apparently felt some obligation to vindicate the former trial, while the defense saw that it might now raise some sympathy by evoking Mrs. Surratt's memory.[14]

As controversy developed around John Surratt's whereabouts at the exact moment of the assassination, the prosecution began to alter its tactics and argue for a doctrine of constructive presence. As Pierrepont said: "It might have been a part of this conspiracy . . . to have a party stationed at that place [Elmira] for the purpose of trying to create confusion by the release of rebel prisoners and by burning the city. . . . He might have been there for the purpose of performing his part in the great drama of this terrible crime, but wherever he was performing it he was as culpable as though he had pulled the trigger that blew the brains out of the head of Abraham Lincoln." The prosecution basically admitted the defense assertion that Surratt was in Elmira on April 13 and then attempted to show that he could have come by railroad in time to be in Washington on the morning of April 14. The defense contended that with the schedule existing at the time and the interrup-

13. *Ibid.*, I, 169, 174, 357, 362, 673, 675, 676, 677, 687–88; II, 930–31, 959–60.
14. *Ibid.*, II, 1111, 1209; I, 530–31. See also I, 161, 178, 334, 340.

tion of service at several places along the line, this would have been impossible.[15]

There was also an endeavor to introduce again some of the same emotion-arousing testimony as at the conspiracy trial, but this time it did not meet with as much success. A controversy arose as to whether the killing of Abraham Lincoln should be regarded as any different in law from that of any other man, as the prosecution contended and the defense denied. An example of the raising of old antagonisms was the prosecution's questioning of James R. Ford as to which side he had taken in the rebellion. For the defense, Merrick tried to damage the prosecution's case by stressing the connection between stable owner Cleaver and the perjurer Conover.

Some of the dubious cipher letters, such as the one found by Mary Hudspeth, and the Duell letter, were also reintroduced as evidence. The defense, however, argued very vigorously that evidence of this nature should not be allowed to stand. Merrick asked exactly what his client was being tried for. Since the prosecution had been successful in having statements made by Mrs. Surratt ruled out, why should not evidence in regard to Paine and Atzerodt be similarly excluded. While Fisher did rule out some testimony against Jacob Thompson and the Duell letter, evidence about Paine and Atzerodt and Surratt's alleged confession to McMillan about shooting Union prisoners were allowed to stand.[16]

This trial also saw the introduction of a bewildering number of character witnesses on both sides. This was the primary means of trying to discredit the testimony of witnesses like McMillan and Ste. Marie, and each side seemed to feel that sheer weight of numbers must be on its side in order to give a little more emphasis to the truth. This type of testimony caused the Washington *Evening Star* to headline its July 24 news about the trial CHARACTER DAY.[17]

There was a great deal of animosity exhibited by the judge, defense counsel, and prosecution. A bitter exchange occurred during the cross-

15. *Ibid.*, II, 1064. See also 771, 916, 927, 935, 940, 1021.

16. *Ibid.*, I, 352–53, 509, 527, 533, 583; II, 1067–68, 1072, 1075, 1076–77, 1092, 1190; *Life, Trial and Adventures of John H. Surratt, the Conspirator: A Correct Account and Highly Interesting Narrative of His Doings and Adventures from Childhood to the Present Time* (Philadelphia: Barclay, 1867), 88.

17. United States Government, *Trial of John H. Surratt*, I, 595–658 passim; II, 847–56 passim, 948–98 passim, 1002–11, 1048–56 passim; Washington *Evening Star*, July 24, 1867, p. 4.

examination of Dye, when Merrick asked him his religion and District Attorney Carrington chided him for such a question. Merrick then declared, "I have no purpose to introduce religious inquisition, nor to follow your example in any particular." On another occasion the following exchange took place: "The court asked if there were any other witnesses to put on the stand. MR. BRADLEY. There are half a dozen out there (pointing to the witness room) in the penitentiary, and have been all the morning. MR. MERRICK. Not in the penitentiary now, but they will be." This reference to the penitentiary led to a bitter clash between Merrick and witness McMillan, and a rebuke to both by Judge Fisher. It also caused Fisher to observe on July 2, "In this connection it may not be improper to observe that I have never, in all my judicial experience, seen a case in which there has been so much trouble with regard to the examination of witnesses, and so much feeling of bitterness displayed."[18]

It is true that during this trial, as at the original conspiracy trial, the government should have had reason to suspect the veracity of some of the prosecution's witnesses. This was especially true of Surratt's former classmate and fellow Zouave Ste. Marie, who had made several contradictory statements. The Canadian minister of public instruction also informed the government in January, 1868, after the trial had ended, that Ste. Marie was a defaulter and absconder who had written him threatening letters. In spite of this, Ste. Marie was awarded the ten thousand dollars. The government also had information from its own detectives that the Surratt handkerchief had been lost on April 20, not April 18, as was testified to by Blinn at the trial. This would make it much more probable that it was lost by Holahan than by Surratt.[19]

Much interest was expressed during the trial as to why the Bureau of Military Justice was involved in the investigation. E. L. Smoot, who was the Surratts' neighbor, among others, admitted that he had been

18. United States Government, *Trial of John H. Surratt*, I, 149, 326, 469–71.
19. United States Court of Claims, *Henry B. Ste. Marie vs. the United States, Amended Petition No. 6415*, 2, 10, 20; Joseph Holt to William Seward, January 23, 1868, in File Folder 44, Seward to Edwin Stanton, January 31, 1868, Transmitting Statement of Chauveau, in File Folder 68, both in RG 153, NA. Holt endorsed this with a glowing account of Ste. Marie's contributions, completely ignoring Chauveau's warnings. Barry Develin, N.d., in Letters Received, File B 47, JAO, 1865, RG 153, NA; Lafayette C. Baker, *History of the United States Secret Service* (Philadelphia: King and Baird, 1867), 555; Eisenschiml, *In the Shadow of Lincoln's Death*, 367; United States Government *Trial of John H. Surratt*, I, 237.

examined before Judge Holt, and the defense bore down hard on this point, for as Merrick said, "Let us deal fairly by this young man, and even if the reputation of Joseph Holt should not have the vindication of innocent blood shed by judicial murder, let us do justice still." It should also be remembered that both Edwards Pierrepont and Albert Riddle were outsiders who were brought in to aid the prosecution. H. S. Olcott had also written to Holt offering his services if he could be paid for them, and a reporter noted that John A. Bingham was quietly aiding the prosecution in an attempt to vindicate himself from the assaults of Congressman Butler.[20]

Although the general public's interest in this trial did not reach the fever pitch of the 1865 trial, Washington interest in it was almost as great as it had been during the conspiracy trial. The same type of comments about ladies being present and the size of the crowd filled the newspapers. The courtroom again became a great spectator affair, though the New York *Times* correspondent constantly reported that the majority of the spectators were rank secessionists and friends of Surratt. The crowd eventually became so large that Judge Fisher withdrew the old passes and issued new ones.

While the bigger city papers, especially in New York City, did carry a fairly full account of the testimony, many smaller papers made little or no mention of the trial. Even in the larger newspapers the trial rapidly faded from the front pages, and there were surprisingly few editorial comments. By June 17, the New York *Herald* reporter was informing his readers that although the newspapers were full of trial news, interest in the Surratt trial was not nearly as great as had been expected.[21]

There were again descriptions and comments about Surratt's reac-

20. United States Government, *Trial of John H. Surratt*, I, 191, 219; II, 1155–56; Albert G. Riddle to Edwin Stanton, May 25, 1867, in File Folder 64, RG 153, NA; Riddle to Joseph Holt, June 3, H. S. Olcott to Holt, June 27, 1867, both in Joseph Holt Papers, LC; New Orleans *Times-Picayune*, July 11, 1867, p. 1.

21. Eisenschiml, *In the Shadow of Lincoln's Death*, 253, 278, 295, and Helen J. Campbell, *Confederate Courier* (New York: St. Martin's Press, 1964), 1–2, both noted erroneously that the public was waiting with great anticipation for the trial which would vindicate Mrs. Surratt. *Life, Trial and Adventures of John H. Surratt*, 43, 56; Baltimore *Sun*, July 9, 1867, p. 1; Chicago *Tribune*, July 6, p. 1, July 1, 1867, p. 1; New York *Times*, July 28, 1867, p. 1; New York *Herald*, June 17, 1867, p. 5.

tions to the trial that could not help but have some effect on opinion. On June 10, the New York *Times* reported, "As the trial approaches, the friends of the prisoner say that he does not express so much confidence as formerly in his ultimate acquittal." The *Herald*, however, commented that Surratt had kept up his spirits very well, lending some credence to the mysterious rumors circulated by his counsel that he would never be tried. On June 11, the *Times* and Associated Press correspondents both described Surratt as careworn and despondent, although he did laugh and converse in a lively manner with his lawyers. The *Times* added that his brother, Isaac, looked much more capable than John of committing evil deeds. When Cleaver testified on June 21, the *Times* reported that Surratt's face was flushed and his teeth and hands were clenched, and that he exhibited great difficulty in controlling his emotions. On June 30, the leisurely attitude with which he viewed the proceedings was noted. "He sits in his chair as though he was a junior member of the Bar, watching the proceedings rather from professional than personal interest in them." The New York *Tribune*, however, said on July 4, after three witnesses had placed Surratt in Washington on the day of the assassination, "For the first time since the trial began, the prisoner, Surratt, showed signs of great anxiety and fear."[22]

There was comment and generally much surprise at the prosecution's attempt to quash the jury and have another panel installed in its place. This also produced complaints that the trial was dragging on too slowly and charges that the prosecution was not really ready and willing to proceed. Some newspapers like the opposition Chicago *Times* expressed apprehension that the jury might be composed of men whose prejudices were against the prisoner, although most newspapers seemed satisfied with the quality of the jury finally selected. Typical of these was the Baltimore *Sun's* comment. "It is conceded, on all sides, that a better or fairer one could not have been chosen. All are well known citizens and trusted business men." However, the Philadelphia *Evening Bulletin* stated that if the jury was as honest as it was reported to be, there would be no problem of obtaining a conviction, showing that for many people an honest jury was one that would act in accordance with their

22. New York *Times*, June 10, p. 1, June 11, p. 1, June 21, p. 1, June 30, 1867, p. 5; New York *Herald*, June 10, 1867, p. 1; New York *Tribune*, July 4, 1867, p. 5.

views. The praise of the jury is interesting in the light of the criticism its decision caused.[23]

Judge Fisher, who presided over the trial and in later years delivered lectures on it, mentioned the difficulties in getting a jury. "For several days it seemed almost impossible to obtain twelve men who had not formed and expressed an opinion in regard to the guilt of the prisoner." Fisher, who is usually portrayed as being venomously opposed to Surratt, further claimed that he had divorced himself as much as possible from the proceedings of the first trial and that his bias, if in fact he had one, was initially in favor of the prisoner. Fisher said that what changed his mind was the testimony of Sergeant Joseph Dye. If true, Fisher's case was the reverse of the majority of the public, for while he began with a belief in Surratt's innocence and ended by believing him guilty, many people had their belief in his guilt shaken after they had heard the defense testimony. The same factors apparently influenced the jury.[24]

Dye's testimony, which has been ridiculed by historians, had an enormous influence on contemporaries. The Chicago *Tribune* said on June 18: "The identification of Surratt was complete. Dye's words and manner were both positive, and he has no doubt evidently on the point. He is an intelligent man, whose evidence cannot easily be overthrown." Several other newspapers reported that Dye had stood up very well under cross-examination, and there seemed very little possibility that Surratt could establish an alibi or be saved from the gallows.[25]

The other testimony placing Surratt in Washington on April 14 also seemed to make a deep impression. Most people felt that an identification made by so many witnesses was beyond contradiction. This was true even when there existed some doubt as to the veracity of certain individual witnesses, for as the Chicago *Tribune* reporter said: "How in the face of all this an alibi can be proved is beyond my comprehension. These witnesses are not swearing falsely—Lee and Cleaver are the only

23. Eisenschiml, *In the Shadow of Lincoln's Death*, 272; Baltimore *Sun*, June 17, 1867, p. 4; Chicago *Tribune*, June 16, 1867, p. 1; Philadelphia *Evening Bulletin*, July 27, 1867, p. 4.

24. George P. Fisher, "The Trial of John H. Surratt for the Murder of President Lincoln, by the Judge Who Presided at the Trial" (Typescript, in George P. Fisher Papers, LC), 8, 15, 17–18.

25. Chicago *Tribune*, June 18, p. 1, June 19, 1867, p. 1; Keene (N.H.) *Sentinel*, June 20, 1867, p. 2.

ones, at least who do so—and it does not seem possible that the other five men can all be mistaken in the man, for, as Dye said, his face is an uncommon one, and not easily forgotten."[26]

As might be expected, Weichmann's testimony also created quite a sensation. As the New York *Times* described it: "His narrative was very clear and connected, and considerably fuller than he gave it on the conspiracy trials, though no new facts were developed. Taken as it stands, it is the most convincing and positive proof yet adduced of the very close intimacy of Surratt and his mother with Booth and the other assassins." The same was true of McMillan, particularly because of his bitter clash with the defense counsel. The New York *Times* said on July 4, "The reproof administered to that impertinent and insulting questioner by the witness Surgeon McMillan was well deserved, though coming from an improper source, and the further scoring he received from the judge on the Bench . . . was a rebuke needed both by the counsel for the defence and the Surratt sympathizers." Union newspapers generally discredited the testimony of Simon Cameron, the major witness in rebuttal to McMillan, calling him a vagabond. As the Chicago *Tribune* said, "No one but rebel sympathizers will believe a word he said."[27]

The attempt to reintroduce sectional hatreds also had its effect. The Chicago *Tribune* said on August 3 that a friend of defense lawyer Merrick repeated a conversation in which Merrick had said during the war that all the people of the Northwest were ready to follow him down to Washington to help hang the despot, Abe Lincoln. On August 11, it added: "It is evident that Washington City is not wholly reconstructed.

26. Keene (N.H.) *Sentinel*, June 27, 1867, p. 2; New York *Herald*, July 5, 1867, p. 4; New York *Times*, June 21, 1867, p. 1. Only one witness, David Reed, had testified to seeing Surratt in Washington on April 14 during the conspiracy trial. See David C. Reed, April 26, 1865, in Letters Received, File R 688, JAO, RG 153, NA; Chicago *Tribune*, June 28, 1867, p. 2. For historians stressing Surratt's guilt, see Lloyd Lewis, *Myths After Lincoln* (New York: Harcourt Brace, 1929), 256; Osborn H. Oldroyd, *The Assassination of Abraham Lincoln, Flight, Pursuit, Capture, and Punishment of the Conspirators* (Washington: O. H. Oldroyd, 1901), 237. For those believing him innocent, see DeWitt, *Assassination of Abraham Lincoln*, 96; Guy W. Moore, *The Case of Mrs. Surratt: Her Controversial Trial and Execution for Conspiracy in the Lincoln Assassination* (Norman: University of Oklahoma Press, 1954), 77.
27. New York *Times*, June 28, p. 1, July 3, p. 1, July 4, 1867, p. 4; Chicago *Tribune*, June 28, p. 1, July 2, p. 1, July 17, 1867, p. 1. See also Boston *Daily Journal*, June 29, 1867, p. 4; New York *Tribune*, June 29, 1867, p. 1; Harris, *Assassination of Lincoln*, 200.

The proper place for Bradley, Sr., is the Dry Tortugas." On the other side, the Charleston *Courier* praised Merrick for his defense of the honor of the South.[28]

It is little wonder then, that as the prosecution's case progressed, those who believed Surratt to be guilty found themselves fully supported in their views. The Chicago *Tribune* and Springfield (Mass.) *Weekly Republican* both commented that the case was even much stronger than had been expected. Again the comment by the New York *World* was significant, for as it said on July 10, "If the testimony which has thus far been given is not shaken by counter-evidence, and is believed by the jury, it will go hard with the prisoner." At the same time the *World* remained implacable in its opposition to military trials even when the individuals hanged were guilty. However, some papers such as the New York *Times* and Springfield (Mass.) *Daily Republican*, which held very strong views about Surratt's guilt, did not change their views very much even after the defense testimony had been concluded.[29]

Nonetheless, it becomes readily apparent that the defense testimony did begin to reshape the views of many people. Opposition newspapers, especially, attacked the interest that the Bureau of Military Justice was taking in the trial and said the evidence appeared to have been manufactured and to have had the hand of Conover behind it. This was particularly true in regard to Cleaver's testimony, for when it became known that he had communicated with Congressman Ashley and perjurer Conover, the Easton (Pa.) *Sentinel* said: "Impeacher Ashley had previously visited him in his cell, and had a talk with him. Radicals— especially Rumpers—work with nice tools—very."[30]

Sergeant Dye's testimony also seemed to wilt somewhat under Mrs. Lambert's story of her encounter with him. The Baltimore *Sun* said on July 12, "The latter is well known in this community and bears a very

28. Chicago *Tribune*, August 3, p. 1, August 11, 1867, p. 2; Charleston *Courier*, August 9, p. 2, August 13, 1867, p. 2.

29. Chicago *Tribune*, June 20, p. 2, July 7, p. 1, July 11, 1867, p. 1; Springfield (Mass.) *Weekly Republican*, June 22, p. 4, July 13, p. 1, July 20, 1867, p. 1; New York *World*, July 9, p. 4, June 22, 1867, p. 4; New York *Weekly World*, July 10, 1867, p. 2.

30. Easton (Pa.) *Sentinel*, June 27, p. 3, July 4, 1867, p. 2. See also Charleston *Courier*, June 11, 1867, p. 1; Memphis *Daily Appeal*, June 27, p. 2, August 15, 1867, p. 2; Roscoe, *The Web of Conspiracy*, 509. See Springfield (Mass.) *Weekly Republican*, June 22, 1867, p. 4, for argument that Stanton's and Holt's zeal was merely a profound desire to bring a guilty party to justice.

high character, so that no one doubts the truth of her statement." Even the New York *Times* was forced to admit that Dye might have been mistaken in this particular, although it did not invalidate the remainder of his testimony.[31]

In similar fashion Kinderhook, a correspondent for the New Orleans *Times-Picayune*, criticized District Attorney Carrington for his change in tactics in relying on constructive presence. "The line of the prosecution is a most extraordinary one. The prisoner is indicted for murder. But he has not been tried for murder. In fact he has not been tried at all. The conspirators have been tried over again, and that is all." The New York *Tribune* also recognized the legal niceties involved. "Morally, his presence or absence is not of the least consequence. If in the conspiracy what difference where he was at the moment of the blow? But, legally, it is vital." Carrington himself admitted in 1889 that there had been no really good evidence that Surratt was in Washington on April 14.[32]

The testimony given by Weichmann and Lloyd was also attacked. The Baltimore *Sun* pointed out on July 2 how the groundwork had been laid to contradict Weichmann by means of Ford's Theatre employee Louis J. Carland (misspelled *Carlin* in the *Sun*) and Surratt family friend John Brophy, and also noted Weichmann's nervous manner on the stand. The New York *World* said that Weichmann's testimony appeared to have been committed to memory. It also noted that very few people had been convinced when Congressman Butler raised the possibility of Mrs. Surratt's innocence, but after the testimony of the drunkard, Lloyd, it appeared that Butler did not lie.[33]

Booth's letter to the Washington *Daily National Intelligencer*, which was supposedly given to actor John Matthews, who read it and then burned it after committing the content to memory, also caused much excitement. Matthews had testified before the committee investigating the impeachment to the existence of such a letter, which he claimed was signed by Booth, Atzerodt, Paine, and Herold, but not Surratt. He was

---

31. Baltimore *Sun*, July 12, 1867, p. 4. See also New Orleans *Times-Picayune*, July 14, 1867, p. 8; New York *Times*, July 12, 1867, p. 5.

32. New Orleans *Times-Picayune*, August 6, 1867, p. 2; New York *Tribune*, July 15, 1867, p. 2; Eisenschiml, *In the Shadow of Lincoln's Death*, 400.

33. Baltimore *Sun*, July 2, 1867, p. 4; New York *World*, June 28, p. 8, June 26, 1867, p. 4. For an extremely unflattering portrait of Lloyd, see Campbell, *Confederate Courier*, 180.

forced to admit that he had not made any mention of such a letter in 1865 but had burned it because he became afraid. When an attempt was made to introduce evidence about this letter during the trial, however, it was not allowed, and as the New York *Times* said, "It will be a new feature in judicial history if one conspirator is allowed to write an acquittance for his confederate." Nonetheless, the gist of his testimony became so widely circulated that it must have had some influence.[34]

The evidence also further divided opinion about Mrs. Surratt's guilt. Many newspapers felt that the strong prosecution testimony during the current trial served to demonstrate her guilt even more substantially than had been done in 1865. Nonetheless, many opposition journals believed that the defense testimony had demonstrated her innocence. The New York *World* said, once the jury had not been able to agree on a verdict: "Here was substantially the same case, most of the same witnesses, substantially the same evidence . . . and . . . the prisoners were promptly convicted. . . . It is clear, therefore, that Mrs. Surratt and the others . . . were murdered."[35]

The bewildering array of character witnesses and witnesses who directly contradicted each other also produced an inevitable confusion. The New York *Times* said on July 25: "The Surratt case continues to become intricate through the difference of opinion regarding the character for truth and veracity of the witnesses on both sides. . . . To-day a dozen witnesses testified that Cameron, the pardoned rebel, was a man of truth and good character, while yesterday a dozen others testified exactly to the contrary, and one expressed the opinion that he was crazy."[36]

There was a report on July 18 that Carroll Hobart, a Vermont Central Railroad conductor who had identified Surratt, had been called

34. John T. Matthews, April 30, 1865, Statement, in Record Book, File M, p. 64, JAO, RG 153, NA; United States Congress, House, Committee on the Judiciary, *Impeachment Investigation, Testimony Taken Before the Judiciary Committee of the House of Representatives in the Investigation of the Charges Against Andrew Johnson*, 39th Cong., 2nd Sess., 40th Cong., 1st Sess. (Washington: Government Printing Office, 1867), 490–91, 532–33, 783; United States Government, *Trial of John H. Surratt*, II, 821–28; New York *Times*, July 8, p. 4, July 19, 1867, p. 5.

35. Philadelphia *Evening Bulletin*, June 20, 1867, p. 4; New York *World*, August 10, 1867, in Eisenschiml, *In the Shadow of Lincoln's Death* 345. See also New York *World*, July 16, 1867, p. 4.

36. New York *Times*, July 25, 1867, p. 5. See also July 11, p. 5, July 26, p. 1, July 30, 1867, p. 4.

back to Washington by Bradley and offered $1,500 to identify someone else. Bradley, of course, denied the charges. There was also a rumor about a plot to manufacture damaging evidence against Surratt. Many people apparently lost all hope of ever discerning the truth, and the Baltimore *Sun* cautioned: "There has been so much contradiction and so much counter-swearing ever since the commencement of this case, that it is quite a puzzle. . . . The jury will certainly have to exercise a wise judgement in reconciling the great conflict in evidence."[37]

Historians have attempted to equate the two trials, but in many ways this is unfair. In some respects the testimony was similar, but given the calmer atmosphere and the fact that most of the damaging anti-Confederate evidence could not be introduced in 1867, there is little wonder that the trial of John Surratt had the outcome that it did.[38]

After the defense had completed the presentation of its case, newspapers that believed in Surratt's innocence summed up the case as it stood and usually concluded that Surratt's alibi had been completely proven.[39] However, what really elicited much comment from the partisan press on both sides was the closing arguments and particularly the rulings made by Judge Fisher.

Fisher's charge to the jury hardly accords with his protestation of friendly feelings toward the prisoner. He began with a biblical injunction that "whosoever sheddeth man's blood by man shall his blood be shed," and went on to explain that killing a president was as bad as killing a king. He also denied the defense claim that the Milligan decision had rendered the military tribunal illegal. If this were so, he asked, why had no application been made to free the prisoners in the Dry Tortugas? The judge also explained that an alibi was a type of defense

37. Montpelier (Vt.) *Freeman*, quoted in Chicago *Tribune*, July 18, 1867, p. 2; New York *Times*, July 21, p. 4, July 24, 1867, p. 5; United States Government, *Trial of John H. Surratt*, II, 893. For rumor of the plot against Surratt, see Charleston *Courier*, August 5, 1867, p. 2; New Orleans *Times-Picayune*, August 3, 1867, p. 1; Washington *Post*, April 3, 1898, p. 11; Baltimore *Sun*, July 24, 1867, p. 4.

38. Helen J. Campbell, *The Case For Mrs. Surratt* (New York: G. P. Putman's Son's, 1943), 270, and *Confederate Courier*, 258; DeWitt, *Assassination of Lincoln*, 194, and *The Judicial Murder of Mary E. Surratt* (Baltimore: John Murphy, 1895), 167–68, 171–72; Eisenschiml, *In the Shadow of Lincoln's Death*, 256. For an extremely perceptive comment by Benn Pitman about this shift in opinion, see Giddens, "Benn Pitman on the Trial of Lincoln's Assassins," 18.

39. Boston *Post*, July 11, 1867, p. 2; Charleston *Courier*, July 15, 1867, p. 1; Easton (Pa.) *Sentinel*, July 18, 1867, p. 2.

usually not regarded very highly by the courts, since it was too easy to procure perjured testimony or for witnesses to be mistaken. He also disagreed with Merrick's contention that the jury might disregard the judge's statement of law in this case. In a more personal vein he was plainly irked at the more than 150 exceptions that the defense had taken to his rulings.[40]

Interestingly, Judge Fisher came in for some fairly severe criticism on a bipartisan basis. The Easton (Pa.) *Sentinel* said, "It is difficult to state which is doing most for the prosecution, Judge Fisher or the Counsel for the prosecution." The Washington *Daily National Intelligencer* took him to task for his defense of military tribunals even after the Supreme Court had declared them to be illegal. Even the New York *Times* felt that Fisher had erred in allowing testimony to stand about Surratt's cruelty to Union prisoners while not allowing the defense to show what he was doing for the Confederate government in Canada. The New York *Herald* criticized Fisher for his apparent assumption that it was not the prisoner's guilt or innocence that was at stake but whether sentimentalism might not save him from hanging. It added that as for liberal use of biblical injunctions, the Book of Kings was "a good book, no doubt, but not often quoted as an authority on criminal jurisprudence."[41]

Similarly, there were comments made about the summations to the jury. The Chicago *Tribune* said: "Judge Pierrepont's argument for the Government in the Surratt trial yesterday is the theme of universal talk in loyal circles. It is conceded to be one of the ablest efforts made before the court in Washington for years. His dignified bearing, and quiet but most impressive delivery—in marked contrast with the disgraceful harangues of the past few days—calls forth praise even from the fair-minded men of the opposition." However, *Frank Leslie's Illustrated* criticized Pierrepont's introduction of everything from the Pope to the

---

40. United States Government, *Trial of John H. Surratt*, II, 1162–63, 1368–70, 1373–76. For a view challenging Fisher's fairness, see Campbell, *Confederate Courier*, 206. For an opposing view, see Harris, *Assassination of Lincoln*, 234. In any case, Fisher came to a conclusion that coincided with the evidence almost exactly as the prosecution presented it. See Fisher, "Trial of John H. Surratt," 5.

41. Easton (Pa.) *Sentinel*, July 25, 1867, p. 4; Eisenschiml, *In the Shadow of Lincoln's Death*, 344; Washington *Daily National Intelligencer*, August 10, 1867, p. 1; New York *Times*, August 12, 1867, p. 4; New York *Herald*, August 9, 1867, p. 4.

Deity, noting that if his statement was true that no man violates a law of God without being punished for it, "what punishment awaits an advocate who distorts truth and appeals to ignorant clamor to obtain a conviction, which is worth nothing, if not procured by undistorted evidence?" The Baltimore *Sun* criticized District Attorney Carrington's speech, in which he also introduced scriptural reference and called for vengeance, for the *Sun* said that it thought the biblical injunction was "Vengeance is mine saith the Lord."[42]

Merrick's plea for the defense drew equal comment. Correspondent Kinderhook told readers of the New Orleans *Times-Picayune*: "The speech of Mr. Merrick . . . was universally acknowledged by the bench and bar to be one of the finest forensic efforts ever heard in Washington. He electrified the court and jury by the boldness of the positions which he assumed and the ability and eloquence with which he maintained them." However, the Chicago *Tribune* spoke of Merrick's "secession harangue." In a more humorous vein, the New York *Times* lightly chided Merrick for his reference to the prosecution playing the gnome and tearing the corpse of Mrs. Surratt from its grave. "Our reminiscences of childhood and fairy lore cry out indignantly at such an imputation cast upon those venerable beings, the Gnomes, who dwell in the recesses of the rocks. . . . Did Merrick mean a ghoul, or a giaour, or a gaul, or merely a 'goak?' "[43]

The jury decision, which was really no decision at all, produced much interest and excitement. After the jury had begun to deliberate and it became apparent that a verdict would be some time in coming, there were rumors that some of Surratt's friends would attempt to rescue him and that these men or some Washington Blacks planned direct action if the verdict was not to their liking. On August 10, the Hartford *Courant* noted, "The members of the Surratt jury were endeavoring, at last accounts, to sing themselves into accord, but with slight hopes of success," adding that "Home Sweet Home" seemed to be one of their

---

42. Chicago *Tribune*, August 5, 1867, p. 1; *Frank Leslie's Illustrated*, August 24, 1867, p. 354; Baltimore *Sun*, August 3, 1867, p. 2. For summation by Pierrepont and Carrington, see United States Government, *Trial of John H. Surratt*, II, 1073–1155, 1247–1366.

43. New Orleans *Times-Picayune*, August 8, 1867, p. 2; Chicago *Tribune*, August 1, 1867, p. 1; New York *Times*, August 1, p. 5, August 2, p. 4, August 3, p. 4. For summation by Merrick and Bradley, see United States Government, *Trial of John H. Surratt*, II, 1155–1246.

favorite melodies. When the jury finally returned, the New York *Herald* correspondent described the tumultuous scene. "There was a decided commotion in the court room at this time and it was whispered about that 'the jury have agreed;' 'they are going to discharge the jury;' 'they can't agree;' 'they have asked to be discharged;' and numberless other remarks of this character."[44]

When it was learned that the jury could not agree, newspapers were quick to comment, sometimes in a decidedly partisan manner. The Boston *Evening Transcript*, which was particularly bitter about the outcome, carried the headline THE DISGRACEFUL TERMINATION OF THE SURRATT TRIAL and said that any impartial jury could have convicted Surratt under Judge Fisher's charge. Generally, however, even among those who reacted in a partisan manner, the outcome was not unexpected. The *Times* said, "There is quite enough in the conflict of evidence, in the doubtful character of witnesses and the consequential character of many of the more positive statements, to suggest doubts and explain the grounds of disagreement." The *Times* even rebuked its own correspondent for his puerile attempt to make it appear that the jury had voted primarily along sectional lines.[45]

There were reports that before the next trial, if one occurred, Congress would pass a bill allowing Negroes on juries and that this might affect the outcome of a new trial. It was also reported that members of the jury had said that if Surratt had been tried merely on a charge of conspiracy, they would have had no difficulty in convicting him. This caused the Boston *Post* to comment that the prosecution had attempted to prove too much, while *Leslie's* remarked that the Scotch system of fifteen jurors and a majority vote might have been very profitably used.[46]

44. Chicago *Tribune*, August 9, 1867, p. 1; New York *Times*, August 8, p. 8, August 9, 1867, pp. 1, 4; New York *Tribune*, August 8, 1867, p. 1; Hartford *Daily Courant*, August 10, 1867, p. 4; New York *Herald*, August 11, 1867, p. 8.

45. Boston *Evening Transcript*, August 12, p. 2, August 26, 1867, p. 4. Eisenschiml, *In the Shadow of Lincoln's Death*, 275, claimed no attacks were ever launched against the jury because of its decision, even though he goes on to cite some! New York *Times*, August 11, p. 4, August 12, p. 4, August 13, 1867, p. 4. Secretary Welles also noted in his diary that the trial's outcome had not been unexpected. Howard K. Beale (ed.), *Diary of Gideon Welles* (3 vols.; New York: W. W. Norton, 1960), III, 166–67.

46. New Orleans *Times-Picayune*, August 16, p. 4, August 17, 1867, p. 4; New York *Times*, August 11, p. 1, August 12, 1867, p. 4; *Life, Trial and Adventures of John H. Surratt*, 135; Boston *Post*, August 13, 1867, p. 4; *Frank Leslie's Illustrated*, August 11, 1867, p. 371.

The trial had also, of course, reopened the entire question of a military trial versus a civil one, and many used the outcome to vindicate their position. The New York *World* said, "The motive of this trial was not the vindication of justice, but the vindication of the government and its famous military commission." And the Chicago *Times* noted, "The present trial is a signal vindication of those constitutional provisions now almost a dead letter, which guarantee to every person accused of crime an impartial investigation by a Grand Jury and impartial trial by a jury of the vicinage."[47]

However, General Harris, who had served on the military commission, also commented on the trial's conclusion and for once made a very incisive observation. "It was just as impossible now, almost two years after the close of the war, as it would have been at the time of the trial by a military commission of Surratt's fellows in crime; and a conviction by a jury in a civil court was just as impossible now as it would have been then because a jury of partisans embracing those of both sides politically can never be expected to come to an agreement in a case that appeals to their partisan feelings."[48] Given the fact that the jury very clearly voted along sectional lines in 1867, who can say that it was really any less biased than the military commission?

Perhaps the most perceptive contemporary comment about the difference between 1865 and 1867 was that made by the New York *Times*.

> When, therefore, the Government, availing itself of the existing state of war, cited the criminals before a Military Commission, which, while respecting their rights, refused all delays and brushed aside the fictions and technicalities usual and useful in common cases, letting in every ray of light from any quarter upon motives and persons, and scanning the widest range of circumstances, most candid persons agreed that a case transcending all experience was rightly tried in modes as extraordinary. . . . John H.

47. New York *Weekly World*, August 14, 1867, p. 2; Chicago *Times*, quoted in Memphis *Daily Appeal*, July 19, 1867, p. 2. For Merrick's comments on the illegality of military commissions, see United States Government, *Trial of John H. Surratt*, II, 1070–71. For historians noting the difference between the biased military commission and the enlightened civil jury that allowed John Surratt to go free, see DeWitt, *Assassination of Abraham Lincoln*, 194, and *The Judicial Murder of Mary E. Surratt* (Baltimore: John Murphy, 1895), 168; Eisenschiml, *In the Shadow of Lincoln's Death*, 285. For a view opposed to the military commission but more balanced, see John W. Curran, "The Lincoln Conspiracy Trial and Military Jurisdiction over Civilians," rpr. from *Notre Dame Lawyer* (November, 1933).

48. Harris, *Assassination of Lincoln*, 233. See also Lewis, *Myths After Lincoln*, 259; *Frank Leslie's Illustrated*, August 31, 1867, p. 369.

Surratt was called to his account in a calmer state of the public mind, after time had appeased its righteous anger and the passion for retribution had been allayed.[49]

While the trial's outcome was not itself unexciting, the near physical combat between Fisher and Bradley generated the most interest. During the trial great bitterness had been exhibited on both sides, and on June 21, the Chicago *Tribune* commented: "Bradley, the senior counsel for the defense, got mad again today. This time he insulted the counsel on the other side. Members of the bar quite generally think, the judge [is] lenient with him." On July 3, it was reported that because of Fisher's rebuke of Bradley for harassing witnesses, Bradley had followed Fisher after the court's adjournment and they nearly came to blows. This caused the New York *Times* to produce an editorial against the practice of bullying and browbeating witnesses for no apparent purpose, while the *Herald* printed an editorial entitled "The Bruiser Bradley."[50]

On July 27, Bradley reportedly said during an exchange with Pierrepont that there was another place where "I can settle these things." Again the *Times* commented that "at all events, he, Bradley, appears to have learned that the Court Room is not the 'place' for brawls, and that is something gained; but what a bore it must be to keep in such a continual freeze in this hot weather." It also called on both sides to stop bullying witnesses, a custom that had long been the dishonor of American courts.[51]

At the conclusion of the trial, Judge Fisher disbarred Bradley from practicing before the Supreme Court of the District of Columbia. Bradley followed Fisher outside to a streetcar and issued him a challenge to a duel. Armed partisans were present, and there were shouts of "He's going to shoot," but the police kept the situation from deteriorating any further. Members of the bar called a meeting at which a resolution was passed to investigate the disbarment. However, another group of lawyers met to protest this action and to support Judge Fisher. Bradley was arrested on August 15 for violation of the law against dueling but

49. New York *Times*, August 12, 1867, p. 4.
50. Chicago *Tribune*, June 21, p. 1, July 3, 1867, p. 1; New York *Times*, June 22, p. 1, July 3, 1867, pp. 1, 4; New York *Herald*, July 4, 1867, p. 1.
51. New York *Times*, July 27, p. 5, July 28, p. 4, July 29, 1867, p. 4.

was released on a one-thousand-dollar bond and never brought to trial.[52]

Sentiment was again divided. The *Times* reported on August 11, "The sympathies of the public are divided in accordance with their political sentiments; Surratt's friends siding with Mr. Bradley, and the more respectable class of people sustaining Judge Fisher." Several other newspapers felt that the rebuke had been well deserved. By this time many people had become disgusted with the conduct on both sides. The *Times* summed up this view when it said: "The unseemly violence of Mr. Bradley must have been of but slight service to the prisoner, while upon himself it brought much discredit. On the other hand, the excess of zeal that has been observable throughout Judge Pierrepont's management of the prosecution, has tended to excite misgivings as to the real strength of his cause." The *Herald*, which titled its editorial "The Arrest of Bruiser Bradley," said that were justice to be done, the entire crew of judges, lawyers, and witnesses should be sent to Botany Bay. The only one who had conducted himself like a gentlemen, it continued, was Pierrepont, and he owed his shining qualities to the fact that he came from New York.[53]

Fisher, in his reminiscences of the dispute, spoke with admiration of Bradley's ability as a lawyer, although he admitted that Bradley reminded him of a line in Horace's "Ars Poetica"—"Imperious, irascible, implacable, bitter." The judge also said that in all of his judicial experience, he had never known of a trial in which partisan feeling was so rampant. Fisher also said that only his illness prevented him from rebuking Bradley sooner and that in making up his mind to disbar him, he let it be known through mutual friends that if an apology were forthcoming, he would not resort to such drastic action. Fisher also claimed that it was his own pleading before the grand jury that had prevented the jury from indicting Bradley on the dueling charge. De-

---

52. New York *Times*, August 11, p. 1, August 15, p. 5, August 16, p. 4, August 19, 1867, p. 4; *Life, Trial and Adventures of John H. Surratt*, 134–35; New York *Tribune*, August 13, p. 1, August 21, 1867, p. 1.

53. New York *Times*, August 11, 1867, p. 4; Chicago *Tribune*, August 23, 1867, p. 2; Hartford *Daily Courant*, August 12, 1867, p. 4; Philadelphia *Evening Bulletin*, August 13, 1867, p. 4; *Frank Leslie's Illustrated*, August 24, 1867, p. 354; New York *Herald*, August 17, 1867, p. 4.

spite this kindness, Bradley brought suit against Fisher for twenty thousand dollars but was unsuccessful. Some three years later he attempted to cane Fisher in the street near the City Hall, also with no success.[54]

The John Surratt trial is an example of a trial wherein public sympathy for the defendant shifted from unfavorable to favorable as the evidence was presented. After the prosecution had closed its case, there existed a fairly widespread belief that he was guilty. However, once the defense testimony was in, the contradiction and confusion had raised equally pervasive doubts.

Historians' arguments that the one overriding factor in the failure to convict John Surratt was his trial before a civil instead of a military court are untrue. Rather, by 1867, public interest had shifted to a variety of issues including Reconstruction policy and Johnson's possible impeachment, amidst rumors of the president's own involvement in Lincoln's murder. The jury did not convict because the evidence against Surratt was inconclusive. By 1867, there was relatively little desire expressed to bring him to trial again, and the public seemed content to leave to historians the task of unraveling whatever mystery still remained in regard to Lincoln's assassination. Unfortunately, historians have often not clearly understood the context in which the events of 1865 and 1867 occurred but have, in fact, created a great deal of the myth and distortion surrounding the Lincoln assassination.

54. Fisher, "Trial of John H. Surratt," 9, 21, 32–35. For approval of Fisher's disbarring of Bradley, see Alfred Ely to George P. Fisher, August 12, 1867, S. J. Bowen to Fisher, August 15, 1867, all in Fisher Papers.

Conclusion

The assassination of Abraham Lincoln, the first murder of a president in our history, occurred at the end of a bitter four-year Civil War that was one of the most traumatic and divisive events in American history. Over one hundred years later we continue to experience the legacy of that conflict.

Given the historical circumstances, it is hardly surprising that the assassination shook the nation to its foundations with grief and rage. There have been similar reactions to nearly all American presidential assassinations, even those taking place in calmer times.

Considering the shock and frenzy of April, 1865, the pursuit and capture of the conspirators proceeded as ably as could have been expected. Officials, such as Secretary Stanton, unsure just how widespread the plot was and frightened for their own safety and that of the government, took measures they deemed necessary to preserve the Union. They hardly needed to conspire to convince the public that the South was behind the assassination, for people naturally looked on the assassination as the last act of a defeated and treacherous cause.

To many contemporaries, although a substantial number disagreed, a military trial was regarded as proper, since, while the war had technically ended, the assassination was viewed as an act of irregular warfare by the South. It was also felt that the wider rules of evidence allowed before a military commission would provide the best means of revealing the full extent of the conspiracy. The trial testimony merely served to reinforce these views.

The military commission, despite some irregularities, reached a verdict that would probably have been very similar to that of a civil jury. Public emotion was at such a fever pitch that few people cared to make fine distinctions between kidnapping and assassination plots and those who could be shown to be associated with Booth in either venture were bound to suffer. In fact, it could be argued that the military tribunal showed a remarkable degree of discrimination because these officers, had their clemency plea for Mrs. Surratt been accepted, decided that only three people should die. The guilt of those three seemed clear beyond a reasonable doubt.

Two years later, the trial of the last of the alleged conspirators, John Surratt, ended in a deadlocked jury. The outcome, however, hardly indicated that a civil jury would have been much more lenient than the military tribunal in 1865. What it did indicate was that with public attention having shifted to other issues, people were in a position to examine the testimony more calmly. Such an examination produced a great deal of contradiction and confusion. The public, therefore, understood the jury's failure to reach a verdict, and there seemed to be a feeling of relief when John Surratt's trial ended.

Unfortunately, historians have acted as if the assassination occurred in a vacuum and have spent a great deal of time discussing erroneous and irrelevant issues. They have been extremely critical of the events that transpired in 1865 and have felt little need to investigate how and why people reacted the way they did.

In addition, they have expended much energy in proposing vast conspiracies involving high-ranking northerners in Lincoln's assassination. However, many of the more extreme claims made by historians are untenable, while others remain merely unsubstantiated speculation. Most of the unresolved circumstances associated with the assassination can be explained far more readily by the nature of man and the irrational behavior of people under such terrible conditions than by any conspiracy theory. There seems to be (as suggested by the 1969 report of the President's Commission on the Causes and Prevention of Violence) some sort of psychological phenomenon that causes people to see conspiracies behind nearly all assassinations. Somehow it is more satisfying to believe that a president died as the victim of a cause rather than at the hands of a deranged gunman. Out of such psychological depths are many conspiracy theories spun. While some areas of mystery remain, those historians who espouse the conspiracy view must be able to place the events in their historical context and present more substantial proof than they have been able to provide.

Index